The Killer Book of Serial Killers

Incredible Stories, Facts, and Trivia from the World of Serial Killers

Tom Philbin and Michael Philbin

sourcebooks

Published by Sourcebooks, Inc.
P.O. Box 4410, Naperville, Illinois 60567–4410
(630) 961–3900
Fax: (630) 961–2168
www.sourcebooks.com

Library of Congress Cataloging-in-Publication Data

Philbin, Tom.
  Killer Book of Serial Killers : incredible stories, facts, and trivia from the world of serial killers / Tom and Michael Philbin.
      p. cm.
  Includes index.
  1. Serial murderers—Case studies. 2. Serial murders—Case studies. 3. Homicide—Case studies. I. Philbin, Michael. II. Title.
  HV6513.P45 2008
  364.152'320922—dc22

                                    2008034035

          Printed and bound in the United States of America.
              VP 30 29 28 27 26 25 24 23 22 21

Contents

PART III: SERIAL KILLERS WORLDWIDE

PART IV: IN THEIR OWN WORDS

PART V: TEST YOUR SERIAL KILLER IQ . . . 309

Introduction

Like our first Killer book—*The Killer Book of True Crime*—this book aims to serve up facts about serial murderers in an entertaining way. As such, some of the information is served up in small bites: quotes, brainteasers, lists, matching games, facts, and factoids permeate the book and make the gruesome information a little more, well, palatable. The meat of the book, chapters 2 to 36, is comprised of long stories that delve deeply into the lives of the most infamous serial murderers, the dark stars of our time and times past.

This book is designed both for people who are relatively unfamiliar with serial killers and their crimes and for those who have already devoured books and websites dedicated to all the grisly details. We think that the quality and depth of the research will enable both groups to enjoy it. *Enjoy* may seem like a strange word to use when talking about murder— particularly serial murder—but the plain fact is that there is a certain subset of ghouls out there (yours truly included) who love reading about it. As in the first book, however, we have drawn a line on the morgue floor: There are some things that are so awful that they are not enjoyable to read. We have tried to exclude that material without taking the bite out of the book. For example, there was one close-up photo that showed a young female victim with her vaginal vault gone, which could make, as they say, a goat barf. If the book were for goats that like to barf, we would have used it, but it isn't.

We hope you enjoy the book and come away with a better understanding of the creature known as the serial killer—and trust us, they aren't really human, not like you and I are.

Yours in blood, death, depravity, and piquer acts,

—Tom Philbin and Michael Philbin

PART I

THE FIENDS AMONG US

"We serial killers are your sons,
we are your husbands,
we are everywhere.
And there will be more of
your children dead tomorrow."

—Ted Bundy

Chapter 1
Meet the
Serial Killer

Serial killers are a lot different from regular murderers. Most people who commit murder do so out of passion and anger. When homicide cops investigate, they usually look at family members as suspects first. There are, of course, people who plan a murder for financial or other gain, but murder is most often a crime of passion. Serial killers are much different; they kill many people, almost all of whom are usually strangers, over a period of time, and usually with some sort of cooling-off period between killings.

According to the FBI, a serial killer is someone who has killed a minimum of three people. We agree that this generally is a true definition, but we would also put firmly into the serial killer category those killers who were stopped from murdering before they reached three victims because they were caught or otherwise incapacitated, but who, because of the way they committed their crimes, would have killed at least three— maybe many more.

The Canadian Paul Bernardo and his masochistic lover Karla Homolka are prime examples of this: They killed three people, but as one of the murders was legally categorized as manslaughter, they aren't "official" serial killers because only two of their killings are considered first degree murder. But a close look at the murderous drive inside the two—a drive that facilitated the rape and murder of young girls, including Karla's younger sister—reveals that there was no way they would have stopped killing had they not been caught. (More on Paul Bernardo and Karla Homolka in Chapter 25.)

Notable Quotable

"In my lifetime I have murdered twenty-one human beings. I have committed thousands of burglaries, robberies, larcenies, arsons, and, last but not least, I have committed sodomy on one thousand male human beings. For all these things I am not the least bit sorry."

—Carl Panzram

The Answer Is Found in Childhood

So, then, what creates a serial killer? Why this compulsion—and it is a compulsion—to kill multiple times?

Some people think that the compulsion to kill may be the result of trauma to the brain. This is what the Tampa, Florida, serial killer Bobby Joe Long thought drove him to rape and murder women; he claimed that, before a motorcycle accident that caused severe head trauma, he never thought about killing women.

Some psychiatrists think it's genetic, that an aberration of some sort occurs and puts people on a homicidal path. Another potential reason is that something dreadful happens to the human psyche when a child is shipped to an orphanage, or given up to a foster care system. Author John Bowlby says in his book *The Making and Breaking of Affectional Bonds* (1979), "In psychopaths the incidence of illegitimacy and the shunting of the child from one home to another is high. It is no accident that Ian Brady of the Moors murders was such a one."

Most psychiatrists are usually vague about exactly what compels someone to kill people, and it's true that there is no definitive answer. However, most doctors believe that serial killers are programmed in their childhoods to be killers—and it's not just doctors who feel that way. Most investigators who are close to these crimes and criminals agree, people like the FBI's John Douglas and Robert Ressler, premier profilers and investigators who have been investigating serial killers since the term was coined in the 1970s.

We believe that to understand the why of serial killers, one has to first accept the existence of the unconscious mind: that things are going on it constantly and that it is capable of controlling behavior. When a child is abused in one way or another by parents, the anger and terror he or she feels is hidden in the unconscious, which becomes like a seething cauldron, and the child starts looking for ways to deal with the terrifying feelings emerging from it. Someone in the family, usually the mother or father, has clearly shown the child that he or she has no value except perhaps as a sex object or someone to hurt. A terrible fear builds up in the child's unconscious that results from feeling constantly under threat, so the child starts to formulate fantasies of being all-powerful, controlling, and able to handle whatever comes his or her way. Then, the child creates symbolic scenarios in which he or she is dominant or acts out, first by showing mastery over animals by abusing them, and sometimes over structures while burning them down. This manifests in adulthood as a powerful sex drive and the abuse of the women or children in the person's life.

Notable Quotable
"I love the sweet, husky, close smell of indoor homicide, the only way I have of reminding myself that I'm still alive."
—Dr. Michael Swango

While all of us are subject to some stress in our childhoods from our parents, the stress we are talking about here is horrendous, and the reaction of the child is equally so. Indeed, this book is full of horrendous things that happened to children who went on to become serial murderers: Ken Bianchi's mother, a prostitute, held his hand over a stove flame to punish him. Edmund Kemper's parents made him kill his pet chicken and forced him to eat it, tears streaming down his face, for dinner.

At some point in serial killers' development—usually when they're in their twenties—the fantasies or the cruelty to animals is no longer enough to satisfy their murderous rages, and their compulsion is satisfied by nothing less than killing people. We believe that serial killers are unconsciously terrified of and furious with people because of their own childhoods, and that they kill to temporarily alleviate that terror.

Notable Quotable
"You feel the last bit of breath leaving their body. You're looking into their eyes. A person in that situation is God!"
—Ted Bundy

As with all murderers, there are more male serial killers than female ones. While it may appear on the surface that some women kill for financial gain—those characterized as "black widows," who benefit from killing family or friends—it's likely that the real reasons they kill are the same as they are for men: to take control, to gain power, and to temporarily conquer the terror inside them. And "temporarily" is a key consideration. At the risk of redundancy, the act of dominance, of killing, must be done over and over again to support the serial killer's delusion that he or she is all-powerful, to reassert superiority.

Strange Trophies

Between killings, some serial killers need something to remind themselves of how powerful they are. Many keep some personal item of the victim as a trophy of the kill, what investigators call "tokenism." This can be a wallet, necklace, driver's license, shoe, or some other object, and the killer handles it when alone to relive the killing and reassert his mastery over his victim. Masturbation usually accompanies tokenism, because it brings the power and satisfaction of the kill back to the murderer.

Some serial killers take body parts as trophies. Jerry Brudos, a serial killer who operated around Salem, Oregon, cut off one victim's feet, mounted them on a base, and kept them on his mantle as a constant reminder of his power. Edmund Kemper took the head of one of his female victims and used it as a masturbatory aid in the shower. Ted Bundy took heads back to his apartment and masturbated on them.

Some serial killers empower themselves by becoming cannibals, as the 1920s killer Albert Fish did with a ten-year-old girl he had abducted. The consumption of human flesh has the same meaning for serial killers as it has for centuries to cannibals in the jungles of South America: As Bellevue psychiatrist George Chase once put it, "they orally incorporate" the powers of the victim via cannibalism, or at least they try to.

And like all insecure people, serial killers are egotists. They want to be known and feted for their achievements as killing machines. And this, as some of the stories in this book will show, sometimes gets them caught.

> ### Notable Quotable
> "I took her bra and panties off and had sex with her. That's one of those things I guess that got to be part of my life . . . having sexual intercourse with the dead."
> —Henry Lee Lucas

The Birth of a Killer

Serial killers, as detailed earlier, do not emerge suddenly—they develop, and there may well be indications that a young person is heading that way. Years ago, psychiatrists established that a serial murderer will have exhibited one or more specific behaviors in childhood: cruelty to animals, setting fires, and wetting the bed. If you know a child who exhibits two of these symptoms, you should consult with a psychiatrist. In particular, cruelty to animals and setting fires are indicative of someone on a power trip: The person lords it over the tortured animals and the houses burned to the ground, and the behavior reassures the person of his or her power.

The Difference between Mass Murder and Serial Murder

Many people confuse mass murder and serial murder, but they are different crimes. In a mass murder, a group of people is killed all at once; serial murder describes the act of killing many people one at a time over a relatively long period of time. An example of mass murder is the March 30, 1975, murders in Hamilton, Ohio, when James Ruppert shot eleven members of his family to death. In contrast, serial murderer John Wayne Gacy killed at least thirty-three young men over a period of six years.

8

Bed-wetting is likely a reaction to the chaotic nature of dreams and is often a symptom of serious abuse—it's maybe the symptom least associated with violence, but coupled with the others, it could indicate mental instability.

Team Killers

While the most common type of serial killer is the person who operates individually, there are also killers who act together as a team. In this instance, one is usually dominant and the other person wants to do anything to please the dominant person. A striking example of this is the Hillside Strangler, who was actually two people: Ken Bianchi, who was trying to please his dominant cousin Angelo Buono Jr. (read more about this killer team in Chapter 13). But while there are two instead of one, they are both sick—although one might be more violent than the other, that does not make the submissive partner innocent or healthy—and just as deadly as any solo killer.

Sociopaths

Unlike regular murderers, serial killers are sociopaths. Sociopaths are missing an essential part of what makes a person human: the ability to empathize with the pain and suffering of others. The confession of the self-styled BTK Killer, Dennis Rader, tellingly demonstrates the mind of a sociopath. While he stood in front of a judge describing the most wrenching acts imaginable, it was clear that he cared as much about the lives he took as someone might care about a discarded napkin. No one showed sociopaths how to love or care for others when they were young.

Q&A

Q. Do serial killers kill only members of their own race?

A. The victims of a serial killer do generally belong to the same race as the killer, but not always.

9

Q. Who was America's first serial killer?

A. H. H. Holmes has been said to be the first serial killer in American history—he confessed to the murders of 27 people in his Chicago hotel during the 1893 World's Fair.

Q. How many victims must a murderer have before he is considered a serial killer?

A. At least three, according to the FBI (most serial killers reach that benchmark with ease).

Q. How many serial murderers are out there?

A. There have been conflicting reports as to the extent of serial murder, but according to the FBI, there may be roughly seventy to one hundred serial killers operating at any given time.

Q. From what profession do the most serial murderers come?

A. The medical profession has produced the most serial killers—primarily doctors but nurses closely follow.

Q. Who is the most famous serial killer of all time?

A. Hands down, Jack the Ripper. This infamous killer slaughtered five prostitutes in the Whitechapel district of London, starting on August 31, 1888, and was never apprehended. To this day—though there are many theories—no one knows his true identity.

One of Jack the Ripper's prostitute victims.

The San Quentin Bridge Club

In the late 1980s, California's San Quentin State Prison was home to four serial killers: William Bonin, Lawrence Bittaker, Randy Kraft, and Douglas Clark. The combined number of victims whom these men brutally tortured and murdered is staggering, yet every day they would sit together and play bridge, just like your grandma did with her neighborhood friends. In 1990 *Vanity Fair* magazine published an article on the men and called them the San Quentin Bridge Club.

The club broke up when William Bonin was executed. Before his execution, Bonin ate a very hearty last meal: two sausage-and-pepperoni pizzas, three dishes of coffee ice cream, and fifteen cans of Coke! It's a wonder he didn't die of gastroenteritis.

Part II

American Serial Killers

In the past forty years or so, serial killers have come into American consciousness in a very big way. Serial killers have been around for all of recorded history, and have been active all over the world, but it could be argued that they've never been more prominent than they are now as part of U.S. pop culture. The following chapters present the stories of some of the most infamous serial killers in America.

Chapter 2
Albert Fish

Notable Quotable

"It took me nine days to eat her entire body. I did not fuck her tho I could of had I wished. She died a virgin."

—Albert Fish, writing to his ten-year-old victim's mother

The infamy of some serial murderers is such that they deserve star treatment in terms of their stories. And if there is a superstar among serial murderers, it is Albert Fish—and if there is a superstar among detectives pursuing serial killers, Will King of the New York Police Department is near the top of the list. His pursuit of Fish is the stuff of legends.

Albert Fish as a young man.

On May 27, 1928, an ad appeared in the Saturday afternoon edition of the *New York World Telegram*:

Young man, 18, wishes position in country. Edward Budd, 406 West 15th Street.

Albert and Delia Budd had placed the ad for the oldest of their five children, Edward. The family lived in a tiny basement apartment, and the idea was that Edward could get a job and help support them. The next afternoon, there was a knock on the door and Delia Budd, who was home alone, answered it.

Framed in the doorway was a small man, maybe 5'5" and 130 pounds. He was very well dressed in a three-piece navy blue suit, blue shirt, black felt hat, and polished black brogues. He had white hair, watery blue eyes, and Delia guessed he was in his sixties. In summary, he looked like a well-to-do gentleman.

Later, Delia Budd would say that the only thing that tarnished the image of the man was his teeth. They were missing, broken, and discolored. They vaguely reminded Delia of an animal's teeth.

He identified himself as Frank Howard and said that he was a farmer and had seen Edward's ad, and that he wanted to talk with him about working on his farm. Delia was excited by the prospect and invited him in. When young Edward came in a short while later, he too expressed interest in working for the well-dressed elderly man. Howard explained to the Budds that he owned a farm in Farmingdale, Long Island, and that business had recently picked up to the point that he needed to hire someone to help. He was willing to pay $15 per week, a large sum at the time.

The Budds were very impressed with Howard, particularly his obvious wealth. At one point in the conversation, he pulled out a roll of greenbacks that would have choked the proverbial horse. For a family who lived on the fiscal edge, it was an awe-inspiring display.

Howard offered Edward the job, and Edward enthusiastically asked him whether he might have an additional position on the farm for his friend Willie Korman. Mr. Howard said yes. He promised to return the following Saturday and pick them both up. On the following Saturday, the Budds waited patiently for Howard to pick up Edward and his friend Willie, but Howard didn't show. That night, they received a telegram from Howard, saying he had unexpectedly had to go to New Jersey on business. He promised to be at the Budds' home the next day.

This time Howard showed up at around eleven o'clock in the morning, again dressed to the nines, ready to take the boys to his Long Island farm. But Howard was early, and they were not ready to go. As Howard and the Budds waited in the living room for the boys, ten-year-old Grace Budd came into the room.

She was a thin, sickly sort of child, but today, Sunday, she was looking her best. She had on her white confirmation dress (she had been confirmed in the Catholic Church just three weeks earlier), her soft, dark brown hair was bobbed, and her large blue eyes twinkled. Howard gushed at what a beautiful child she was. Grace took to the old man immediately, walking over and sitting on his lap. And Howard took to her. He engaged her in a game of counting his money. He had $91 on him, an impressive amount, and rewarded her counting ability by giving her a half-dollar for candy. Then Howard had an idea. His niece was having a birthday party at her home at 137th Street and Columbus Avenue. They had a few hours before they needed to leave for the farm. Might it be OK to take Grace to the party?

Delia Budd resisted the idea, but her husband Albert championed it. How often, he said, did Grace get a chance to get away from their cellar apartment? Grace put on a gray coat and left with Howard, who said he would have her back in a few hours.

The Budds accompanied the pair out of the apartment and watched as Grace walked, hand in hand, with Howard as he walked along in his bowlegged, rolling gait toward Ninth Avenue. Later, Delia Budd would admit to having an almost subconscious concern for her daughter as she watched them walk away. But she did nothing. Just before they turned the corner, Grace turned and yelled something, but they could not hear what she said.

If only the Budds had known a simple fact, Grace Budd might have lived. Columbus Avenue ended on 105th Street. The intersection of 137th Street and Columbus did not exist.

Howard did not return with the little girl at the appointed time. The Budds wondered where they could be, and Edward and Willie were anxious to get going to their new jobs. Maybe, the Budds thought, Howard and Grace had been in an accident. Incredibly—and this is something that has never been explained—the Budds did not contact the police about their daughter until the next morning.

At the time of Grace's disappearance the NYPD had recently formed the Missing Persons Bureau, which dispatched two detectives to see the Budds and try to determine what had happened. One of the detectives was Will King. King was a gruff-talking, heavy smoker who believed in order and discipline and whose life was being a cop. He was also gutsy, patriotic, and had that most important attribute of a great detective, determination. Frank Howard would have been better off if Sherlock Holmes and not Will King had come to investigate the case.

Word of what was then regarded as an abduction spread fast, and soon newspapermen of the day were assaulting 406 West Fifteenth Street, swarming all over the Budds for tidbits about Howard and the little girl. Under immense pressure to solve the case, the head of the Missing Persons Bureau assigned fifty detectives to it, forming a task force with King as the head. People of the day said that the only case that rivaled it in intensity was the kidnapping of Charles Lindbergh's baby.

To King, there was little question that Grace Budd was dead. But it riled him that a man could walk in off the street, take a little girl, and never return. King pursued the case with a withering ferocity.

The detectives spread out and talked to hundreds of people. They dusted the entire house for prints, they questioned Western Union at length about the telegram Howard had sent the Budds, they went to Farmingdale to question farm owners. They followed every lead possible, but after a few months they had come up with nothing, and the task force members were reassigned to new cases. It remained an open case, but the police department started to forget about it.

However, Will King did not forget. He handled other cases, but in a mind-boggling display of determination, not a single day went by that he did not pursue one lead or another in the Budd case.

Some of the earliest leads came from ordinary folks. When the case first hit the media, the Budds were deluged with mail both sympathetic and crank, and from time to time they would receive letters that seemed to contain actual leads and would turn them over to the police. Will King doggedly tracked them all down.

Mail leads continued even after the police had stopped actively investigating. King specifically instructed the Budds to turn the mail on Grace over to him unopened, but invariably when he got it, it would be open. His relationship with the Budds became less than cordial—while King understood that they just wanted to find their daughter, the Budds were contaminating evidence.

Weeks turned to months, then to years. Soon it had been more than six years since Grace Budd had disappeared with the kindly old Howard, and not a single day had gone by when Will King had not worked on the case. In fact, his superiors started to worry about him—and their worry proved well founded.

In early 1934, Will King, working night and day on his other cases as well as on the disappearance of Grace Budd, collapsed and was confined to a hospital for three months. Before he was discharged, his doctors warned him about overexerting himself. The police department, concerned for his health, assigned him to a desk job.

But, of course, he did not stop. He pursued every lead, however thin, that turned up, and continued his awe-inspiring pursuit of the kidnapper. Besides the overall frustration of not solving the case, there were also the promising leads that didn't pan out. To King, each lead was a new hope, a new road that could lead him to the kidnapper—and each was a dead end.

Then, on November 2, 1934, Will King got a telephone call from Delia Budd. She had received a letter from someone, and it looked like it was about Grace. Did he want to see it?

He did. Edward Budd brought over the letter—this one unopened—and King carefully opened it and read it. The contents of the letter were later to be read into the court record and would stun and repulse people, but King was excited: It was the handwriting. He did not have to be a graphologist to know that the spidery-inked handwriting in this letter to Delia Budd was written by the same man who had written the telegram to the Budds six years ago, telling them that his arrival would be delayed because of business in New Jersey—Frank Howard.

The letter read, in part:

On Sunday June 3 1928 I called on you at 406 W. 15th St. . . . Grace sat in my lap and kissed me. I made up my mind to eat her: On the pretense of taking her to a party. You said Yes she could go. I took her to an empty house in Westchester I had already picked out. When we got there, I told her to remain outside. She picked wild flowers. I went upstairs and stripped all my clothes off. I knew if I did not I would get blood on them. When all was ready I went to the window and called her. Then I hid in the closet until she was in the room. When she saw me all naked she began to cry and tried to run downstairs. I grabbed her and she said she would tell her mamma. First I stripped her naked. How she did kick-bite and scratch. I choked her to death, then cut her in small pieces so I could take my meat to my rooms, Cook and eat it. How sweet and tender her little ass was roasted in the oven. It took me nine days to eat her entire body. I did not fuck her tho I could of had I wished. She died a virgin.

A Break in the Case

What followed was a masterpiece of detective work on the part of Will King. He noticed that the legal-sized envelope the letter arrived in had an emblem and some initials on it, and that someone had attempted to scratch them out. But by holding the envelope up to the light, he could read them clearly enough: NYPCBA.

A check of the phone book revealed that NYPCBA stood for the New York Private Chauffeur's Benevolent Association, at 627 Lexington Avenue in New York City. King went to the headquarters and explained his business to the president of the association. The president was concerned that King suspected one of his members, but King reassured him that he just wanted to check handwriting samples.

Working more than seven hours, until past midnight, King checked the handwriting samples on applications for membership in the NYPCBA. None was close to the handwriting of Frank Howard. King tried another tactic. A few days after reviewing the applications, he spoke in front of the seventy-five-member group and asked whether anyone had used any of the NYPCBA envelopes or had taken any for personal use. He made it clear that no one would get in trouble if they had, but he was vague about why he wanted to know.

After his speech, he waited in the president's office until a small, red-haired man named Leo Sicoski came in. After being reassured by King that there would be no punishment, Sicoski admitted that he had taken some of the envelopes and used them while he lived at a rooming house at 622 Lexington Avenue. He said he might have left some around.

King immediately shot to the rooming house, where he was disappointed yet again—no one had rented Sicoski's room since he had left it. It was boarded up tightly, and a canvas of the neighborhood proved fruitless: No one knew anyone who looked like Frank Howard.

Stymied, King went back to Sicoski to find out whether he remembered anything else. Sicoski said that, before 622 Lexington Avenue, he had lived at 200 East Fifty-second Street. He had left some NYPCBA envelopes there on a shelf behind a bed. King hurried over there. It was a flophouse, and this time he found something.

He spoke with the landlady and asked her whether she knew anyone who looked like Howard. She did—and said it sounded like Albert Fish, who was staying in No. 7. King looked at his signature on the register. Albert Fish and Frank Howard were the same man! King asked where Fish was. The woman didn't know, but she said he periodically returned to the flophouse to pick up a check from the Civilian Conservation Corps sent by his son, John.

King checked it all out, and then he set up a stakeout, taking a room at the top of the stairs that gave him a view of the intersection at Fifty-second Street and Third Avenue. He smoked, he exercised, and he ate canned food. He stayed awake for more than twenty hours a day. Fish did not show.

On December 12, 1934, King decided to take a break from his routine and went Christmas shopping. He was away for two hours, and as soon as he returned to his room there was a rapid-fire knocking on the door. It was the landlady. Excitedly, she told him that Fish was back: He had come by a half hour ago, and she had told him his check wasn't in (it was). He was waiting, but she didn't know how long he would stay.

King strapped on his .38 and went to Fish's room. He knocked. The person inside invited him to come in. Inside, sitting on the bed, was a man who perfectly fit the description of Frank Howard: a little white-haired, baggy-eyed man with watery blue eyes. King identified himself as a policeman and told Fish that he wanted to talk to him about some letters he had written, and that Fish needed to accompany him to headquarters. Fish agreed mildly.

King brought him downstairs and then, just as they were about to exit the building, Fish whirled, straight razors in both

Albert Fish in the custody of Will King.

hands. King quickly subdued and shackled him; he had gotten a glimpse of the real Albert Fish. At the police station, for whatever reason, Fish started to speak. He expounded on the horrendous letter for the detectives. He said that after he killed Grace, he positioned her neck on a one-gallon paint pail and cut her head off, letting her blood drip into the pail. He tried to drink the warm blood but vomited. Then he used a knife and a cleaver to cut her in half at the navel, and proceeded to cut her into pieces. He planned on eating all of her except her head, guts, and skeleton.

And it was all true. Later, at his trial, he admitted that as he ate Grace Budd over the nine days specified in the letter he was in a state of continual sexual excitement, and the memory of eating her during the day led him to masturbate at night.

Ultimately, Fish led the police to the house where Grace's murder had occurred, the abandoned Wisteria Cottage (as the locals called it) in Greenburgh, New York. He showed detectives where he had buried the parts he didn't eat, and they used pickaxes and shovels to break through the frozen ground until they found Grace's head and various bones.

There was some jurisdictional dispute, but Fish was eventually tried for the murder of Grace Budd in White Plains, New York, and after a nine-day trial in March 1934 he was convicted of her abduction and murder and sentenced to death in the electric chair. He described his upcoming death as the "supreme thrill" of his life; apparently, for a sadomasochistic psychopath, the thought of being electrocuted is quite enticing.

The trial produced some interesting background on Albert Fish—he had some quaint habits. He engaged in coprophagy (he ate human waste), and he liked to stick needles into himself. Indeed, on one occasion he tried to stick needles into his testicles but had to stop. It was too painful, he said. However, when doctors took X rays of Fish at Sing Sing Correctional Facility, they found numerous long pins that had been driven into his abdomen in a kind of gruesome acupuncture. Technically, doing such a thing is known as a Piquer act: jabbing sharp objects into yourself or others for sexual gratification.

On the day Fish was to be electrocuted, January 16, 1936, three of his six children visited him. Less than a year after his trial, Albert Fish had his last meal at eleven o'clock at night. His children were there when the switch was thrown; it was said that it took two full jolts to kill him because of all the needles and pins he had stuck into his body.

'X' marks the spot where Fish murdered Grace Budd.

Will King knew that Fish, who had roamed the country as an itinerant house painter, had killed other children; in fact, a number of children had disappeared from neighborhoods where Fish had been working. However, he never officially confessed to any killings except the murder of Grace Budd, which was plenty enough to send him to his death.

The Boy Behind the Monster

Albert Fish was pretty much doomed to a life of crime and sadism from the start. He was born on May 19, 1870, in Washington, D.C. When Fish was five years old, his seventy-five-year-old father died in New York's old Penn Station, leaving only his mother (who, in a striking age difference from

her husband, was just in her early forties) to take care of little Albert. She could hardly afford to support herself, so she had no choice but to place Albert in St. John's Orphanage in Washington, D.C.

When Fish was nine years old, his mother was a little more stable and able to take care of him, so she took him back. However, the orphanage had been a training ground for Fish in the perverse, sexually

The skull of Grace Budd, found outside the abandoned cottage where she was killed.

and in every other way. And, of course, because of his psychological makeup, Fish was ready to use what he had learned.

A Long List

In his book *Deranged*, the author Harold Schecter lists the peculiar obsessions of Albert Fish. There are fifteen of them, including *undinism*, a sexual preoccupation with one's own urine. The only thing that seems to be missing from Fish's list is bestiality.

Chapter 3
Bobby Joe Long

Notable Fact

Bobby Joe would have sex with his wife two or three times a day—and masturbate an additional five or six times a day.

The sexual drive of Bobby Joe Long can be described in one word: unbelievable. But for a number of women in Florida, it became all too believable—and deadly. Bobby Joe Long believes that his troubles began in 1974, when he was involved in a very nasty motorcycle accident. He was speeding down a street in Tampa, Florida, when a car suddenly appeared in front of him. He slammed on the brakes, but it didn't help. He was thrown into the car hard enough to crack his helmet. From then on, Bobby Joe says, strange things happened to his sex drive. He started to think about sex all the time—and to do it all the time, becoming almost satyrlike.

Before the accident occurred, he would have sex with his slim, pretty wife, Cindy Jean, two or three times a week. After the accident they would have sex two or three times a day, and Bobby Joe masturbated an additional five or six times. (This kind of sex drive is reminiscent of that of another murderer, Albert DeSalvo—who claimed to be the Boston Strangler—who used to have sex with his wife more than thirty times a week.)

Soon enough, sex with his wife was not enough for Bobby Joe; he wanted other women as well. Starting in 1980, Bobby Joe started to look at the want ads in the Miami and Ocala areas in Florida. He would find ads for furniture or televisions for sale, and then, during the day—always during the day, when it was less likely that a man would be home—Bobby Joe would go to the home, ostensibly to look at the item for sale. Once he was inside and sure that no one else was there, he would tie and gag the woman, then rape her.

Long did this more than fifty times between 1980 and 1983, and he became known in the area as the Want-Ad Rapist. Local task forces and the FBI went after him, but he eluded capture. As the rapes continued, he felt a rising sense of anger. He started to feel anger as never before. The slightest thing triggered a towering rage, which he would act out in bizarre ways.

Once, for example, his mother Louella was visiting and said something that displeased Bobby Joe. He grabbed her and spanked her like a child, an absurd, painful, and humiliating event for her. Noise also started to bother Long. The slightest noise would set off an explosive reaction.

Whatever was cooking inside him, in 1983, Long converted from rapist to killer—and then to serial killer. His first victim was a Vietnamese woman named Ngeon Thi Long. He somehow lured her into his car, then tied her up, took her to an isolated spot, raped and killed her, and dumped her body on the side of the road.

Prosecutor Mike Bonito would later say that Long set up his car to particularly serve his murderous ends. The passenger seat could be pushed back flat. He would have the victim sit in the seat, tie her up, and then push her back so her head would be lower than the back window. With his free hand he would molest her as they drove, then he would rape and strangle her at their destination.

Almost any woman was fair game for Long, but he particularly liked prowling the strip joints, bars, and assorted dives along Nebraska Avenue in North Tampa to look for victims. However, there was one thing that all of his victims shared: They had to come to him, pick him up, or otherwise approach him. This was the way he rationalized killing them—if they picked him up, he considered them as manipulative, detestable whores, people who should be killed.

Bobby Joe Long

Loss of Desire

With eight victims behind him, something strange happened to Long. Following his usual pattern, he picked up a big, sexy woman named Kim Sann in North Tampa. As soon as she was in the car, he started to assault her. But Sann was a fighter, and she fought back—and screamed. There followed a series of skirmishes inside the car during which he managed to choke her into unconsciousness, only for her to awaken and scream and fight.

Finally he strangled her to death, and it was then that he discovered the curious thing: He had no energy to violate her sexually. To some degree, his frantic sexual energy had dissipated.

But an encounter two days before the one with Kim Sann was even stranger. On the prowl, he picked up a seventeen-year-old girl—and didn't kill her. The girl couldn't know it, but the reason, in Long's mind, was that she was not a whore, not a manipulator of men. Rather, she was homeless, rejected by her own family. Not that this kept him away from her sexually. He took her to his own apartment and raped her, but he did not kill her. Rather, he was with her for more than twenty-four hours and then simply dropped her off where he had picked her up.

The really strange thing about this abduction was that he gave the girl the opportunity, though he kept her blindfolded throughout the rape and for much of her ordeal, to see him at various points, to glimpse his apartment, to see him at an automated teller machine. He knew he was putting himself in jeopardy but did nothing to stop it.

In fact, because of leads that the girl provided, the police tracked down Bobby Joe Long and arrested him for murder. He said later that his capture did not surprise him, that he wanted to be caught and knew he would be. As time had gone by, he had gained more and more a sense of revulsion—though not remorse—at what he was doing.

Less than a year after he was arrested, Long was tried on multiple homicide charges. There was a mound of evidence against him, including the testimony of the girl he had raped and held at his apartment. His defense counsel tried mightily to establish

Growing Breasts

On top of the various emotional burdens that Bobby Joe Long had to carry, he suffered, like some other members of his family, from a disorder of the endocrine system that had a devastating side effect. When he was about twelve, he began to develop breasts. He was terrified that he was becoming a woman. This certainly would have a traumatic effect on a twelve-year-old boy, particularly one who already must have had severe doubts about his sense of worth and self. Eventually he had to have an operation and doctors removed several pounds of tissue from his breasts.

a medical reason for his actions: Medical experts presented evidence that the motorcycle accident had caused trauma to his brain and that his injuries were the precipitating factor in his assaults on women. Before the brain injuries, his counsel argued, there had been no offenses. After, there had been the fifty-plus rapes of the Want-Ad Rapist and nine homicides.

There was no question he had brain damage. Brain tests showed it, and he also had physical symptoms: His face felt dead on one side and he walked with a limp. But the defense counsel did not effectively establish a connection between his injuries and his actions, or maybe the jury just didn't think it reason enough for his crimes. They found him guilty, and in early 1985, he was sentenced to death in the electric chair. He is still—after all these years—on death row in Florida.

An Only Child

Although the defense couldn't prove that Long's head injury had caused his crimes, there were some things in his childhood that likely contributed to how he turned out.

Bobby Joe Long was an only child raised by his mother, an attractive woman who was a waitress who lived on the edge of poverty after divorcing her husband. Until he was twelve, Long and his mother shared the same bed in a series of hotel rooms she rented. As reported in *Serial Killers: The Growing Menace*, by Joel Norris, she said, "We just didn't have the money for two bedrooms." However, she also said that she never undressed in front of him or in other ways acted improperly.

When she got finished with her waitressing jobs, she would go out on dates rather than stay home with her son, whom she had neighbors watch. Bobby Joe apparently went into rages over his mother's lack of concern or caring for him. Her work and dating schedule also angered him in terms of the times she would come home: five or six in the morning, when Bobby Joe would be getting ready for school. They spent almost no time together.

As mentioned earlier, when Long was twelve, he stopped sleeping with his mother. But whatever damage there was had already been done. Perhaps sleeping with a grown woman diminished the young boy. Indeed, in studies conducted with serial killers, psychiatrists have found that the most savage are those who feel sexually diminished by women. Feelings of shame also might have been a factor. Such feelings coupled with the terror and rage he felt over his mother neglecting him may have made for a murderous combination.

Chapter 4
Ted Bundy

Notable Quotable

"You feel the last bit of breath leaving their body. You're looking into their eyes. A person in that situation is God!"

—Ted Bundy, on the joy of murder

The old joke goes:

Q: What's the leading cause of death in Florida?
A: The electric chair.

The state of Florida has no problem at all letting bad guys ride the lightning. And it may well be that Ted Bundy, one of the most infamous serial murderers of this century, wanted to ride it—at least subconsciously. Consider this 1976 conversation Bundy had with his lawyer while in jail in Aspen, Colorado, on multiple murder charges, as reported in *Bundy: The Deliberate Stranger*, by Richard W. Larsen:

"What's going on with executions now?" Ted asked. "Where are most people likely to be executed now?" "I suppose it might be Georgia. . . . No," Bundy's lawyer corrected himself. "It'd probably be Florida now." "Florida?" repeated Bundy.

> The lawyer said the constitutionality of Florida's death penalty had recently been upheld by the U.S. Supreme Court.
>
> "Florida," murmured Bundy, "Florida. Hmmm."

It makes you wonder, then, why, knowing this, Ted Bundy would travel all the way across the country from Colorado to Florida to kill somebody. Why not one of the other forty-nine states, where he was less likely to be executed?

Although we may not understand his motives, one thing is for sure: Ted Bundy ranks as one of the most malevolent serial murderers of the twentieth century, mainly because he was a con man supreme. If you were pretty girl who had long, dark hair parted in the middle and you met Ted Bundy, you were in deep trouble.

Looks That Could Kill

Bundy was a trim man about six feet tall with wavy brown hair, penetrating eyes, and even features, born in November 1946. He was handsome and articulate. Bundy graduated from the University of Washington, went partway through law school, and was active in both politics and community activities in Seattle, where he was raised—he even worked for the governor, Dan Evans. Ironically, he was one of the volunteers on Seattle's crisis hotline, counseling people who were contemplating suicide or had other problems.

It was hard to imagine that behind this polished exterior lurked a monster. Indeed, Ann Rule, one of the top true-crime writers in America, had befriended Bundy at the crisis hotline and never suspected that it was he who was responsible for the host of women being killed or disappearing in Washington and, later, all across the Pacific Northwest. (Ann

Rule went on to write a riveting book about Bundy called *The Stranger Beside Me*.)

The serial killer in the motion picture *The Silence of the Lambs*, who lures a woman into his van by pretending his hand is broken and that he needs help carrying a piece of furniture, portrays a good example of Bundy's cleverness. Bundy did that at least twice in one day in Lake Sammamish State Park in Washington. He approached one woman in the morning and one in the afternoon, and asked each for her help loading his boat on to his Volkswagen bug. The women went with him, and that was the last anyone saw them alive.

He tried it on other women, too, some who, fortunately, did not fall into the trap. One woman in Tallahassee, Florida, told a local newspaper about coming out of the Florida State University library one night and encountering a scruffy-looking man whose arms were loaded with books. He seemed to be in obvious pain and was struggling to carry his books with one arm. The woman offered to help him carry them, and she walked along with him in the darkness.

But there was something about him that turned her off, and by the time they arrived at his car—a VW with the rear seat missing—she was scared. When he asked her to get in, then ordered her, she ran away—an action that undoubtedly saved her life.

There is no way to tell just how many women Bundy killed—bones buried in some godforsaken woods don't talk—but police conservatively estimate at least forty. Invariably, as mentioned earlier, Bundy's victims were pretty, with dark hair that was parted in the middle. Most of the killings occurred in the Pacific Northwest, but three occurred in Florida, and two of those in the Chi Omega sorority house at Florida State University.

A few of Bundy's many female victims.

The Great Escape

Bundy was ensconced in jail in Aspen, Colorado, while a number of murders in the state were being investigated. In December, against the advice of his attorney, Bundy filed a motion with the judge for a change of venue—mysteriously, because his lawyer advised him that Aspen was one of the most liberal towns in the state and that he was likely to get a lighter sentence there. The judge obliged Bundy and moved the trial to Colorado Springs.

Too late, Bundy realized that his trial would be held in probably the most conservative, law-enforcement-conscious city in all of Colorado, a place in which four of the five murderers on the state's death row had been tried.

Bundy realized that he had to break out of prison to avoid being tried and sentenced in Colorado Springs. He plotted various means of escape before discovering a metal plate directly above the ceiling light fixture in his cell that had been improperly welded and was loose. By prying and probing, he was able to push it off, leaving an opening of about one square foot. Bundy had been dieting to lose weight in preparation for escape, and he was down to a very lean 150 pounds. He realized that he could wriggle through the hole into the area above.

The jail was a one-story building with a low attic, and crucially, the attic was connected to other rooms. A few times Bundy stealthily crawled up into the ceiling to explore, and he finally found an escape route—he could break through a plasterboard ceiling into a closet in the jailer's house. One night when the jailer and his wife went to the movies, Bundy dropped down and made his escape. He was not discovered missing until noon the following day, when jailers went in to wake Bundy and discovered that he had bulked up books and other objects under his blanket to make it appear that he was sleeping there. In the meantime, Bundy was busy stealing cars and taking public transportation across the country until he arrived in Florida.

Bundy the Lothario

From the television writer Tom Towler:

Bundy, of course, portrayed himself as a Lothario who could attract women at will. In fact, he always used a ruse to get them to his VW, a fake cast on his arm, a crutch, etc. He'd removed the back seat from the VW and hidden a tire iron by the rear wheel. He'd knock them out with the tire iron, load them into the car, then take them to a wooded location of his choosing where he killed them and then had sex with them. He, like the Green River killer, returned often to his victims for sex and to watch them change colors.

Murders in Florida

Bundy had always liked college campuses, so when he got to Tallahassee, Florida, after escaping from jail, he took a room—he had about $700 in cash on him—on West College Street in a big rooming house called the Oak. The Oak housed a number of people who went to Florida State University and was about a block and a half away from the campus. Using the name Chris Hagen, Bundy started to hang around the campus and join in the activities. On the night he began to kill in Florida, he went to a local bar frequented by students, and at least one girl there had a very close brush with death. He danced with her and then asked her if she wanted to take a ride. She almost did but demurred because of a certain look in his eyes that she didn't like. Her life had been saved because she caught a glimpse of a madman.

The author Richard W. Larsen has aptly described Bundy's visit to the Chi Omega sorority house as a day on which a "tornado of violence touched down." The sorority house, a small brick apartment building, had an entrance on West College Street and another on the side. One of the sorority sisters, a pretty strawberry blonde named Nita Neary, was returning to the house with a date a little after three in the morning after an uncharacteristically cold night for north-central Florida. She came in through the side door, which she opened by dialing a combination lock.

She walked inside quietly and heard a loud thump from upstairs, and then the sound of someone running. Then she heard someone racing down the stairs and caught a glimpse of a person moving quickly across the foyer toward the front door. He was wearing a dark cap, a dark coat, and in one of his hands he was carrying a club of some sort or a rough, thick piece of lumber.

Neary went upstairs to her room and woke up her roommate, Nancy Dowdy, and told her to get up, that something strange was going on. Together they woke up the president of the sorority, Jackie McGill, and they were standing in the hall when the first victim of the night found them.

Bloody Result

Sorority sister Karen Chandler staggered out of one of the rooms, and the girls were taken aback—Karen's head was

38

soaked with blood. They rushed to her aid, and then went into her room and found her roommate, Kathy Kleiner, sitting on the edge of her bed in a daze, her head also soaked with blood.

Someone called the police, and they were there in minutes. A description of the man with the club went out over the police airwaves. The officers started to check the other rooms, one of which belonged to Lisa Levy. They entered the darkened room and called for Lisa to wake up, but she didn't respond, and when they turned on the lights, they saw blood all around the woman. Levy was lying prone on the bed, covered with a sheet. An officer pulled the sheet back and saw that her buttocks were bloody, and when he rolled her over, he saw that she was already cyanotic—her lips purple and her eyes covered with the grayish film of death.

In the hall someone was screaming that she hadn't seen another of the sorority sisters, Margaret Bowman. Where was she? With trepidation, one of the officers opened the door to her room and turned on the light. It was as if someone had hosed the place with blood. The bed was covered with blood and the walls spattered with it, as was the victim, Margaret Bowman. As he got close, the officer saw something that made him gasp: A ligature had been pulled around Margaret's throat with such ferocity that it looked as if she had been decapitated.

Kathy Kleiner and Karen Chandler were taken to an area hospital. They survived, but with physical and psychological wounds that would last all their lives. Lisa Levy and Margaret Bowman were dead.

An hour and a half after the assault on Chi Omega, Bundy struck again, six blocks from the first scene, at 431 Dunwoody Street. One young woman was awakened from her sleep by a rhythmic pounding noise, which she quickly realized was coming through the wall of the adjoining apartment, whose single occupant was Cheryl Thomas. She awoke her roommate and they heard Cheryl, a pretty dance major from Richmond, crying and moaning.

One of the women called Cheryl's number, and when the phone started to ring they heard the sound of someone running away, banging into things. Bundy was frightened off. The girls next called the police, and medics who had recently worked on the sorority sisters now had to minister to the savagely beaten Cheryl Thomas.

This time the police found the weapon—a length of a two-by-three near the bed. They also found a large semen stain on Cheryl's pillow. As they would learn later—and this says much about Ted Bundy's mind—he had been rhythmically beating her on the head with the club while masturbating with his free hand.

The police issued an all points bulletin, and it was one officer's alertness that snared Ted Bundy. On February 15, 1978, Officer David Lee was on car patrol, tooling down Cervantes Street in Pensacola, when he noticed a yellow VW bug idling in an alley behind a restaurant. It was late and the restaurant was closed; it seemed suspicious that someone was there. Lee went past it but watched the car in his rearview mirror. It pulled out of the alley and headed in the opposite direction.

Lee turned around and followed the car; as he went, he radioed in the car's license plate number. It came back as stolen, and Lee started going after the car, which sped up and began a series of evasive maneuvers. Finally the car stopped. Lee drew his gun and approached the car cautiously.

Ted Bundy reacted with characteristic slickness, wondering aloud why he had been stopped. Lee ignored Bundy's protests, took him out of the car, and had one cuff on him when Bundy suddenly assaulted Lee and tried to escape. Lee quickly subdued him, and Bundy was brought into the station.

Because Bundy had false identification on him, it was a while before the Tallahassee police realized they had hooked as large a fish as anyone could imagine.

The Trial

Bundy's trial was a circus. It was televised, and Bundy represented himself. The consensus was that he did a bad job, though not a lot of lawyers could effectively fight the amount of evidence the prosecution had against him. For one thing, they had an eyewitness who could place Bundy at the scene: Nita Neary, the woman returning to the sorority house from a date. And then there was the forensics evidence, the centerpiece of which was expert testimony from a forensic dentist. He was able to testify—using huge close-ups of Bundy's teeth—that bite marks found on Lisa Levy's buttocks had been made by the teeth of Ted Bundy.

In July 1979, Bundy was found guilty of the murders of Lisa Levy and Margaret Bowman and the assaults

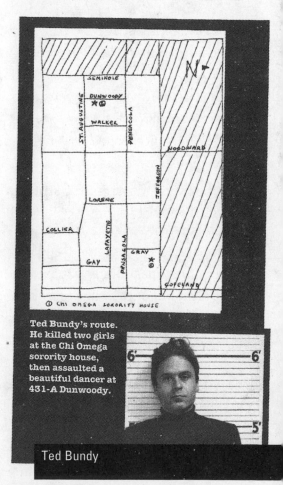

Ted Bundy's route. He killed two girls at the Chi Omega sorority house, then assaulted a beautiful dancer at 431-A Dunwoody.

Ted Bundy

Close Call

From television writer Tom Towler:

The detective who got [Bundy] to confess, Bob Keppel, got a letter one day from the [Florida] state slam. It was from Bundy, who offered his services in finding who he called "The Riverman," who was eventually known by the name Green River Killer. In the letter, Bundy told Keppel that he was incarcerated with some serial killers and so knew a bit about them.

Keppel, by the by, was put on the Seattle area Bundy murders as a young cop. Just before he got to Bundy's file, Bundy left for Utah to go to law school and the murders stopped.

on the other women. For the assaults, he received sentences totaling 270 years. For the murders, Judge Edward Cowart invited him to ride the lightning.

Birth of a Monster

How did Bundy get to be the way he was? There are only hints. His mother Louise had him out of wedlock in November of 1946 at a home for unwed mothers in Vermont, and for a time Louise and Ted lived with his maternal grandfather in Philadelphia. This grandfather was purportedly a strict and forbidding figure and—it is alleged—was Bundy's blood father. In 1951, when he was nine years old, Louise moved with Ted to Tacoma, Washington, and married a man named John Bundy. It's difficult, though, to track exactly what forces drove Bundy to the point in life where he loathed women with dark hair parted in the middle to such an extent.

Notable Quotable
"Sometimes I feel like a vampire."
—Ted Bundy

42

Afterword

Ted Bundy, still his own lawyer, was granted a number of last-minute stays of execution, but on January 25, 1989, he went to his death in the electric chair. (A reporter told one of the authors of this book that Bundy had once come very close to getting murdered himself before his trial. The father of one of his victims, twelve-year-old Kimberly Smith, spotted Bundy being transported in a police car and, for a millisecond, contemplated driving his car into the police car to kill Bundy—but he was able to control himself).

Bundy maintained his innocence until the end of his life, but of course he wasn't innocent. The authors Steve Michaud and Hugh Aynesworth provided plenty of circumstantial proof: They interviewed

Hope You Don't Meet Someone Like Me!

From television writer Tom Towler: "I spent a couple of days with a professor in [Florida]—an anti-death-penalty advocate—who became friends with Bundy and got the last words Bundy wrote (he also was responsible for Bundy's 'wife' getting pregnant while Bundy was in the [Florida] slam). Bundy closed his last letter to the prof[essor] with, 'Be careful. There are a lot of crazies out there. Peace, ted' (small t on his name was the way he signed it).

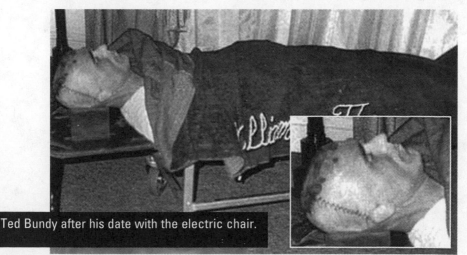

Ted Bundy after his date with the electric chair.

Bundy hundreds of times over four years, compiled hundreds of tapes, and published the book *The Only Living Witness*. Bundy talked freely with the authors about the murders but in the third person, distancing himself from the crimes and never admitting anything directly to them. However, of all the books written about Ted Bundy, none is as horrendous as theirs—Bundy brings the readers into the scenes as he killed his witnesses.

Getting Ready to Ride the Lightning

In his final jailhouse interview with the psychologist James Dobson, Ted Bundy was agonizing over how his addiction to hardcore pornography had ruined his life and how much it had contributed to his violent sexual urges. Midway into the conversation, the prison lights dimmed. Bundy reassured Dobson that the lights would be back on momentarily. Bundy knew the reason that the lights had dimmed. They were testing the electric chair that he would be sitting in at seven-fifteen the next morning.

Chapter 5
Dean Corll

Notable Fact

In preparation for what was to happen to the boy, Corll would always place a sheet of plastic under the plywood to catch the excreta, blood, and vomit that would invariably be discharged from the victim while Corll had his fun.

On August 8, 1973, the police received a call from a young man who requested that they come to a house in Pasadena, a suburb of Houston, Texas. As John Godwin reports in *Murder U.S.A.: The Ways We Kill Each Other*, the caller, in a voice that was young and slurred, said: "Listen, yah better come over. Ah killed a guy here." He identified himself as Wayne Henley and said that the address was 2020 Lamar Drive.

A patrol car responded, and on the street outside the ordinary-looking, white, ranch-style house, they found two teenage boys and a teenage girl who were obviously high on drugs. Henley identified himself as the one who called, and then led them inside.

The few rooms were sparsely furnished and had a heavy, sickening smell. On the floor of the bedroom the cops found the corpse of a tall, pudgy man with sideburns that Henley said was Dean Corll. Henley said that he had shot him in self-defense—six times—because he had feared for his life and the lives of his friends.

Henley laid out the whole story for the stunned cops. It seems that Henley had met Corll about two years earlier, and Corll had given him money, food, a place to stay, marijuana, and plenty of other drugs. All Henley had to do was troll the streets of Houston for young boys and reel them in for Corll. Corll would then rape them, but also, Henley came to learn, sometimes torture and kill them, too. Then Henley explained exactly how he usually found the victims and exactly what Corll did to them.

Henley and another boy, David Owen Brooks, would cruise the streets, and when they found a likely candidate for "partying" they would invite him to get in the car. They would proceed to Corll's house, introduce the boy to Corll, and then start to party. The boy would be encouraged to drink, smoke marijuana, and sniff acrylic paint that Corll stole from his job as a relay tester at the Houston Lighting and Power Company. Eventually the boy would pass out, and more than occasionally when he awoke he would be spread-eagled and pinned to a sheet of plywood, his hands and feet restrained by nylon cord and handcuffs.

In preparation for what was to happen to the boy, Corll would always place a sheet of plastic under the plywood to catch the excreta, blood, and vomit that would invariably discharge from the victim while Corll had his fun. Corll would use knives and other implements to work his victims over, sometimes castrating them. He would crank up the radio full blast while working on someone so that his screams could not be heard.

"What followed then," Godwin says in *Murder U.S.A.*, "lasted ten minutes to half a day, depending on Corll's mood and spare time. In conclusion he usually shot or strangled the boy, sometimes with the help of his young assistants." It was this same fate that Henley feared when he shot Corll, Henley explained.

While he'd lived off Corll, Henley had another life, complete with a fifteen-year-old girlfriend named Rhonda Williams, and he lived at home. His family thought of him as a normal wild kid, his only vice being the propensity to drink too much beer. In the early morning hours of August 8, Henley, his girl-friend Williams, and a male friend named Kerley showed up at Corll's house, and this precipitated real problems.

Corll was enraged at Henley for bringing a female into his male den, but after a while he relaxed, and the four of them started to drink, smoke, and sniff acrylic paint. Eventually everyone seemed to pass out, but then Henley gained consciousness and adrenaline snapped him totally awake. Dean Corll was just finishing handcuffing Henley to the plywood sheet; the other two people had already been immobilized, and Corll was muttering angrily that he was going to kill them all.

Henley spoke rapidly, and he spoke for his life. He told Corll not to do it, and that if Corll would release him, he would kill Williams and Kerley. This appealed to Corll.

"OK," said Corll. "I'll take the guy and you take the chick."

Corll released Henley, who immediately grabbed Corll's .22 caliber pistol and shot Corll six times. Then he called the police.

When the police asked Henley how many people Corll had killed, his answer floored them: "Thirty, I think."

The police asked Henley whether he knew where the bod-ies were, and Henley said he thought they were under the floor of a rented boat shack at Southeast Boat Storage, which was about ten miles south of the city proper near the power company. Henley led detectives and four convicts—who were to do the digging—to the shack, one of a number of metal storage units about thirty-four feet long and deep enough to handle large boats. The floor was earthen, and Henley said that after Corll buried the bodies there he poured crushed limestone over them to destroy them.

The trek to the boat shack had attracted the attention of the media, and they arrived in force: newspaper reporters, magazine writers, and television reporters, complete with their equipment. It was a media circus.

The digging began, and it wasn't long before things started to show up: a random sneaker, a watch, some money. Then the first body was unearthed. It was the decayed remains of a young man in a plastic bag, accompanied by a stomach-wrenching odor.

Then another body was unearthed, and another. The convicts dug down, sweat pouring off them in the hot, muggy weather. Another body, and another. Each was a young man in a plastic bag, but the lime had also done its work. The diggers started to come across body parts—feet, hands, legs, bones— human remains in a boggy mess.

The smell was atrocious and so was the sheer horror of what the convicts were uncovering, body after body after body. Then one convict could not go on: He simply started to weep, his psychological defenses broken down, and then another had to stop because he could not stop retching. It was all too much.

At around ten or eleven in the evening, some burly detectives took over, with the scene illuminated by high-wattage lights secured to fire trucks that had parked at the scene. More bodies were found, and then more after that. All one detective could say—and it seems to sum it all up so perfectly—was "Christ . . . Jesus Christ."

Dean Corll

There was one particular horror. One of the detectives at the scene had a nephew who had been missing. The boy was the tenth body to be unearthed.

After a while, close to vomiting, the detectives donned gas masks, but soon afterward they stopped. They were exhausted, disgusted, and traumatized by the digging. "It's worse," said one of them, "a lot worse than a plane crash."

When they were formally finished, they had not uncovered the thirty bodies Henley spoke about. Only twenty-seven.

Corll's Story

Originally Corll had lived in the Heights neighborhood of Houston, a poor area of the city riddled with worn-out houses, junkyards, empty lots—a classic example of urban blight. That is where he met Henley—Henley and his family lived there—and it's where Henley and another boy would cruise for potential victims.

Henley was not subtle about the pickups, and when families started to complain to police about missing sons, it should not have been that difficult to make a connection between the missing boys and Henley. But at the time, the Houston Police Department was woefully understaffed; there were only some 2,200 cops to handle a population of 2 million people. It was also charged that the cops were poorly trained, unmotivated, underpaid, and their efforts misguided. They never made the connection, and the abductions and killings continued unabated.

Apparently, Corll first killed in August 1970. At the time, people who knew Corll said that his personality underwent a change. Before 1970, he was described as a hardworking man—he worked at the power company and at a candy company he and his mother owned—with very little outward expression of emotion. But something changed, and he became quick to get angry and seemed ultrasensitive to things, particularly his age: He loathed the idea of getting old. He also started to drink, and in conversations with his mother, Mary West (their names were different because she had been married a number of times), he seemed very depressed, on the verge of suicide.

Don't Accept Candy from Strangers

One of the things we're all taught when we're young is not to accept candy from a stranger. Too bad Dean Corll's victims didn't follow this advice—he often gave away candy to charm potential victims.

As with other serial and mass murderers, Corll's background was chaotic. He was born in Waynesdale, Indiana, on Christmas Eve in 1939. At the time, his parents, Mary and Arnold Corll, were twenty-four years old. Arnold worked in a factory, and Mary stayed home to take care of the kids.

There was trouble in the marriage almost from the start. One of the problems, West said, was that Arnold didn't like or appreciate kids. He was distant from Dean and his younger brother, Stanley. Shortly afterward, Arnold and Mary Corll were divorced, and Mary was suddenly on her own with two small children, though Arnold did make child support payments. Mary Corll went out to work, and a variety of people took care of Dean and his brother—sometimes they even took care of themselves.

When a child is left alone for long periods of time, it can be frightening and cause anger, and the child will try to scurry for safety. Psychotic people, however, build worlds that look safe

More Victims?

Author Jack Olsen wrote about Corll in *The Man with the Candy* and claimed that there may be more victims buried around Corll's candy shop. But the Houston police have shown no inclination to investigate that.

and habitable and try to live in them. To do this they might assume different identities that help them cope with the stress. And sometimes, as the Houston psychiatrist Harvey Meader said, "Safety can mean assuming an identity of the parent perceived as having the strongest persona."

The child may not like the new identity that he or she takes on—especially if it is an identity with another gender, such as Dean adopting the identity of his mother. Indeed, unconsciously the child may loathe the identity. This may well have been the case with Dean Corll. Consciously he loved interaction with young boys, but unconsciously he loathed it; it frightened and diminished him. "And the way to handle that, in the psychotic mind," says Meader, "is to kill it."

And he did, at least twenty-seven times. And you couldn't find a Houston cop who will say that there aren't more bodies buried somewhere else.

Afterword

Elmer Wayne Henley was tried for his murderous participation in the Houston killings and was found guilty. He was sentenced to 594 years. Then, on December 21, 1973, the verdict was reversed on appeal, with the appeals court declaring that Henley's defense attorneys did not get enough consideration on a change of venue. A short while later, though, Henley was retried and found guilty again. He is still in jail.

Chapter 6
Gary Heidnik

Notable Fact
Indeed, Heidnik was cooking something;
it was not his dinner but the rib cage
of a human being.

With a little luck, lives might have been saved.

On November 26, 1986, Sandra Lindsley, a mildly mentally disabled young African American woman who lived in
northern Philadelphia, went to the corner drugstore to pick
up a package of Midol. Hours went by and she didn't return,
and her mother, Jeanette Perkins, went searching for her. She
spent an anxious weekend trying to find her daughter.

On Monday, Perkins contacted a close friend of Sandra's,
Cyril "Tony" Brown. Brown didn't know where Sandra was,
but he asked Jeanette whether she had tried the home of Gary
Heidnik, a white man in his early forties who was a friend of
both Sandra and Tony. Sandra had been to Heidnik's house on
numerous occasions.

Jeanette Perkins went over to Heidnik's house at 3520
North Marshall Street, a run-down house in a neighborhood
that vaguely resembled Berlin after World War II and was
nicknamed "OK Corral" because of the numerous gunfights
drug dealers had there. Heidnik had only paid $15,500 for the

single-family home, and it would be appraised at only $3,000 less than a year later.

When Jeanette knocked on Heidnik's door, no one answered, so she went away. She returned a couple of times that day, but there was still no answer. In fact, as she knocked, her daughter was inside the house. If only Sandra had screamed, or if Jeanette had called the police.

Gary Heidnik

And then, later, there was the smell. An atrocious, gagging kind of smell was coming from the house on Marshall Street, and it was so powerful that it could be smelled along the entire block. Because Heidnik had not been seen for quite some time, the neighbors assumed that the smell might be his rotting corpse. They called the police, and a Detective Aponte went to the house. He pounded on the door, and this time Gary Heidnik, a good-looking man with dark hair and eyes, opened up.

Aponte inquired as to the stench. Heidnik said that he had just burned his dinner.

Astonishingly, Aponte accepted this explanation, even though the stench had been permeating the neighborhood for days. If only he had not accepted the explanation, but instead had insisted on being let in.

Indeed, Heidnik was cooking something; it was not his dinner but the rib cage of a human being.

The Colony

The details, as they were revealed later, were to be some of the most shocking that Philadelphia could ever have imagined. In essence, Gary Heidnik ran a mini-slave colony of African American women in his basement, keeping them chained, abusing and beating them, feeding them a blend of dog food and human flesh—which the starving women were ultimately forced into eating by their hunger—and sexually abusing them.

It all started with Josefina Rivera, a slim prostitute with a pretty, hard face. On November 26, 1986, she was working the corner of Third and Girard streets and hoping to meet a john. All told, it had been a miserable night for Josefina. She had had an argument with her boyfriend, Vincent Nelson, she was broke, and in an hour or so it would be officially Thanksgiving Day. The night, too, was miserable, cold, damp, and windy. She was wearing a thin jacket and her thin legs were encased in skin-tight jeans.

She hoped she would turn at least one trick, but as time went by, her prospects got dimmer; there were few johns cruising by that night. Then she noticed that a Cadillac Coupe DeVille stopped. The window lowered electronically and the driver, a middle-aged white man, asked her what she charged.

She gave him a high figure, and they eventually settled on $20. He invited her into the car and she got in. He was dressed in a fringed leather jacket and wore a Rolex. The car was fairly new and heavily customized with chrome. Josefina figured that the man had money to spend. He told her he was going to take her to his house. They stopped to buy coffee, and then he drove at Daytona 500 speed through the empty, wet streets to his house on North Marshall.

Heidnik's house was different from many homes in the area. Although the house was also run-down, it stood alone from most houses, which were attached to another home on one side, and it had a dilapidated garage, which other homes did not. Astonishingly enough, in that garage was a 1971 Rolls-Royce. The garage doors were lined with steel to protect the car against errant shots from drug dealers' shoot-outs. A few years earlier Heidnik, who had a genius IQ and was brilliant at playing the stock market, had paid $17,000 cash for it, a withdrawal that hardly dented his money market account with Merrill Lynch of more than $500,000.

In the house, Heidnik brought Josefina upstairs to a bedroom, the dominant feature of which was a waterbed. He paid her the agreed-on $20, then took off his clothes and got in bed with her. They had intercourse for a while, and then suddenly Heidnik changed: He grabbed Josefina around the neck and started to choke her. Terrified, she said she would do whatever he wanted her to do if he would let her live.

He led her downstairs to the first floor, then down another flight of stairs into the basement, a dark and dingy place with a dirt floor. Suddenly, he had cuffed her hands; the cuffs were secured to a chain, which in turn was linked to a metal bar that ran the length of the ceiling. She was like an animal in a pen. Then he went upstairs and went to sleep.

Three days later, Heidnik brought another woman downstairs. She was African American, too, and plump. Her name, Josefina learned, was Sandra Lindsley. Like Josefina, he cuffed and chained Sandra to the metal bar.

Then the sex started. Every day from that point on, Heidnik had sex with both of them, including intercourse and other acts. He seemed insatiable and liked humiliating and dominating the women. A particular favorite was forcing one to fellate him while the other watched. He also abused them physically, beating them for no apparent reason with his hands and sticks. It wasn't long before the women were totally cowed and completely terrified of him.

He didn't exactly lay out a regal repast for them, either. Sometimes he gave them oatmeal for breakfast, or Pop-Tarts, or crackers. For lunch there would be sandwiches—sometimes. A special treat was take-out chicken. He also offered them sandwiches made with dog food, which they rejected. But then, as their hunger deepened because Heidnik refused to feed them, they accepted the dog-food sandwiches.

To compound their grief, it was winter and the basement was chilly and damp, and neither woman was dressed warmly. Indeed, at one point they were bare from the waist down.

More Prisoners

Three days before Christmas in 1986, Heidnik captured a new girl. Her name was Lisa Thomas, and she was nineteen years old, a nice-looking young woman. She was walking down Lehigh Street when her life intersected with Heidnik's. He was cruising along in his Cadillac and pulled up beside Lisa and asked ingenuously, "You want to see my peter?" Lisa responded that she was no prostitute, that she was just on her way to her girlfriend's house.

Heidnik assured her that he was not dangerous and that he would be happy to give her a lift. After some discussion, Lisa decided he was harmless and got into the car.

Before they got to her destination, Heidnik took her to a restaurant for a cheeseburger and fries, flashed a roll of bills, and asked her if she wanted to accompany him to Atlantic City.

When she responded that she had nothing to wear for such an outing, Heidnik said he would be happy to buy her whatever she needed. He took her to a store and bought her an armful of jeans and blouses. After that they went to his house and had sex on his waterbed, where eventually she fell asleep.

When she awoke, she asked Heidnik to take her to her girlfriend's apartment. Again Heidnik changed from a seemingly harmless man to something else. He grabbed her around the throat and choked her. (Later, court wags would dub this the "Heidnik maneuver.") Lisa begged him to stop and said she'd do whatever he wanted. So he took her down to the cellar and introduced her to Josefina (who had told Heidnik her name was Nicole) and Sandy.

Then he humiliated Lisa in front of the other women. He told her to kiss his behind, which she did, and he then forced her to "suck my balls," which she also did, then to "suck my peter," which the girl also complied with. Afterward, Heidnik served peanut butter and jelly sandwiches, something of a treat, and completed his day's work by cuffing and chaining Lisa to the metal bar.

Heidnik's fourth captive was Deborah Dudley, and his fifth was eighteen-year-old Jacquelyn Askins, taken just four days after Dudley. Askins was a prostitute; Dudley was not.

It was midday when Heidnik, driving a blue Dodge van with imitation-fur interior, picked Askins up. When he got her to his house, he dragged her into the basement and, with the other captives watching, thrashed her with a plastic switch and then chained her up. He now had five African American female prisoners in his basement, and some of them had been in there for months.

Sometime during all this, Heidnik had devised a special punishment for the slaves who did not obey him—or whom he decided did not obey him. He dug a hole in the cellar floor and covered it with a plywood panel. To discipline someone, he would make her get into the hole; he would then cover the hole with the plywood and weigh it down with sandbags. It was an ordeal within an ordeal. (It also may have served as inspiration for the author Thomas Harris, who had his fictional psychopath in the book *The Silence of the Lambs* hold women captive in a deep well-like hole in his basement.)

Heidnik's sexual activity continued, and it often involved humiliating the women. For example, he would occasionally force the women to have sex with one another while he watched. Dog food eventually became a staple in the women's diet, but all still lost weight. And, of course, hunger was with them all the time.

They certainly didn't lack for music. Heidnik kept the radio blasting rock music twenty-four hours a day. This was one reason why they had determined screaming would not have helped them—no one would be able to hear them above the music.

Despite all of Heidnik's sexual activity, none of the women became pregnant, though there were a few false alarms when two missed their periods (Heidnik had been forced to buy tampons for all the women). Later it would be determined that Heidnik's main goal was to impregnate them—he viewed the basement as a kind of baby farm—but he was unable to achieve that goal. There is no telling how he would have reacted if one of them had become pregnant.

A Death

Something eventually occurred that made the situation in the basement particularly terrifying for the abused women: Sandra Lindsley died. On February 7, 1987, she had a fever and was feeling very washed out; she seemed to have no energy. Heidnik tried to force her to eat, and he suddenly realized that she was not moving—in fact, she had died.

If the event bothered him, he didn't show it, merely commenting that she had choked on a piece of bread. But he had to get rid of her body. He carried it out of the room, and the next thing the prisoners heard was the sound of a power tool. They imagined he was cutting Sandra up, and they were right; Heidnik dismembered Sandra Lindsley, packed parts of her in white plastic bags and put them in the freezer, and used a food processor to grind up some of the body. The parts he couldn't use—the head, feet, hands, rib cage, and bones—he tried to cook away. (It was this burning-flesh smell that neighbors had complained about.)

The cooked flesh did not go to waste. He started mixing it with dog food and fed it to his two dogs, Bear and Flaky—and to the prisoners. It is not known whether they knew that they were eating human flesh.

Of all the girls, Deborah Dudley was the most rebellious, and she battled Heidnik's dominance daily. Heidnik realized he needed a "special" lesson to get Dudley to obey him. So one day he took her upstairs, opened the freezer, and showed her Sandra Lindsley's head and other body parts. He told her that if she didn't acquiesce, she would end up the same way. But Dudley was tough. She continued to fight his will, and Heidnik finally devised a special torture for her.

One night he put her in the hole, which he had partially filled with water, then plugged a wire into a wall outlet and touched her hands with the bare end of the wire. The pain was excruciating, and he repeated the torture as often he wished. Ultimately, the pain ended her life; Deborah Dudley took one too many shocks and died. Instead of cutting her up, Heidnik dumped her body in the pine barrens in a New Jersey park, far from North Marshall Street.

Dudley's death had a softening effect on Heidnik. He started to treat the women better and supplied them with blankets, pillows, and a television.

This did not mean he stopped kidnapping, though. On March 23, 1987, he captured twenty-four-year-old Agnes Adams. Heidnik had paid Adams for sex on two prior occasions. The first time he could not get her into his house because someone had parked their car in front of his driveway, and the second time he paid her $35 for oral sex and, for some unaccountable reason, let her go. The third time they met, she was working Fifth and Gerard streets. This time he brought her home and she was forced to stay.

An Escape

During the women's captivity, Heidnik's first prisoner, Josefina Rivera, using all her street-smart ways, had gradually won over Heidnik's trust. Indeed, she had shown her loyalty when he abducted Agnes Adams—Josefina was in the car when Heidnik encountered Adams for the third time. Agnes knew Josefina as "Vicki" from the Hearts and Flowers strip joint. Josefina made no attempt to warn Agnes that she was dealing with a madman, so Agnes felt that it was safe to go with them.

So when Josefina asked Heidnik if she could see her children and family, he said she could, but that if she didn't return all the other women would die. Heidnik drove her into town, and she agreed to meet him at a gas station at midnight at Sixth and Gerard streets. She also promised to bring another woman with her.

After Heidnik released her, Josefina Rivera immediately ran four blocks to the apartment of her boyfriend, Vincent Nelson.

He was there. Hysterically, she blurted out the story of where she had been and the horrors at 3520 North Marshall Street.

The boyfriend was skeptical, but after a while he began to believe her and told her to come with him—he would confront Heidnik at the gas station and beat him up. On the way over, though, he had second thoughts about the solidity of this plan, and they called 911. The responding uniformed officers doubted Rivera's story, too—until she showed them the marks made by the chains and cuffs. They all went to the gas station and found Gary Heidnik in his car. He was arrested without incident.

On March 25, 1987, Philadelphia detectives, armed with a search warrant, entered Heidnik's house. Downstairs they found three women in the basement. Two of them (Lisa Thomas and Jacquelyn Askins) were huddled under a blanket trying to keep warm. They screamed hysterically, and when they stood up, the blankets dropped off and revealed that they were nude from the waist down. The cops found Agnes Adams in the hole. She was nude, her hands cuffed behind her back. During the search of Heidnik's house, one detective got an unpleasant surprise. He found the packaged human flesh, the human fatty remains in a burned pan, and on a shelf in the freezer, a human forearm.

Heidnik's Story

Heidnik was born in Cleveland in 1943 and had one sibling, a younger brother Terry. His mother, Ellen, a nice-looking woman who was part Native American, was an alcoholic who slept around. When Gary was two years old, his parents divorced. After the divorce Gary and his brother lived with their mother, but she soon seemed incapable of taking care of them. Around the time they entered the first grade, the boys went to live with their father, Michael, who had remarried.

They would not live with their mother again, who married three more times before committing suicide by ingesting mercury in 1970.

Gary had described his father as cold and uncaring, a strict disciplinarian, but a psychiatrist who spoke to Gary said that this description of his father is a gross understatement. For example, when Gary or his brother wet the bed, his father would hang the sheets out the window to show the world what "piss asses" they were. Or he would paint bull's-eyes on the brothers' pants to show the other boys at school where to kick them. And if Gary or Terry were really bad, punishment could be just about anything, including being hung out the window by the ankles.

Gary's father was totally uncaring when it came to his sons. Indeed, when Gary was arrested his father acted as if Gary had brought all his troubles on himself. And when Gary was sentenced to death, his father—who had not talked to Gary in twenty-five years—said, "I'm not interested. I don't care. It don't bother me a bit. All I want is for you people to leave me alone. I don't care what happens."

Gary and Terry were in and out of mental institutions throughout their lives, and both brothers had tried to commit suicide on a number of occasions. Terry had tried it just a few times, but Gary had tried it thirteen different times, using everything from driving his motorcycle into a truck to stockpiling Thorazine while he was in the hospital and trying to overdose on it.

Growing up, Gary was extremely interested in the military and finance. He actually attended a military high school for a couple of years. He had been reading the financial pages since he was a kid, and as an adult, he used his intellect and experience to amass a small fortune in stocks.

He was arrested a few times for assault and did prison time, but overall he spent the bulk of his years in mental institutions, and just about everyone who examined him considered him dangerous—schizophrenic and incurable. One particularly startling symptom was that he sometimes went mute—did not utter so much as a word—once for almost two years.

Afraid of Women

Heidnik also seemed to be afraid of women who were his intellectual equals, and even women of average intelligence. Except for a brief marriage to a woman of average intelligence, for years before he abducted women to be his slaves he became involved with women only who were very intellectually inferior to him. One, for example, had an IQ of 49; a person with an IQ of 70 or below is considered to have mental retardation.

This was part of a broader pattern of constantly getting involved with people whom Heidnik could feel superior to. Where his father had power and superiority over him, Gary associated with people over whom he could feel powerful.

Afterword

Gary Heidnik was found guilty of murder and was sentenced to die in the electric chair. Before his execution, he was housed in the State Correctional Institution at Pittsburgh because of a change of venue granted to the defense during the trial. Since the age of fourteen, Heidnik had been in twenty-one different mental institutions and had tried to kill himself thirteen times. People who knew him well predicted that he would go for number fourteen, but he never got the chance. He was executed on July 6, 1999.

Chapter 7
John Wayne Gacy

Notable Fact
The most dangerous situation
for young boys to be in with
John Wayne Gacy was at his home.

There are three images that jump to mind about John Wayne Gacy, who ranks as one of the worst serial killers in the United States during the twentieth century:

- A photo of the portly Gacy, dressed and painted as a clown, with a big clown smile on his face—and a certain chilling light in his eyes.
- A picture of Gacy standing next to Rosalynn Carter in 1978, which she autographed, "To John Gacy, Best Wishes, Rosalynn Carter."
- And finally, when the cops searched his house, they found a two-foot-long dildo, one of his torture implements, eighteen inches of it covered with dried excreta and blood.

Growing Up Gacy

Like most serial murderers, John Wayne Gacy was able to disguise the savagery inside him, the compulsion that made him kill. Part of his disguise included marrying—twice—and having children.

John Wayne Gacy

John Wayne (after the movie star) Gacy was born in 1942 in Edgewater Hospital in Chicago, the only boy in a family with a younger and older sister. In Gacy's family there were not the obvious ruptures so common in the childhood of other serial killers, such as a father who abandons the family or a history of insanity. Gacy's family, for all intents and purposes, was a lot like yours or mine. They lived a middle-class existence in middle-class Chicago.

But while Gacy grew up, something terrible was happening between him and his father. His father seemed obsessed with punishing "Little John," criticizing him, never allowing that his son could do anything right. For years they were at odds, and it was a lifelong regret of Gacy's that he could never please his father. Indeed, Gacy's father died while Gacy was in jail; Gacy couldn't even get permission to attend the funeral.

Gacy was an ordinary kind of student in grade school and high school, and he never got into much trouble. His personality, however, developed a couple of noticeable quirks. He was a glad-handing kind of person, with an aggressive style that turned some people off.

But his biggest problem was that he was a liar. He was always lying about his accomplishments, as if what he really did do was not good enough; to make himself feel good, he had to exaggerate. He never seemed to notice that many people knew he was lying. Indeed, his tales were often so tall that it would have been impossible for him to have crowded into his life all the things he said he did.

After high school Gacy briefly attended business school, and then he became a salesman for the Nunn-Bush Shoe Store in Springfield, Illinois. While working there, he met a pretty young woman named Marilyn Myers. They started to date and he eventually popped the question. While Gacy was no matinee idol—he was short, 5'8", and always had a weight problem complete with large belly—he was persuasive and generous and nice to be around. She said yes. They were married in September 1964.

Undone in Iowa

Marilyn's parents bought a string of Kentucky Fried Chicken stores soon after Marilyn and Gacy's wedding, and they wanted the young couple to manage them. They agreed and moved into the elder Meyers's home in Waterloo, Iowa.

They seemed blessed. Marilyn bore a son and then a daughter. They lived comfortably and worked hard. Gacy also became active in the Waterloo chapter of the Jaycees, a civic group devoted to bettering their communities with a wide variety of activities; he had first done this in Springfield, achieving quite a lot of success and earning a number of awards from the Jaycees for his work.

Although this sort of life would be more than enough to satisfy most people, Gacy kept lying. He worked hard at the job—seven days a week until ten or eleven at night—but he continued his self-aggrandizement; at one point he claimed to be a relative of the person who founded the fried chicken chain. He not only liked to seem important but also liked to look the part. One manifestation of this was his car, which he equipped with a siren and police lights. Later, his more sinister purpose would be revealed.

The Rumors

But there were problems. There were some nasty rumors circulating, claiming that Gacy was propositioning and having sex with some of the teenage boys who worked in the restaurants he managed. It was charged that he gave the best-looking boys—he seemed to like light-haired boys with muscled bodies—rides home and favored them in other ways as well.

Then a boy named Mark Miller brought charges against Gacy. Miller said that Gacy had forced him to perform "deviant" sexual acts with him. Gacy denied it, but an investigation showed that they had been involved with each other and that there were other boys too. One of those boys, James Tullery, detailed a terrifying ordeal in the book *The Man Who Killed Boys*, by Clifford L. Linedecker. Tullery had been at Gacy's house and, after plying Tullery with booze and pornographic films, Gacy had tried to force him to perform sexual acts. To do this,

Gacy had threatened Tullery, cut him with a knife, shackled him, and choked him almost to the point of unconsciousness. Nothing happened, and Gacy released the boy—he was lucky to get out alive.

The judge in Miller's case, mindful of Gacy's perverse patterns, sentenced him to ten years at the Iowa State Reformatory at Adamosa. At the tender age of twenty-six, John Wayne Gacy was in jail. Marilyn filed divorce papers soon after, and ultimately he was to lose her, the house, and his two kids. That didn't seem to matter too much to him, however, because he apparently never contacted her or the kids again.

Gacy brought the same verve and vigor to the prison world that he brought to his fried chicken restaurants, and prison officials regarded him highly. After only eight months, he received parole. Freed, he moved into a house in Chicago with his sixty-one-year-old mother and his sister and got a job as a fast-food cook. He then asked the Iowa parole board for permission to move to Chicago. Because of his seemingly stable life, including a job, the board granted his request.

Suburbia

He moved around as a cook but was doing well for himself—so well that he decided to buy a house. With the help of his mother, who provided half the financing, he bought a small two-bedroom ranch at 8213 West Summerdale Avenue in Norwood, a middle-class suburban community not far from the Northwest Side of Chicago. The house was on a one-way westbound street and did not get a great deal of traffic; most of the people traveling down it were heading home. It was a typical suburban brick house, with a garage and front and back yards: The most significant feature of the house (as it turned out) was the crawl space underneath. It had four-feet-high concrete walls and a dirt floor, and to gain access to it there was a trapdoor on the floor of the bedroom closet. John Wayne Gacy passed through that trapdoor many times.

Gacy made friends with his neighbors at the new house, particularly the Grexa family directly next door, which had six children. They noticed that he was always working around the house; he seemed to like that type of work very much.

Gacy didn't stay a bachelor for too long. On June 1, 1972, he married Carole Hoff, a divorcée with two kids, and settled into a suburban life at his home on Summerdale. In 1974 Gacy formed PDM Contractors—the letters stood for painting, decorating, and maintenance—and started remodeling commercial properties.

But all was not blissful at home. Soon his relationship with his wife had deteriorated to the point that she filed for divorce. Later she was to explain that he was sexually impotent and had a quick, dangerous temper. One minute he would be cool, calm, and collected, and the next he would be in a rage and breaking furniture.

Gacy had also told his wife a minor detail about himself: He said he liked boys as well as women. While unsuccessful in marriage, however, Gacy's contracting business was doing quite well. He worked extremely hard, finishing jobs early and making sure customers were satisfied. His work crews consisted of two kinds of people: experienced older craftsmen and teenage boys as laborers. He often invited the better-looking boys home to watch stag films, where they could drink and smoke marijuana.

From time to time Gacy had brushes with the law, but no convictions ever came of them. One boy complained to the police that Gacy had ordered him into his car one night saying that he was a deputy sheriff, and then had forced him to perform oral sex. After Gacy demanded that the boy fellate him again, the boy refused and jumped out of the car. Gacy tried to run him down, but he escaped. Luckily for Gacy, Iowa parole authorities didn't find out, and soon he didn't have to worry: On June, 18, 1976, his parole from the Iowa prison was up and he could not be brought up on parole violation charges.

Gacy was too old to work for the Jaycees in Chicago, but he was not too old for politics. He got himself involved in local politics, ingratiating himself with politicos by providing the services of PDM free of charge. Perhaps the high point of his political achievements was when he posed with Rosalynn Carter.

House of Horrors

At one point after Gacy moved onto Summerdale, his neighbors, the Grexas, noticed an objectionable odor around his house that never really left during all the time Gacy lived there. It was a thick, foul smell; when they asked about it, Gacy said it was probably something wrong with the sewer lines. Because the Grexas had also had trouble with their sewer lines, they didn't pursue it. The smell, of course, was not sewage: From time to time, Gacy would kill a young man, then carry his body through the trapdoor in the closet and bury it in a shallow grave. He hastened decomposition by covering the bodies with lime.

Later, investigation would reveal that Gacy trapped his victims in a variety of ways. One method was by posing as a police officer, as he did with the previously mentioned young man. He had purchased a black 1978 Oldsmobile Delta equipped with a searchlight on the side, and he would often cruise the gay neighborhoods of Chicago. Young men—particularly young gay men—felt they could not say no to a police officer

71

and would obediently get in. Or he would simply pick up street hustlers and pay for sex—and sometimes kill them.

The most dangerous situation for anyone to be in with John Wayne Gacy was at his home. He had a couple of ways to trap young men there. One was chloroform; he would catch the person off guard and hold a chloroform-soaked rag to his nose until he collapsed. Once the boy was incapacitated, Gacy would cuff the victim.

Another way he got them was the handcuff trick. Gacy would produce what he said were toy handcuffs and challenge the person to put them on and escape. Of course, they were real handcuffs and his victim couldn't escape, and then Gacy would rape and torture and perhaps kill him, though not always. A street hustler named Jaime described a very close call with Gacy in *The Man Who Killed Boys*:

Jaime's husky host led him to the bedroom, where both of them stripped. Gacy told Jaime to get busy doing what he was paid to do, but before the youth could comply his head was jolted with a sudden slap. Suddenly Jaime was being beaten. He tried to scream but the powerful hands that closed around his throat smothered the noise. The boy managed to wriggle free, then Gacy did something that terrified him even more. From somewhere Gacy produced a pair of handcuffs. Jaime picked up a vase and shattered it over the man's head. Moments later Jaime was lifted off his feet and heaved onto the bed. The man threw his heavy body onto that of the youth, smashing him into the mattress. Jaime couldn't move. He was smothering.

Then, for some unaccountable reason, Gacy got off the boy and sent him on his way with $50—$20

72

more than he had agreed to pay—and seemed to regard the whole thing as a joke. Jaime, terrified, left. He had been a prostitute since he was twelve, but he was so shaken by the event that he didn't go back on the streets for a month.

In retrospect, it is amazing that Gacy wasn't caught before he was. Young boys were disappearing at an alarming rate, and Gacy's name even came up in various investigations at different police stations. However, there was often no communication between different police jurisdictions, and none of them thought to see whether he had a criminal record. If they had, they would have discovered his conviction in Iowa for sodomy and might have saved many lives.

It is amazing, too, that none of the neighbors suspected anything. One woman living in a home a block away said she would occasionally hear faint screams coming from the house in the dead of night, but neither she nor anyone else did anything about it. And of course, there was that sickening odor that never really went away.

A Break in the Case

It took the murder of Robert Piest—and the determination and skill of one police officer—to derail Gacy's murderous train.

Robert Piest was a sixteen-year-old, all-American high school boy who, in December 1978, was working in the Nisson Pharmacy in Des Plaines, Illinois, for $2.85 an hour. His mother came to pick him up one night at nine o'clock, and Robert asked her to wait in the store while he talked with a contractor about a job that would pay him $5 an hour for the summer. Piest was saving to buy a car, and the job was quite attractive.

73

Piest went out a few minutes after nine and never returned. When his mother went outside the pharmacy to check on him, she found he had simply vanished. The next day Lieutenant Joseph Kozenczak was looking over missing-person reports and came across that of Piest. He spoke with Piest's mother, ascertained that Piest was not a runaway, and launched a full-scale investigation.

One tentacle of the investigation led to Gacy, who denied even having seen the boy. However, unlike other police officers before him, Kozenczak had done a routine background check of Gacy, which included a check for any prior criminal record. The check revealed the Iowa sodomy conviction and prison sentence. Kozenczak convinced a judge that there was probable cause to issue a search warrant, and soon thereafter cops descended on the house at 8213 West Summerdale.

They found pornographic gay films, literature, and other material. And in the trunk of his car, the black Oldsmobile, they found hair that matched that of Robert Piest.

The hair found was not sufficient for an arrest, so police started open surveillance on Gacy that drove him crazy. Then came another break: Police had taken a roll of film from Gacy's house during their search, and when they developed it, they discovered that it belonged to Robert Piest.

An Unusual Collection

Jonathan Davis, the lead vocalist for the heavy rock group KoRn, is an avid collector of crime memorabilia and has a special interest in items relating to serial killers.

Davis, a former mortuary science student, admits that he has always been drawn to the dark side, and at one time he planned to open a museum dedicated to crime items with a special emphasis on serial murder. He personally owns a great deal of memorabilia, including original artwork from John Wayne Gacy and Richard Ramírez. The highlights of his collection, however, are two "Pogo the Clown" suits once owned by Gacy when he entertained at children's parties and the yellow VW Ted Bundy drove when he was out looking for victims.

Kozenczak was sure that Gacy was his man. And when one of his investigators entered Gacy's house with a second search warrant, he got lucky: Before he was a police officer, the detective had long worked in a place where the smell in Gacy's house was routine: the morgue. The police obtained another warrant and started taking up floorboards and digging into the earth in the crawl space.

The digging took place over a two-week period, very carefully, as if it were an archaeological dig. When it was over, the police had uncovered twenty-seven bodies and Gacy had confessed to killing another five, which he had dumped in the Des Plaines River. That was the final resting place of Robert Piest, who was found in the river some months later. An autopsy revealed paper towels jammed in Piest's throat; he had suffocated.

It was questioned whether Gacy was mentally fit to stand trial, but Judge Louis B. Garippo determined that he was. A psychologist for the defense testified that Gacy was a paranoid schizophrenic and did not have control over his actions, but that wasn't enough: Gacy was found guilty of the murder of thirty-three young men and was sentenced to die by lethal injection. He was shipped down to the Menard Correctional Center in Menard, Illinois, where for a time he was the only inmate in the death-row cell block. Illinois authorities said they received hundreds of

Creepy Reenactment

The first season of the FOX television channel's hit series *Prison Break* was filmed at the now-closed Joliet Correctional Facility in Illinois. Some of the scenes during the first season were filmed in a cell actually occupied for a time by John Wayne Gacy. Gacy was at Joliet before his execution in 1994. Actor Lane Garrison, who played Tweener, a young convict, commented, "We do some stuff here in Gacy's cell, which is really scary."

requests from citizens all over the United States asking for the pleasure of injecting him.

Afterword

The Menard prison in southern Illinois, about fifty miles south of St. Louis on the Mississippi River, has a panoramic view of the river and surrounding countryside. In fact, it may have the most scenic view of any prison in the Illinois system.

Gacy became a portrait painter during his time on death row; his subjects were mostly clowns. He would paint clowns in all kinds of scenes, and he sold them for a handsome price until prison officials cracked down on the practice. He was executed by lethal injection on May 10, 1994.

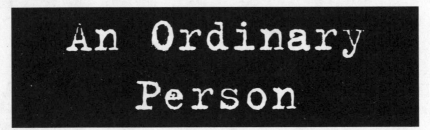

An Ordinary Person

Below is a questionnaire filled out by serial murderer John Wayne Gacy, who killed at least thirty-one young men. When he filled it out he was in prison, waiting to be executed for his crimes. His answers make him seem like a very ordinary person. Misspellings and other errors have been left as is (certain answers are partly illegible).

Full name: John Wayne Michael Gacy
Date of birth: March 17, 1942
Age, Ht., Wt: 50, 5′9″, 208
Home: Menard Deathrow, Chester, Ill.
Marital status: Twice Divorced
Family: 2 sisters, 5 children

Most treasured honor: 3 times son of the year Jaycees 3 different cities

Perfect woman or man: independent thinker, self starter, mind of her own.

Man: Bright, bold, honest dependable says what he is thinking

Childhood hero: J.F. Kennedy, R.J. Daley.

Current Hero: M Cuomo, Donald Trump

Favorite TV shows: Unsolved Mysteries, National geographic Specials

Favorite movies: Once Upon A Time in America, Good fellas, Ten Commandments

Favorite song: Send in the clowns, amazing grace

Favorite singers: Judy Collins. Bob Dylan, Neil Diamond, Roy Orbison, Shan a na

Favorite Musicians: REO Speedwagon, Elton John, Zamfir

Hobbies: Correspondence, oil painting, study of human interests

Favorite meals: Fried Chicken, deboned lake perch drawn in butter, salad. Tea

Recommended reading: Texas Connection, Question of Doubt

Last book read: naked Lunch and wild boys William S Burroughs

Ideal evening: Dinner and concert or live show, drinks and a quiet walk by lake

Every Jan 1st: resolve: Correct things that I go year before

Nobody knows: I'm a character who love to tease and joke around

My biggest regret: being so trusting and gullible. Taken advantage of.

If I were president I'd: make sure the people of this country had jobs and a place to live before worrying about other countries

My advice to children: Be yourself, think positive respect parents

What I don't like about people: Phonies, people who don't keep their word.

My biggest fear: Dying before I have a chance to clear my name with truth

Pet peeves: People who say things they have no intention of doing.

Superstitions: none its for negative people

Friends like me because: I am outspoken and honest, fun loving dependable

Behind my back they say: The bastard got it made and he grandiose

People in history I'd like to have met: Michelangelo, Leonardo DaVinci

If I were an animal I'd be: a Bear or Eagle

Personal goals in life: To see to it that my children are provided for.

Personal interests: Reading, Writing meeting people, classic movies and music

Favorite color: Red

Favorite number: nine

I view myself as a: positive thinker, self starter, open minded, non judgmental.

What I think of this country: Great, if people would work for it instead of against it, pointing fingers at others, the problem takes all races to [illegible]

Political views: semi-liberal Democrat, that one party doesn't have all winners.

Thoughts of crime: Too much political corruption, and allowed drugs by governed has set off the balance of the judicial reform and punishment.

Thoughts on drugs: Make some legal to avoid crime [illegible]

I consider myself to be Conservative ____ **Moderate** ____ **Liberal with values**: Liberal with values

What I expect from friendships: lighthearted, fun loving, dependable [illegible]

Religious thinking: My faith is in God. Churches need to work on the family unit.

What you're thinking now: why the hell did I fill this out and who cares what I have to say.

Your artistic interests: To please myself first and hope that expression is enjoyable to others. Art as in life is a journey not a destination. If you don't like it move on. Just like music to the ear, food to the smell and taste.

Chapter 8
Albert DeSalvo

Notable Fact

He would usually rape the woman while she was dying or dead, and violently assault her with various objects, among them a wine bottle and a broom handle.

Of all the serial murderers in the history of the United States, none has ever evoked more widespread terror than the man who became known as the Boston Strangler. From 1962 to 1964, women of all ages and backgrounds who lived in Boston and the surrounding towns lived in fear. The police were in a state of anxiety and frustration. The only people who likely welcomed the presence of the Strangler were those who ran home security and personal defense businesses.

On June 14, 1962, the body of Anna Slesers, a young-looking fifty-five-year-old woman, was discovered in her apartment at 77 Gainsborough Street in Boston by her son Juris. She was lying on her back in the hall, a little blood underneath her head and a rope around her neck with the loose ends forming a sort of bow. Juris, unaccountably, assumed that she had hanged herself on the bathroom door and fallen. A police officer at first concurred, but subsequent investigation determined otherwise. In fact, she had been murdered, and her body had been arranged in a certain way. Her legs were spread very wide, with one leg hiked up at the knee. And she had been both sexually assaulted and a foreign object forced into her body. The police knew that they were dealing with someone bizarre.

A Second Victim

Two weeks later, on a very hot June 30, the body of sixty-eight-year-old Nina Nichols was discovered in her apartment on Commonwealth Avenue in Boston. The gray-haired physiotherapist, who was in good physical condition, was found posed in a similar position to Anna Slesers. She was on her back with her legs spread and had been sexually assaulted with a foreign object. She had been strangled, ferociously, with a pair of her own stockings, and the loose ends of the excess stockings on the floor had been arranged in a bow shape.

The police immediately suspected that the person who had killed Anna Slesers had also murdered Nina Nichols. Some officers were holding their breath, wondering whether—but mostly when—the killer would strike again.

They didn't have too long to wait. On July 2, two women who lived at 73 Newhall Street in Lynn, a suburb north of Boston, decided to check on their neighbor Helen Blake. They had not seen Blake for a couple of days and feared that perhaps she was sick, though Blake, a sixty-five-year-old ex-nurse, had not complained of any maladies.

They decided to go into her apartment, number 90, directly across the hall from them. They got the key from the superintendent of the building and entered the apartment. Almost. They took one look at the apartment, which had been ransacked, and, too scared to go farther, called the police.

The police found Helen Blake on her bed, facedown. She had been violently strangled with her own stockings, her legs were spread wide, and her brassiere had been placed under her neck with the ends arranged to form a bow. She had been violated with a foreign object. Police theorized that she had been killed in the kitchen, then carried into the bedroom and her body assaulted there.

At the time, Boston and Lynn had different police departments with separate jurisdictions, but they were aware to some degree of what was going on in adjacent areas.

When the police commissioner heard about the body found in Lynn, he articulated what every officer was feeling. "Oh, God," he said, "we've got a madman loose."

Q&A

Q. Who played Albert DeSalvo in the movie *The Boston Strangler*?

A. Tony Curtis

The media started to fan the flames of public panic about the Strangler over the summer, but it appeared that the killer might have stopped—the rest of July passed without a killing, and the city relaxed a bit.

Then, the body of seventy-five-year-old Ida Irga was discovered on August 21 in her apartment on Grove Street in Boston. It was clearly the work of the Boston Strangler: Irga's body was lying on her bed, her legs spread, a pillow under her buttocks, and her foot propped on the rungs of a chair and tied there. She had been sexually assaulted with a foreign object and her body had been placed so it faced the door and would be the first thing the person entering would see. The medical examiner calculated that she had been dead for two days.

Boston shivered despite the summer heat. The Strangler was back, and women started taking extraordinary precautions: not going anywhere without a companion, not letting anyone into their apartments, using three and four locks on their doors.

The Murders Continue

The police were under great pressure to solve the case and catch the killer, and in desperation they called in the FBI to educate their detectives on murders involving sexual assault. There was also a distinct feeling, almost 100 percent certainty on the part of the police, that the Strangler would strike again and would continue to kill until he was caught. They had to get the guy.

On August 30, the body of Jane Sullivan was found in her apartment at 435 Columbia Road in Dorchester, far away from Ida Irga's apartment. Sullivan, a heavyset person, was found facedown in six inches of water in the bathtub in a half-kneeling position, her housecoat was thrown over her shoulders, her girdle pulled up on her back, her panties down about her ankles, and her buttocks exposed. She had been strangled with her own stockings. Her body was too decomposed to determine whether she had been sexually assaulted, but the way the body was found as well as the similarities to the other murders led police to believe that she had been.

It was also determined that she had died on August 20, which had a chilling implication. Ida Irga had been killed on August 19. The Strangler had killed both women in less than twenty-four hours.

The police efforts to track down the Strangler intensified, and police work went on around the clock. All the stops were pulled out: Hundreds of known sex offenders were rounded up, psychologists were called in to profile the killer, fifty detectives worked on the cases full-time and went door-to-door trying to get some sort of lead. They also had to track down numerous leads from Boston citizens: The crimes had brought out the slightly insane, the attention seekers, and what one officer called "the ray people"—they were sure they knew who the killer was because rays from outer space told them.

All the work seemed to be paying off—there were no killings in September or October, and Thanksgiving passed tensely but uneventfully.

Then, on December 5, 1962, the Strangler struck again—and this time, Boston's anxiety level went through the roof. His victim deviated sharply from the profiles of his previous victims: She was not elderly and white but young and black. Serial killers rarely if ever deviate from their victim type, but the crime scene bore the

Desperate Times

Police were so desperate to solve the Strangler case that they even tried a psychic, Peter Hurkos. But it didn't help.

unmistakable modus operandi (MO) of the Strangler: Sophie Clark was lying on the living room floor and her legs, in black stockings, were wide apart. She had been strangled with three pairs of her own stockings, knotted under the neck. There was a gag in her mouth. She had been sexually assaulted and, for the first time, police found seminal stains outside the body, on the floor next to it.

There were other scary differences. She did not, like other victims, live alone. In addition to the apartment being ransacked, there was evidence that there had been a struggle. Moreover, Sophie Clark was aware of and very scared of the Strangler—she had had an additional lock installed. Since there was no sign of forced entry, it meant that she had let the killer in.

How? Why? If he could get past the defenses of a person who was so prepared, maybe defenses didn't work.

A Near Miss

This time, though, there was some luck, a possible solid lead. Police, as usual, were canvassing the neighborhood when they came across a woman who lived in another wing of the same apartment building as Sophie Clark. She said that on December 5 her doorbell had rung and she had opened the door to a man who identified himself as Thompson, who told her that the super had sent him to paint her apartment. The woman protested that she wasn't due for painting, but the man brushed by her and entered the apartment. He told her she had a nice figure and that maybe she should get into modeling.

The woman thought fast: She put "her finger warningly to her lips," as Gerold Frank wrote in his book *The Boston Strangler*. When "Thompson" gruffly asked what that was for, she said her husband was asleep in the bedroom. The man—whom she later described to police as having honey-colored hair, being perhaps twenty-five to thirty, and wearing a dark jacket and green work pants—quickly exited with no further discussion of painting.

It could have been the Strangler. As investigation revealed, the super hadn't sent anyone to the woman's apartment—but the police, hopeful though they were, couldn't manage to track him.

The next Strangler victim was strangled with hosiery entwined with one of her blouses: Patricia Bissette was murdered on New Year's Eve in 1962. She was in her locked apartment at 515 Park Drive in the Back Bay area, the same area where the first victim, Anna Slesers, and the most recent victim, Sophie Clark, had both lived. She was found in the bedroom, face up, but her legs, instead of being spread wide apart, had been placed close together by the killer. Her pajama top was pushed up to her shoulders and she was naked from the waist down. She had been sexually assaulted.

The Strangler's longest killing gap occurred between the murder of Patricia Bissette and the next victim, Beverly Samans. Samans's body was discovered in her apartment at 4 University Road on May 6, five months after Bissette's murder. This crime was across the Charles River in Cambridge, meaning the Boston police, under siege from the media and the public, breathed a collective sigh of relief that the body hadn't shown up in their jurisdiction. Samans, who was a rehabilitation therapist, was an atypical kill: She was the first and only victim who had been stabbed to death, innumerable times in the neck and chest. The killer had directed the knife thrusts into one breast in a bull's-eye pattern.

Three more killings were to occur before the Strangler was through, with the same random victims and locations. On September 8, 1963, the body of fifty-eight-year-old Evelyn Corbin was found in her apartment on the first floor at 224 Lafayette in Salem. On November 23, the body of twenty-three-year-old Joann Graff was found in her home at 54 Essex Street in Lawrence. And on January 4, 1964, the youngest victim of all, nineteen-year-old Mary Sullivan, was found in her apartment at 44A Charles Street in Boston.

Catching the Strangler

The unraveling of the killer began in an unlikely place—with a prison snitch, a man named George Nassar. Nassar, who had been committed to Bridgewater State Hospital for the criminally insane, notified his attorney, the famed F. Lee Bailey, that one of the inmates was more than hinting that he was the Boston Strangler. Nassar wanted to talk with Bailey, who was in the process of making a big name for himself—he had just won a Supreme Court appeal reversing the conviction of Dr. Sam Sheppard for killing his wife—about getting Nassar a deal for snitching.

The man Nassar fingered was Albert DeSalvo, a dark-haired, dark-eyed, well-built man who had been a middleweight boxing champion in the army. DeSalvo was twenty-nine years old, and in the institution for observation for having tied up and sexually assaulted a woman.

Bailey was doubtful; Bridgewater was for crazies. Nevertheless, one time when he was visiting Nassar, he decided to talk with DeSalvo. This first talk led to a second, when Bailey came armed with questions about the crimes to which answers had not been published. When Bailey repeated DeSalvo's answers to the detective who gave Bailey the questions, the detective was impressed. Bailey became convinced that DeSalvo was, in fact, the Boston Strangler.

Some of the doctors at the hospital weren't convinced, however—they thought Nassar's psychological profile fit better with the crimes, and this led to a sort of debate over which one was the Strangler. Finally, DeSalvo agreed to talk with John Bottomly, a special assistant to the state's attorney general, who had taken overall charge of the case.

Despite their differences—Bottomly was a child of privilege, while DeSalvo was a product of Boston's mean streets—the two men got along well, and DeSalvo eventually detailed his crimes for Bottomly. Anyone reading the transcripts of what DeSalvo said could hardly doubt that he was, in fact, the Boston Strangler. He described in gruesome detail how he would talk his way into an apartment, posing, for example, as a handyman or plumber, and once inside would maneuver things so he could get behind a woman and choke her with his arm, then finish the job with her stockings or some other article of clothing. Then, he would arrange the body so the legs were wide. The bow left in the ligature, he said, was just a way of tying; it had no special significance. DeSalvo would usually rape the woman while she was dying or dead and violently assault her with various objects, among which were a wine bottle and a broom handle.

When Bottomly started to talk with DeSalvo, he assumed there were only eleven victims—but DeSalvo revealed two more that the police didn't know about because the case did not include evidence of strangling.

Q&A

Q. Who played John Bottomly in the film *The Boston Strangler*?

A. Henry Fonda

One other victim was Mary Brown of 319 Park Avenue in Lawrence. For some reason—he had no idea why—on March 9, 1963, DeSalvo had battered her to death with a pipe he found on the premises.

The other murder seemed, for some reason, particularly savage and sad, a standout even among all the other savagery DeSalvo had wrought. He had talked his way into the apartment of eighty-five-year-old Mary Mullen of 1435 Commonwealth Avenue in Boston. He described to Bottomly how he got behind the elderly woman and grabbed her around the neck, and the next thing he knew, she slumped in his arms and he knew she was dead. And she was, having expired of a heart attack. He put her on the couch and left, and no one had ever suspected that it was a murder.

The Life of Albert DeSalvo

An investigation into DeSalvo's background revealed a predictably unsavory past. He came from a family of three boys and two girls; the boys were in and out of reform school and prison, as was his father, a savage brute who beat his wife and kids and openly hired prostitutes. The family was always on welfare.

Albert DeSalvo

Albert DeSalvo married a German immigrant named Irmgard, and they went on to have two children, a boy and a girl. They lived a typical suburban life in Malden, a suburb of Boston. DeSalvo called Irmgard frigid, but in the face of his sex drive a nymphomaniac would have been frigid. He would have sex with her in the morning, on his lunch break from his job, in the early evening, and before they went to sleep. On weekends he would have relations with her five or six times a day. They had sexual relations more than thirty times a week. This did not stop DeSalvo from making lascivious comments to attractive women while he and his wife were together.

Strangulation: A Highly Popular Means of Murder among Serial Killers

Strangulation ranks high on the list of how serial murderers finally kill their victims (often preceded by various rituals of torture, sexual savagery, and/or mutilation). It can be done manually with bare hands or with a ligature, such as a cord, rope, or piece of clothing, looped around the victim's neck and tightened to an impossible degree.

Manual strangulation is often seen in murders involving female victims and male perpetrators, where there is a large disparity in size and strength; the female is simply overpowered. Ligature strangulation is seen with all manner of killers and victims. Death generally results from one of two causes or a combination thereof. The first is asphyxiation, the cutting off of air to the body (oxygen deprivation). Asphyxiation creates a condition known as hypoxia, where the oxygen level decreases and the carbon dioxide increases until it reaches a lethal point. The terrifying feeling of not being able to breathe (commonly referred to as "air hunger") will cause the body to struggle violently—literally fighting for life—as it attempts to get back its oxygen supply. Unchallenged compression of the air passages will result in unconsciousness in ten to fifteen seconds, and basic neurological functions will shut down rapidly and eventually result in death if oxygen deprivation continues. The other fatal result of strangulation is cerebral ischemia, or the cutting off of blood to the brain. Compression of the carotid arteries and jugular veins interrupts blood flow and causes unconsciousness, brain damage, and ultimately death. Strangulation (and smothering, the covering of the mouth and nostrils with the hands, a pillow, or another object to block the air supply) is a very unpleasant way to die.

Afterword

For a time there was a debate not only over whether DeSalvo was the Strangler but also over whether he was insane. Despite his confession, the prosecutors were worried that a jury might find him insane and not responsible for his crimes. After all, all they really had was DeSalvo's own incriminating statements—there was no physical evidence. F. Lee Bailey's goal was not to free DeSalvo but to get him treatment, so a compromise was finally reached. DeSalvo was tried on other sexual assault and robbery charges and was found guilty. The judge remanded him to Bridgewater State Hospital until his appeal was heard.

His hospitalization did not put an end to the debate on whether Albert DeSalvo was the Boston Strangler, but one significant thing did happen when DeSalvo was out of the picture that convinced police they had the right man: No one else was killed with the Strangler's modus operandi.

In January 1968, Boston got a brief scare from Albert DeSalvo—just a month after being convicted and sent to Bridgewater, he and two other inmates escaped. His attorney, F. Lee Bailey, said that DeSalvo had left a note at Bridgewater saying he was escaping to make public officials admit that he was the Boston Strangler. This could only mean one thing: He was going to kill again. Fortunately, he was recaptured a few days later in Lynn and was shipped off to Walpole State Prison.

In all his confessions, DeSalvo did not display a great deal of remorse—except once, when he spoke of the old woman Mary Mullen, and how he had grabbed her and she had died in his arms. Indeed, he wept bitterly over it. On November 26, 1973, prison officials discovered the body of Albert DeSalvo in his cell. He had been stabbed sixty-eight times.

Chapter 9
Jerry Brudos

Notable Fact
He cut off the young girl's left foot, slipped her shoe on it, and stored it in the freezer.

Jerry Brudos, who stalked Salem, Oregon, and the surrounding area in the late 1960s, kept a gruesome photographic record of his victims. He carried out all of his murders while ostensibly carrying on a normal life (well, at home, he and his wife walked around in the nude). His wife, Darcie, would later say that she had no idea what was going on.

Jerry Brudos

Brudos is also one of the physically strongest serial killers on record. As a six-foot, freckle-faced man with eyes turned down at the corners and a moonish face, at 190 pounds, he may not have looked terribly imposing—but it was said that he could lift a three-hundred-pound freezer by himself.

First Victim

Brudos's first victim was a woman who was selling encyclopedias door-to-door. In January 1968, the slight, short-haired nineteen-year-old Linda Slawson, who lived in the suburb Aloha, got off the bus in Portland at Forty-seventh and Hawthorne streets. She was unclear as to what address she was going to; it was raining, and the paper with the address on it had smeared. As she walked down the block, she saw Brudos in his yard and asked him whether he was the person who was looking to buy encyclopedias. Brudos invited her into the house, told her that his mother and daughter were upstairs playing, and suggested that they go down to the basement where they wouldn't be disturbed.

Slawson willingly agreed to go downstairs while they chatted about the encyclopedias and how good they would be for his two kids. When they reached the basement, Brudos pulled up a stool for her to sit on. She sat, then Brudos came up behind her and slammed her on the head with a two-by-four. She fell off the stool, unconscious. Brudos got on top of her and finished her off, choking her to death with his bare hands.

While all this was going on, his mother and young daughter really were upstairs playing. He decided to get them out of the house so he could have fun with the corpse. He went upstairs and suggested that his mother pick up some hamburgers for supper, and he gave her the money to do so. She left the house, and Brudos went back downstairs.

He undressed the young woman, getting a thrill out of her lacy and colorful undergarments—women's undergarments had always thrilled him—and stripped her completely. Then he redressed her, like a child playing with a doll. He then did something he had wanted to do for a long time: He dressed and redressed her in various other undergarments that he had been stealing for years. (In fact, Brudos had been stealing undergarments since he was a teenager. When he first started, he used to snatch them off clotheslines, but then he gradu-ated to something far riskier: He would invade apartments and steal undergarments while the women were in the house. Occasionally they awakened and he would rape them.)

When his mother and daughter returned from the restaurant, Brudos was not deterred. He had a beer, then went back into the basement to continue his games—all in a state of pulsating sexual excitement. Before he was finished with the body, Brudos decided to take something to remember her by: He cut off the young woman's left foot, slipped her shoe on it, and stored it in the freezer. Brudos had a deep fetish for women's shoes.

As he was getting rid of the body, Brudos displayed both his cleverness and his strength. He tied part of an engine to her body and, under the cover of darkness, carried

Shoeaholic

Jerry Brudos's foot and shoe fetish manifested itself when he was quite young. He was stealing shoes from his sisters by the time he was sixteen years old.

her out to his car and stored her in the trunk. He then drove out to a bridge that spanned the Willamette River, parked, and slyly broke out his tire-changing gear as though he had a flat. A car or two went by, and when the coast was clear he opened the trunk and lifted Linda Slawson out with ease, despite the weight of the engine, and dropped her into the water. She sank immediately and stayed down.

Linda Slawson's disappearance didn't shock the community. Because of the transient nature of door-to-door sales, when a young person like Slawson didn't show up back at work, no one gave it a second thought—she had just quit, they assumed. Happened all the time.

Second Victim

Brudos's second victim was Jan Susan Whitney, a dark-haired, pretty girl who was 5'7" and weighed 130 pounds. She disappeared

95

on November 26, 1968. As information gathered later would show, Whitney had left her friend's house in Eugene, Oregon, and was traveling on Interstate 5 toward her apartment in McMinnville when her car had problems and she had to stop. Jerry Brudos was the one who stopped to help her.

When she disappeared people were very concerned, particularly when her car, a red and white Rambler, was found locked and intact, parked in a rest area just north of Albany, Oregon. But though this was highly indicative of foul play, it seemed to be an isolated disappearance and no one connected it to the disappearance of Linda Slawson nine months earlier.

Then a girl named Karen Sprinker failed to show up for lunch with her mother on March 27, 1969. They had plans to eat and then shop at Meier and Frank's Department Store, where they were going to pick up clothing for Karen's spring semester at Oregon State University. After a few hours and a fruitless search for Karen, her mother reported her missing to the Salem police. She explained to the police that Karen was definitely not a runaway, that she was someone special—and indeed she was. At nineteen she had been class salutatorian, a brilliant student, a lovely girl who one day hoped to be a doctor.

Despite this, all the police could do was take a report and wait the required twenty-four hours before instituting a search. They do this because most of the time the missing person will show up within the first twenty-four hours with a logical explanation, and the wait saves time and effort on fruitless investigations. But the next day, when Karen still had not appeared, they started the search.

Eventually the trail led to Meier and Frank's Department Store, where police made an unnerving discovery: On the top floor of the gray concrete garage was Karen Sprinker's car—

without Karen, of course. There was no evidence of foul play, no sign of violence, blood, or semen and nothing to indicate that someone had assaulted or fought with Karen. Her books were on the seat; it was as if she had vanished into thin air.

Since it was broad daylight when Karen entered the garage, and quite a few people passed through it, it was difficult to envision how she could have been abducted. But then one of the detectives theorized that an abduction could have taken place if all the circumstances were right. To get from her car to the store entrance, Karen had to walk down a flight of concrete stairs, then pull open a heavy door to get into the store. Maybe someone was waiting for her at the bottom of the stairs and grabbed her? If she cried out, she wouldn't have been heard through the heavy door, and the traffic noise would drown out her cries for anyone on the street. It was later discovered that this was exactly what happened.

The police interviewed people who were around the department store after they found Karen's car in the parking garage, as they now knew this was where she had disappeared. Two young girls who had been in the parking garage a couple of weeks before Karen Sprinker reported seeing something bizarre. As reported in the book *Lust Killer*, by Andy Stack (the pseudonym for ubiquitous crime writer Ann Rule), "We saw this tall, heavy person. All dressed with high heels and a dress. 'She' was just standing there in the garage, as if she were waiting for someone. She was tugging at her girdle and fixing her nylons."

The girls did not think it was a woman but a cross-dressing man. Some of the investigators wondered whether the transvestite could be linked to Sprinker's disappearance, but as it was purely speculation that this person might be involved, there was nowhere to go with the lead.

Another young woman disappeared on April 23, the perky and pretty blonde Linda Salee. She failed to show up at a meeting with her boyfriend, who was a lifeguard. And the next day, when she didn't show up at her job at Consolidated Freightways, alarm bells sounded. A subsequent search by police, who now knew of the other missing girls and were aware of what to look for, unearthed Linda Salee's bright red VW bug on the top floor of a parking garage. The similar MO to that of the disappearance of Karen Sprinker was all too obvious.

Linda Salee's abduction and murder was confirmed on May 10: A man was fishing in the Big Tom River, about twelve miles south of Corvallis, Oregon, when he spotted a body floating just under the water—Linda Salee. Investigators found that she had been weighted down with a transmission tied to her body with nylon cord.

After this discovery, the police decided to search the river for the missing girls. They didn't find any more bodies, but two days later, a fisherman discovered the corpse of Karen Sprinker. It had been weighted down with a transmission.

The cops knew this about serial killers with this kind of output and MO: They would not stop. This man would kill, and kill some more, until he was caught or killed. The cops were imbued now with a sense of urgency.

The Salem police, led by Lieutenant Jim Stovall, launched an intensive and widespread investigation. As part of their investigation, Stovall and his team made an assumption: Maybe the killer had tracked Karen Sprinker. Maybe she wasn't a random victim but someone who had been selected and then captured and killed. They decided to question people at Oregon State University who knew Sprinker, and ask them whether anyone unusual seemed to be hanging around lately or whether they had seen anyone with Sprinker who seemed unusual.

But they didn't stop there. The team questioned hundreds of coeds at the university, hoping to come up with anyone at all.

"Vietnam Vet"

After weeks of interrogation, the police came across something promising. Three women had received calls from someone who addressed them by their first names and identified himself as a Vietnam veteran. He had asked the girls if they were available for "Coke and conversation." Two of the girls refused, but one didn't. She met with the man, who said his name was Jerry.

She didn't like him. She described him as being about thirty, with red hair and freckles. He was around 6'0" and on the pudgy side.

The cops were very interested. In a separate prong of the investigation they had learned of a big man with red hair and freckles who had recently tried to wrestle two young girls into a car. The cops told the woman that if the man ever called her again, she was to try to stall him until they could get to her. One night a couple of weeks later the man called and asked the woman if she could be ready to meet him in fifteen minutes. She stalled, saying she would—but it would have to be in an hour. He agreed, and as soon as she hung up she called the police.

An hour later, the man showed up and was greeted by the police. He identified himself as Jerome Henry Brudos. The police had no reason to hold him, but they decided he was worth looking into. When they checked his past, they found he had a troubled history, including a record for sexual assault. They started to "look at him hard," as the police say, and the more they saw, the more interested they became. They put a trail on him for two reasons: to learn more about him and, if he was the killer, to perhaps save someone's life.

The officers trailing Brudos caught him loading up his car with luggage on May 30, 1969. It looked like he might be running away, so they made their move. They arrested him.

A Gruesome Confession

The case was broken during interrogation by Lieutenant Jim Stovall. Brudos, despite the warnings of his attorney, just kept talking. He eventually admitted his first murder of the encyclopedia saleswoman, and the floodgates opened. He admitted killing the other girls and added some gruesome details: He had made paperweights out of the breasts of some of them.

But the method he used to kill them was the real horror. He took them to his garage, trussed them, tied a noose around their necks, and, with the rope secured to an overhead beam, winched them off the floor and strangled them. He also liked to photograph them as they died. Indeed, when police examined the picture of Jan Susan Whitney being hung, in a corner of the picture they saw a face reflected in a mirror—the face of the photographer, Jerry Brudos.

The investigation into his background provided some interesting information, from the days when he would steal women's underwear and shoes to the days of invading apartments to steal the items, and finally to the point where he stole their underwear, their breasts and feet, and their lives.

Afterword

Brudos was convicted of the killings and sentenced to consecutive life terms. In 1969, he was confined to the Oregon State Penitentiary, a maximum-security facility. He was sentenced under the old system, which meant that he had a parole eligibility hearing once every two years; the new "matrix" system today is based on the severity of the crime and the background of the perpetrator.

Penitentiary authorities say Brudos was a model prisoner, but there was little chance of his parole. Said Kay Hopkins, the cousin of one of the victims, "Being a model prisoner doesn't mean anything to us or to his next victim." But no need to worry: Brudos died in 2006.

Not Prom King

While prison authorities thought Jerry Brudos was a model prisoner, he was hardly popular with other inmates. During the years he spent in prison he had a number of "accidents," including one that left him with a fractured neck

Chapter 10

Henry Lee Lucas and Ottis Toole

Notable Quotable

Toole enjoyed crucifying his victims, after which he would often barbecue and eat them. Lucas said he never joined Ottis in these unholy feasts. When asked why not, he replied, "I don't like barbecue sauce."

If serial murder has a poster child, Henry Lee Lucas is surely a candidate. It has been said that he killed more than three hundred people, and while this is undoubtedly false, one thing is for sure: He murdered a lot of people. There's no question he was a very dangerous man. His compatriot and lover, Ottis Toole, was no slouch in the murder department, either. Lucas and Toole traveled across the country in the 1970s and 1980s, committing many of their murders along Interstate 35, which stretches from Laredo, Texas, to Gainesville, Florida.

The Clearance Factor

There has been some debate over whether Lucas was actually the perpetrator of all the murders he confessed to. The Texas Rangers, a law enforcement organization that assists local police departments in a kind of "have expertise, will travel" capacity, say that Lucas was a genuine serial murderer, and in the mid-1980s he cooperated with law enforcement departments all over the country. The Rangers let Lucas travel to various states and be interviewed by various departments, and he helped "clear," as they say in police parlance, hundreds of murders by confessing to them.

Henry Lee Lucas, right, and Ottis Toole

But there are local law enforcement groups, such as the Texas state attorney general's office, that say that Lucas the serial killer is more myth than fact. In 1986, Texas Attorney General Jim Mattox published the "Lucas Report," a thick document that examines a number of murders Lucas confessed to and that allegedly proves how Lucas couldn't be the killer.

There are also ordinary people who do not believe Lucas is the killer he confesses to be. One family, the Lemonses of Lubbock, Texas, went to great lengths, including selling their house, to finance an investigation of Lucas's claims that he had killed their newly married daughter, nineteen-year-old Deborah Sue Williamson. Their conclusion, as reported by Ron Rosenbaum in a September 1990 article on the controversy in *Vanity Fair* magazine, was that Lucas was not the killer; they claimed that Lucas did not know details of the case, such as the layout of the house, and believed the killer of their daughter was still at large. The Texas reporter Hugh Aynesworth also analyzed Lucas's confessions. The result was a report in the *Dallas Times Herald* that discredited dozens more of the murders Lucas claimed.

At the core of the controversy seems to be the "clearance" factor. Detectives like it when cases are cleared or solved—it makes life easier and makes them look good. In this case, it would also make the Rangers look good, because they "owned" the clearance weapon in so many cases from the 1970s and 1980s: Henry Lee Lucas and his confessions. So it could be possible that there are other murderers involved in these crimes and the police just don't want to solve them.

It's impossible to know for sure how many murders he actually committed, but Henry Lee Lucas was beyond a doubt a serial killer, and a most active one. It's definitely possible that he lied about some confessions or was somehow cajoled or coerced or conned into giving them—or perhaps he was the con, confessing to more and more crimes to boost his notoriety or just mess with the authorities. But lies aside, there have to be other murders he confessed to—many murders—that he did commit.

A Horrific Childhood

There is no doubt that Lucas had a childhood that could incite a murderous rage. He was raised, as Ron Rosenbaum reports in *Vanity Fair*, "in a fairly primitive log-cabin-like dwelling in an isolated backwoods county in western Virginia, the kind of hillbilly milieu that produced the predators of *Deliverance*." Appropriately, the name of the town was Blacksburg (the same town, in fact, where a gunman went wild at Virginia Tech and killed thirty-two people in April 2007).

But it wasn't the town that did Henry Lucas in. It was mainly his mother. "I was brought up like a dog," Lucas told Rosenbaum in a death-row interview. "No human being should have to be put through what I was."

His stepfather, nicknamed "No Legs" by townsfolk, was an alcoholic who had lost his legs to a slow-moving freight train. For whatever reason, perhaps lack of money, he did not buy prostheses for his limbs—instead, he slid around the bare dirt floor of the shack the Lucases called home, propelling himself on his stumps. Said Lucas of his father, as stated in Joel Norris's book *Serial Killers*, "He hopped around on his ass all his life."

Lucas's mother, Viola, was part Cherokee—and all monster. She was a part-time prostitute who used to service men in the cabin and liked to force "No Legs" to watch. The legless man would watch as long as he could and then get sick. On the final occasion he watched, a winter day in 1950, he was so overwhelmed by what he was seeing that he dragged himself out into the cold, snow-covered landscape and lay there all night. Within a week he was dead of pneumonia.

Viola Lucas also made Henry Lee watch her practice her profession, from the ripe old age of eight until he was fourteen. To add to the event, she liked to dress him as a little girl when he watched. She also dressed Henry Lee as a little girl when he went to school, taking pains to curl his then-long blond hair. When he wasn't dressed as a girl, he went to school dirty and smelly and dressed in ragged clothes. One teacher there remembered that he was particularly pathetic among a group of students who came from poverty-stricken families and that the other children constantly taunted him, particularly for his glass eye (Henry Lee had lost an eye to an accident when he was seven).

One would have to search very hard to find a mother who was crueler to her son than Viola Lucas was. She relished her cruelty, even reveled in it. She was the antithesis of warm and nurturing, what we expect a mother to be. Verbally, she constantly tore him apart, detailing what a worthless person he was, what a burden. Physically, she was a savage. She beat him constantly with anything that was handy—including two-by-fours. Years later, the damage from her beatings would show up in CAT scans taken of Lucas's brain.

Viola's cruelty was not only constant but also inspired. For example, Henry Lee came to love a mule on the farm, and one day Viola asked if he liked it. He told her he did, very much. That was enough for Viola. She went into the shed, came out with a shotgun, and killed the mule as Henry Lee watched. Then she beat Henry Lee for burdening her with having to pay for the animal's removal.

His diet was minimal. He suffered from malnutrition and later, as Joel Norris reports in *Serial Killers*, there were excessive amounts of lead and cadmium found in his body. Henry Lee would often try to supplement what he got at home by foraging through garbage cans.

The effects of his mother's savagery started showing up fairly early. In Henry Lee's case it was cruelty to animals, a typical symptom of a budding serial murderer. Henry Lee and his half brother got into the habit of killing farm animals and then having intercourse with them, a practice Henry Lee would continue years later with human beings.

Henry Lee would also pleasure himself by skinning small animals alive. By the age of ten, he was drinking like a fish and had become an accomplished thief.

By his own admission, Henry Lee started to kill people when he was fifteen. He attempted to rape a girl in the county and she resisted, so he strangled her and buried her body.

Later he would state that it was his "worst murder"—not because he felt remorse, but because he was afraid the police would track him down. They didn't, and Lucas eventually left home and began his pattern of crime, which was usually to steal cars, money, whatever, get caught, and be incarcerated. He served time in Virginia State Penitentiary and a federal reformatory in Ohio.

Killing Mom

The year 1959 was a good one for Henry Lee; he murdered his mother. At the time, Viola was staying in Michigan with Lucas's sister, and Lucas, freshly discharged from the penitentiary in Virginia, met her there. He introduced his mother to a woman he had met named Stella, whom Lucas said he was going to marry.

Viola didn't approve of Stella—and she also accused Henry Lee of molesting his sister's children. They argued. Both were drunk, the argument got physical, and Henry Lee stabbed her in the chest. She lay on the floor for half a day, bleeding, before her daughter found her; she subsequently died.

Henry Lee was sentenced to forty years for his mother's murder and was to spend the time at the Michigan State Penitentiary. Prison changed him, but not in the way law enforcement would have liked. Before prison, he had killed out of fear or rage. After, he was bent on killing anything with a heartbeat.

In prison, Lucas heard his mother's voice ordering him to kill himself. He pulled a razor across his abdomen and wrists to comply but failed. It was to be one of many suicide attempts. And he heard other voices that told him to do bad things. Prison doctors diagnosed him as schizophrenic, a sexual psychopath who felt potent—and became physically potent—only when he was having sex with dead bodies. (An FBI agent once asked Lucas why he only had sex with women after he killed them and his answer was, "I like peace and quiet.").

Lucas knew he was dangerous, and when he was granted parole in 1970, he begged Michigan authorities to keep him caged up. He knew he would kill. But they let him out anyway, and he fulfilled his own prophecy by murdering a young woman the very same day in Jackson: She lived only a few blocks from the state prison.

A Match Made in Hell

After the murder in Jackson, Michigan, Lucas was on the move, and soon he met Ottis Toole—a man who always seemed to be smiling. Ron Rosenbaum, in his *Vanity Fair* article, described Toole as "a six foot tall occasional transvestite with a build like a linebacker's and a voice like Truman Capote's." Born in Florida, Toole grew up with a skewed sexuality helped by the fact that his sister Drusilla had raped him. Years later he would enjoy watching Drusilla's young daughter Betty have sex with men that Toole picked up. Among other claims to fame for Toole was the abduction, murder, and decapitation of Adam Walsh, the seven-year-old son of John Walsh, host of the television show *America's Most Wanted*. This could be a Lucas-like faux confession—Toole was never charged with or convicted of killing Adam Walsh, though he confessed to it a number of times (and retracted his confession almost as often).

> ### The Warm One
>
> Henry Lee Lucas's eyes struck a reporter interviewing him in the Huntsville death house. "The glass one," the reporter said, "is the warm one."

Precisely what Lucas and Toole did and didn't do is debatable, but it's a safe assumption that their life together was a spine-tingling amalgamation of sodomy, strangling, stabbing, cutting, shooting, necrophilia, dismemberment, and cannibalism. Lucas told Rosenbaum that Toole enjoyed

Henry Lee Lucas, far right, showing police where to unearth one of his victims.

crucifying his victims, after which Toole would often barbecue and eat them. Lucas said he never joined Ottis in these unholy feasts. When asked why not, he replied, "I don't like barbecue sauce."

A Film about Henry Lee

Henry: Portrait of a Serial Killer was a film dramatization of Lucas and Toole's relationship. However, it didn't have much to do with their lives. Despite the gore, it was much too tame.

The duo's main murder scene was Interstate 35. During the 1970s and 1980s the highway was virtually littered with bodies, hundreds of them. As Joel Norris points out in *Serial Killers*, there was no consistent MO in the murders, so police could not be sure whether they were dealing with one perpetrator or many. The victims were sometimes sexually assaulted, sodomized, shot, strangled, beaten, and/or dismembered.

Although the number of murders may be debatable, everyone agrees that Lucas killed Kate Rich, an elderly woman who lived in Wichita Falls, Texas. Rich lived near the House of Prayer, a chicken farm that had been converted into a church that housed homeless people and others down on their luck in the former chicken coops. Two of these people were Ottis Toole and Henry Lee Lucas, and the House of Prayer is where they would carry out many of their crimes. Lucas stabbed Kate Rich to death, chopped her up, and destroyed her remains by burning them in a stove on church property. He also burned her house to the ground.

Another murder Lucas definitely committed, and the one that put him on death row, was the killing of "Orange Socks," an unidentified young woman, found facedown on the side of Interstate 35, strangled, and nude except for some long, pumpkin-colored stockings that were pulled down around her ankles. She was an attractive young woman with reddish brown hair, perfect teeth, a nice body, and a venereal disease.

Lucas said she was hitchhiking; he picked her up in Oklahoma City and they drove toward Texas. At one point they stopped and Lucas made an exception for her: He had sex with her while she was still alive. Then they continued on, and Lucas wanted to make it an even rarer day: have sex with her again. She told him, "Not now." Lucas did not take no for an answer. Joel Norris describes what happened in Lucas's words in *Serial Killers*:

> **She tried to jump out of the car and I grabbed her and pulled her back. We drove for a little piece further than that, and I pulled off the road because she was fighting so hard that I almost lost control of the car. After that I pulled her over to me [and] I choked her until she died.**

Then he had sex with the corpse and dumped the body in a culvert.

Lucas was tried for Orange Socks's murder in San Angelo. He was quickly convicted and sentenced to death by lethal injection. He did not seem chagrined by the idea. He had tried to take his own life many times, and now he would give the state a crack at it.

However many people Lucas and Toole killed, they were

Would You Believe?

Henry Lee Lucas had been sentenced to death for his murder spree, but Texas Governor George W. Bush commuted his sentence to life in prison. It was the only one of 153 death penalty cases in which Bush intervened, and it involved the killing of Orange Socks. Bush explained: "The first question I ask in each death penalty case is whether there is any doubt about whether the individual is guilty of the crime. While Henry Lee Lucas is guilty of committing a number of horrible crimes, serious concerns have been raised about his guilt in this case."

clearly capable of scores and perhaps hundreds of killings. Indeed, how many people would want to go for a ride with them along Interstate 35 on a moonless November night? Chances are that not many folks would be clamoring for seats.

Q&A

Q. Where are Lucas and Toole now?

A. Taking a dirt nap. Ottis Toole died of cirrhosis of the liver in September 1996 while in prison in Florida and Henry Lee Lucas died in prison in Texas on March 13, 2001.

Chapter 11
Jeffrey Dahmer

Notable Quotable
"There's a fucking head in the refrigerator!"
—Police officer during the initial investigation
of Jeffrey Dahmer's apartment

Jeffery Dahmer was born in Milwaukee in 1960; when he was six years old, his family moved to Ohio. There is not a great body of detailed evidence on what happened to create Jeffrey Dahmer, but it is known that, as a child, he was subjected to his mother and father's blistering arguments. There were also reports that a male neighbor had sexually molested him. Whatever the confluence of forces, by the age of ten, Jeffrey was clearly showing the signs of a future killer—he delighted in violating the bodies of dead animals, such as mounting the head of a dog on a stake, decapitating rats and mice, and bleaching chicken bones.

In June 1978, when he was eighteen years old, he killed his first human being. His mother and father, who had separated by this time, had gone off somewhere on separate journeys and had left him alone in the house. He had a car, and he picked up a hitchhiker named Steven Hicks and took him home in hopes of having sex with him. But when Hicks wanted to leave, Dahmer prevented it by smashing him in the skull with a barbell, and then cutting him up and burying the parts.

For a while after this there were apparently no more murders; it was a time when Dahmer enrolled in college, unsuccessfully, and then signed up for a six-year stint in the army. He was discharged after two years for alcoholism.

Notable Quotable

"I couldn't find any meaning for my life when I was out there, I'm sure as hell not going to find it in here [in Wisconsin's Columbia Correctional Institution]. This is the grand finale of a life poorly spent and the end result is just overwhelmingly depressing . . . It's just a sick, pathetic, wretched, miserable life story, that's all it is. How it can help anyone I don't know."

—Jeffrey Dahmer

In 1982, Dahmer moved in with his grandmother in West Allis, Wisconsin. In August of that year, he was arrested for exposing himself at a state fair. In September 1986, he was charged again with public exposure after two boys accused him of masturbating in public. This time he was sentenced to a year in prison, and he served ten months. On September 25, 1988, he was arrested for fondling a thirteen-year-old Laotian boy in Milwaukee, for which he served ten months of a one-year sentence in a work-release camp. He was required to register as a sex offender. He convinced the judge that he needed therapy, and he was released on good behavior with five-year probation. Shortly thereafter, he began a string of murders that would end with his 1991 arrest.

Dahmer's first kill in this string of murders occurred on September 15, 1987. Steven Tuomis disappeared, and people found out he had been murdered by Dahmer only when Dahmer confessed to his crimes in 1991. He killed three more men, and he was also experimenting with his victims, particularly with their body parts. The odor proved too much for his grandmother, who threw him out of her house on September 25, 1988. Dahmer took an apartment on Milwaukee's North Twenty-fifth Street, and there at least eight killings took place. Dahmer's MO was particularly horrible: He wanted to create "zombies" that would be at his beck and call, and to do this, he drilled holes in his victims' skulls and poured caustic solutions into the holes to make them unconscious. The method didn't work, though it did succeed in killing the victim every time.

In the early morning hours of May 30, 1991, fourteen-year-old Konerak Sinthasomphone (the younger brother of the boy Dahmer had molested in 1988) was discovered on the street, wandering nude and under the heavy influence of drugs. Dahmer convinced police that they had an argument while drinking, and that Sinthasomphone was his nineteen-year-old boyfriend. Against the teenager's protests—which the police likely didn't understand, as Sinthasomphone didn't speak English—police turned him over to Dahmer. Later that night, Dahmer killed and dismembered Sinthasomphone, keeping his skull as a souvenir.

Should Have Been Paying More Attention

John Balcerzak and Joseph Gabrish, the two police officers who returned Sinthasomphone to Dahmer, were fired from the Milwaukee Police Department after their actions were widely publicized, including an audiotape of the officers making homophobic statements to their dispatcher and laughing about having reunited the "lovers." In fact, they had allowed a murder to occur and a murderer to continue.

115

By the summer of 1991, Dahmer was murdering approximately one person each week. He killed Matt Turner on June 30, Jeremiah Weinberger on July 5, Oliver Lacy on July 12, and finally Joseph Brandehoft on July 18. On July 22, 1991, Dahmer lured another man, Tracy Edwards, into his home.

Jeffrey Dahmer

According to the would-be victim, Dahmer struggled with Edwards to handcuff him. Edwards escaped and flagged down a police car, with the handcuffs still hanging from one hand. Edwards led police back to Dahmer's apartment, where Dahmer at first acted friendly to the officers, only to turn on them when he realized that they suspected something was wrong. As one officer subdued Dahmer, the other searched the house and uncovered multiple photographs of murdered victims and human remains, including three severed heads and penises. All told, the police found the remains of eleven people, with parts divided between acid vats and the refrigerator. And it was not that Dahmer wasn't religious: In his bedroom they found an altar festooned with candles and skulls of his victims, as well as photos of people he had killed.

The Trial

On January 30, 1992, Jeffrey Dahmer faced fifteen counts of murder in a Wisconsin court. The murder cases were already so notorious and Dahmer so clearly guilty that the authorities never bothered to charge him with the attempted murder of Edwards. His trial began in January 1992. With evidence overwhelmingly against him, Dahmer pleaded not guilty by reason of insanity. The court found Dahmer sane and guilty and sentenced him to fifteen consecutive life terms, totaling 957 years in prison. At his sentencing hearing, Dahmer expressed remorse for his actions, also saying that he wished for his own death.

Notable Quotable
"I really really screwed up this time."
—Jeffrey Dahmer, to his father

Dahmer served his time at the Columbia Correctional Institution in Portage, Wisconsin, where he ultimately declared himself a born-again Christian. This conversion occurred after viewing Evangelical material sent to him by his father. A local preacher, Roy Ratcliff, met with Dahmer and agreed to baptize him.

On November 28, 1994, Dahmer and another inmate named Jesse Anderson were beaten to death by fellow inmate Christopher Scarver with a bar from a weight machine while on work detail in the prison gym—ironically, just how Dahmer had killed his first victim. Dahmer died from severe head trauma in the ambulance en route to the hospital. Before his death, Dahmer had already survived one attempt on his life: After attending a church service in the prison chapel, an inmate tried to slash Dahmer's throat with a razor blade. Dahmer escaped the incident with superficial wounds.

Chapter 12

David
Berkowitz

Notable Quotable
"The demons were howling for blood."

On July 26, 1976, Donna Lauria, a pretty, petite eighteen-year-old, sat in an Oldsmobile chatting with her friend Judy Valenti. The car was parked in front of Donna's apartment building at 2860 Buhre Avenue in the Bronx, New York, one of a number of apartment buildings that lined the quiet street in the middle-class neighborhood.

At about one in the morning, Donna's father, who had been out, returned to the building and spotted Donna and Judy in the car. He suggested Donna come in soon, and she said she would be right up. Less than a minute later, the two women were distracted by the appearance of a dark-haired man wearing a denim jacket and jeans and carrying a paper bag. They watched as he calmly walked to the passenger side of the car where Donna was sitting. Donna turned to Judy, "What does he want?"

Suddenly, a pistol emerged from the bag and the man dropped into a squatting position, the gun held in both hands. He was in the classic combat shooter's pose and fired five shots through the passenger window, shattering it—and shattering Donna Lauria. Upstairs, her father was startled by the rapid-fire crescendo and thought a car was backfiring. He went downstairs and was assaulted by the horrendous sight of his daughter covered with blood, her friend shrieking hysterically.

Soon Donna Lauria would be dead, the first victim of the Son of Sam, a name that would terrorize New York City.

David's Demons

Berkowitz believed that demons talked to him. The killing of Donna Lauria had a calming effect on those demons, but gradually the demands began again. The demons wanted more blood, more shooting, more death. Soon the demands were so strong that Berkowitz, who tried to fight them, could no longer refuse.

On October 23, 1976, he went to Queens, again on the hunt. In the Flushing area, he spotted a red Ford Galaxie and followed it in his white Ford. Berkowitz saw that there were two people in the car, but he couldn't tell whether they were male or female. One had long, dark hair, a favorite of the demons. Soon the couple parked the car near the corner of 33rd Avenue and 159th Street. Berkowitz parked behind them.

Inside the car was Carl Denaro, a young man who was soon to enter the air force. Driving the car was Rosemary Keenan, eighteen years old, whose father was a New York City police officer. Berkowitz approached the car, concealing the heavy gun under a denim jacket. He went to the passenger side of the car and, without further ado, fired five times through the window.

Denaro was shot in the head, but miraculously Rosemary Keenan was not hit and bolted from the car screaming. Despite being shot five times, Denaro amazingly survived, but required a metal plate in his head to replace the bone fragments blown away in the shooting.

The demons were howling for blood again in less than a month, and on the chilly, windy night of November 26, 1976, Berkowitz was back in his predatory mode. Two girls, sixteen-year-old Donna DeMasi and eighteen-year-old Joanne Lomino, had returned to Queens after seeing a movie in Manhattan. They got off a bus at 262nd Street and Hillside Avenue and started walking home. Joanne had a twelve-thirty curfew, and it was almost midnight. As

David Berkowitz

they walked, they noticed a man starting to follow them. They were worried and walked faster, but by the time they got to Joanne's home, he was nowhere in sight. Then they saw him coming toward them, and Joanne searched her bag for her keys. The girls were nervous, but the man—dark haired, stocky, wearing a denim jacket—didn't seem terribly threatening.

In the next instant he was firing at them, and he hit both. Then he was gone. The girls both lived, but Joanne Lomino paid a terrible price: one of the bullets had severed her spine and she was paralyzed from the waist down.

Unconnected Crimes

Unfortunately, the police did not assume that one shooter perpetrated all of these assaults, simply because they didn't have any physical evidence that tied the crimes together. These assaults were in the days before computers were in common use, which help immensely in making connections between apparently unconnected cases. Without looking at all the evidence side by side, why would they assume someone was shooting complete strangers for no apparent reason?

The next shooting resulted in another death. A young engaged couple—Christine Freund, age twenty-six, and John Diel, age thirty—had gone out to see the movie *Rocky*. They returned to their car, which was parked at Station Plaza on Continental Avenue near the Long Island Railroad line in Queens. In fact, they had to walk under a railroad bridge to get to the car, a blue Pontiac Firebird.

It was a bitterly cold night, just five or six degrees above zero, and they had just gotten into the car when out of nowhere shots smashed through the passenger-side window. Christine Freund was shot twice in the head and once in the chest, but, miraculously, Diel was not hit at all. Someone called 911 after hearing the shots, and within four minutes the emergency service team was on the scene. But it was too late for Freund. She died at St. John's Hospital at four in the morning, never regaining consciousness.

After Christine Freund's murder, panic set in over New York. Police put out word across the city to find out whether there were any similar homicides, and the random shootings of six people were finally lumped together. The cops knew that a large-caliber revolver was involved in them all. A homicide task force was formed.

On March 8, 1977—a little more than a month after Freund was killed—there was another shooting. Virginia Voskerichian, an honor student at Barnard College, was walking to her home in Queens along Dartmouth Avenue near Seventy-first Street when she spotted a man coming toward her. No one will know what she thought, but it might have been that he was over-dressed for the day: It was unseasonably warm and he was wearing a ski coat.

The Son of Sam had been searching the area for a pretty girl to shoot and kill for the last hour, as his demons had ordered. Virginia fit the bill; she was slim and pretty. When he was within twenty-five feet of her, he pulled out the revolver. Instinctively, Virginia pulled the books she was carrying up to her face to shield herself. Berkowitz fired once, the bullet entering Virginia's head above the lip. She fell into the bushes that flanked the road. Virginia was rushed to St. John's Hospital, but she never regained consciousness and died at four the next morning.

If the police had any doubts as to whether there was a psycho loose in the city, the investigation into Virginia's death erased those doubts. A .44 caliber bullet was recovered from the scene, and the New York Police Department's ballistics unit matched it to one of the bullets used to kill Donna Lauria only six months earlier. They now knew beyond a shadow of a doubt that there was a serial killer on the loose.

Police Commissioner Michael Codd called a press conference on March 10 and announced to the world that a crazy man was on the loose, and that women—particularly pretty girls with dark hair—were at risk. Panic spread and then deepened. The .44 caliber killer was front-page news, and more shootings—and a frightening letter—whipped the city's fear into a frenzy.

On April 17, a young couple, Alexander Esau, age twenty, and Valentina Suriana, age eighteen, were shot dead while parked just a block short of 1950 Hutchinson River Parkway in the Bronx—only three blocks from where Donna Lauria had been killed. The killer was getting better: fewer shots and more deaths. Only four shots had been fired this time, two into each victim. Along with the bodies that displayed the killer's newfound marksmanship, there was another new development with these murders—police found this letter at the scene (shown as written):

Dear Captain Joseph Borrelli, I am deeply hurt by your calling me a wemon hater. I am not. But I am a monster. I am the 'Son of Sam.' I am a little brat.

When father Sam gets drunk he gets mean. He beats his family. Sometimes he ties me up to the back of the house. Other times he locks me in the garage. Sam loves to drink blood. 'Go out and kill,' commands father Sam. Behind our house some rest. Mostly young—raped and slaughtered—their blood drained—just bones now. Papa Sam keeps me locked in the attic too. I can't get out but I look out the attic window and watch the world go by. I feel like an outsider. I am on a different wavelength then everybody else—programmed too kill. However, to stop me you must kill me. Attention all police: Shoot me first—shoot to kill or else keep out of my way or you will die! Papa Sam is old now. He needs some blood to preserve his youth. He has had too many heart attacks. 'Ugh, me hoot, it hurts, sonny boy.' I miss my pretty princess most of all. She's resting in our ladies house. But I'll see her soon. I am the 'Monster'—'Beelzebub'—the chubby behemouth. I love to hunt. Prowling the streets looking for fair game—tasty meat. The wemon of Queens are prettyist of all. It must be the water they drink. I live for the hunt—my life. Blood for papa. Mr. Borrelli, sir, I don't want to kill anymore. No sur, no more but I must, 'honour thy father.' I want to make love to the world. I love people. I don't belong on earth. Return me to yahoos. To the people of Queens, I love you. And I want to wish all of you a happy Easter. May God bless you in this life and in the next. I say goodbye and goodnight. Police, let me

haunt you with these words: I'll be back! I'll be back! To be interrupted as—bang, bang, bang, bang, bang—ugh! "Yours in murder Mr. Monster."

Now the newspapers had an official name for the killer: the Son of Sam.

More Shootings

On June 26, two months after the killings of Esau and Suriana, the killer struck again, this time shooting Judy Placido, age seventeen, and Salvatore Lupo, age twenty. They had been at the Elephas dance club, and their car was parked across the street at 4539 211th Street in Queens. Ironically, the young couple was talking about the Son of Sam when suddenly there was a booming echo inside the car. Unbelievably they both survived the shooting, though Placido was shot in the temple, near the spine, and in the shoulder. Lupo was hit in the arm.

A Brush with Danger

The Son of Sam's next foray personally touched this author, Tom Philbin, in a chilling way. On July 31, 1977, my two young daughters wanted to go to a teen club in the mall in the town of Huntington, Long Island, where I lived. I discussed the possible danger of the Son of Sam with my wife, Catherine, who was worried that the killer might go there. I pooh-poohed her fear, but the end result was that the girls didn't go. Later, when Berkowitz was captured, it turned out that he had gone to Huntington that very night planning to kill someone, but as reported in Son of Sam, by Lawrence D. Klausner, he decided not to do it because the place didn't seem right—his demons demurred.

So the Son of Sam made his way into Brooklyn on the night of July 31, 1977, looking for people to shoot, and he found them: Stacy Moskowitz, a pretty twenty-year-old blonde, and her date, twenty-year-old Robert Violante. The couple had parked on Shore Parkway, next to a cyclone fence, after another very lucky couple had pulled out of the area just moments before. It was just after two-thirty in the morning, and the Son of Sam fired five shots into the car. The shots made Robert Violante blind. They killed Stacy Moskowitz.

A Break in the Case

As often happens in matters of great consequence, the thing that ultimately resulted in the capture of Son of Sam was something utterly pedestrian: a traffic ticket. It was fortunate timing, because as he would later report, the killer was getting bored with these types of homicidal forays and wanted to do something a little more dramatic and climactic—a mass murder. In fact, he almost did it.

On Saturday, August 6, he decided that he would slaughter a bunch of people at a campground in Southampton, Long Island, a place he knew because he had camped there the year before. The campground was at the peak of its season, loaded with young people. Berkowitz showered, dressed in fresh clothes, and loaded his revolver and a .45 caliber semiautomatic rifle.

Rich Girl

David Berkowitz once claimed that the No. 1 song "Rich Girl," by Hall and Oates, was the motivation behind the murders he had committed, but because the song came out after the killings had begun, it was in all likelihood just more disinformation Berkowitz enjoyed telling the investigators

It was a two-and-a-half-hour drive to Southampton, and the weather, which had started out fine, changed as he went. Great thunderheads dominated the gray sky, and before he knew it, raindrops spattered on his windshield and soon turned into a torrent. The sky shredded with lightning. It got so bad that Berkowitz pulled off to the side of the road to wait out the storm and await word from his demons. The demons decided that the storm had cleared away too many potential victims. They instructed Berkowitz to go home. A summer shower had prevented a bloodbath.

Then the demons turned on him. In his apartment in Yonkers, a community just north of the Bronx, they ripped at him for not being able to fulfill his mission. They didn't accept rain as an excuse, even though they had ordered him to abort the plan. Berkowitz's punishment was simple: He had to die. But while the Son of Sam wrestled with his demons, forces were combining that would result in his capture.

The night he killed Stacy Moskowitz and blinded Robert Violante, Berkowitz had parked at 290 Bay Seventeenth, only a block and a half from the scene of the crime. During the investigation into the deaths of the young couple, a woman who had been walking her dog said that she spotted a police-man writing a ticket for a cream-colored car parked in that spot. But none of the officers could remember it, and the ticket seemed to have vanished. Then, about two weeks later, some-one found the ticket squirreled away with some others in the backroom of the precinct where it had been issued. The car belonged to David Berkowitz, of 35 Pine Street, Yonkers, New York. Some detectives went to Berkowitz's address and found his car parked in the street—and spotted something inside that electrified them. Sticking out from under a gunnysack was the butt of a machine gun. They also saw two letters, in handwriting that resembled the handwriting that Son of Sam had used in the terrifying letters he had been writing to *Daily News* columnist Jimmy Breslin.

Soon there were three hundred police officers surrounding Berkowitz's building, and the district attorney had gone on a frantic foray for a search warrant. They waited and waited and waited, and finally Berkowitz appeared. The cops weren't sure what to do. Should they grab him? Arrest him before the search warrant arrived? Then, perhaps with the idea that he was leaving to go kill again, they acted when Berkowitz got into his car: Guns drawn, they tapped on the car window and shouted at Berkowitz to freeze. Berkowitz looked at one of the detectives, Bill Gardella. "He had that stupid smile on his face," the detective was to say later, "like it was all a kid's game." But that could hardly describe what Berkowitz had done. He was put under arrest and the killing finally stopped.

Fifty-six Stitches

On July 10, 1979, David Berkowitz was attacked and nearly killed in the segregation block of Attica Correctional Facility. A fellow inmate used a homemade knife to attack Berkowitz from behind and slash his throat. The wound required fifty-six stitches to close. Berkowitz felt that the attack may have been retribution for talking about the satanic cult that he claimed took part in the Son of Sam murders.

Chapter 13
Kenneth Bianchi and Angelo Buono Jr.

Notable Fact

Bianchi's mother was a bona fide psychopath who used to scream at him constantly and discipline him by forcing his hand into stove burner flames.

Mass murderers usually operate alone. Rage and pain ferment in them until they explode in solitary savagery. But the same is not true of serial murderers—there are team killers in the world of serial murder, and they can be just as deadly as any killer who acts alone. Sometimes these team killers are lovers, sometimes they're friends or relatives, and sometimes they're husband and wife; usually there is a dominant partner, though left to their own devices, both are killers in their own right.

One of the deadliest of these dual death dealers operated in the Los Angeles area during the five months from October 1977 to February 1978. The media dubbed the killer the "Hillside Strangler" because the bodies were invariably found dumped on hillsides adjacent to freeways.

The first victim of the Hillside Strangler was the nineteen-year-old part-time prostitute Yolanda Washington. There was a collective ho hum from the Los Angeles citizens and police when her body was found near 6510 Forest Lawn Drive, next to a cemetery where many stars are buried. Who cared? She was a prostitute, part of society's debris.

Then the body of a fifteen-year-old runaway named Judith Lynn Miller was discovered on October 31, 1977, on the side of a road near 2833 Alta Terrace, La Crescenta. Later, authorities would learn that Judy Miller was the first of ten victims of the Hillside Strangler to be killed in a similar manner. (Washington had been killed in a car, and her body dumped from it; clearly, the Strangler hadn't perfected his process yet.) Miller had been tied to a chair, tortured, sodomized with animate and inanimate objects, then strangled. First, though, as with all the victims, she was forced to go to the bathroom so that, in death, when her bladder and sphincter muscles failed, she wouldn't soil the floor.

On November 20, 1977, two young girls, fourteen-year-old Sonja Johnson and twelve-year-old Dolores Cepeda disappeared, last seen strolling in the area of Dodger Stadium. Neither of these young girls was a prostitute or runaway—they were just normal young girls taking a walk. When their bodies were found that same day in the 1500 block of Landa Street, in Elysian Park, the alarm went out. Both girls bore the traces of the same savagery that had been perpetrated on Judy Miller.

If the police needed any confirmation that a serial murderer was on the loose, another body turned up: Kristina Wackler, age twenty, whose corpse was found in the 4100 block of Ramons Way, in Highland Park.

Terror in the City of Angels

Los Angeles, like any big city, has known its share of horror, but perhaps it was particularly sensitive to extraordinary murder in 1977—just ten years earlier, Charles Manson and his followers had terrorized the community with their savage killings.

Los Angeles reacted to the Strangler with the same kind of terror that Manson had triggered, reminiscent of the terror incited by the Boston Strangler.

Overnight, self-defense courses became very popular, prostitutes started to work in pairs—with one writing down the license plate of any car her partner got into—and some people who committed traffic and other minor violations refused to stop when flagged by police because it had been reported that the killer was posing as an officer. A task force was formed, but the killing continued: just three days after the young girls were found, the body of Jane Evelyn King, age twenty-eight, was discovered in Los Feliz, her body tossed like so much garbage on the off-ramp from the southbound Golden Gate Freeway.

On November 29, the body of Lauren Rae Wagner, age eighteen, was found at 1217 Cliff Drive, in Glassell. A little more than two weeks later, on December 14, the body of Kimberly Diane Martin, age eighteen, was found at 2006 North Alvarado, in Echo Park. Then, almost as if the killer were respecting the holidays, the killings stopped, and the fears of the police abated a bit.

Those fears came roaring back with the discovery of Cindy Lee Hudspeth, age twenty, who was found in the trunk of a car off Angeles Crest Highway on February 17, 1978. The MO was different—the victim was in a car trunk—but her body bore the terrible signature of the killer: ligature marks around her ankles and wrists, and horrific damage to her organs caused by inanimate objects. Fear of the Hillside Strangler was at fever pitch, and the task force of some eighty-five detectives was working night and day and had no leads at all. The pressure to solve the case was excruciating, but they just weren't getting anywhere.

Movin' on Up

Then the killings appeared to stop, which, as it turned out, they had—at least for Los Angeles. After February 1978, no more victims turned up. In total, there had been ten. Despite the fact that the killings seemed to have ended, the task force slogged on frustratingly without results. And then, in January 1979, almost a year after the Los Angeles killings had ceased, task force detective Phil Bullington got an electrifying call. As reported in *Mass Murderers: America's Growing Menace*, by Jack Levin and James A. Fox, the call was from the Bellingham, Washington, police. The Bellingham detectives explained that there had been a dual homicide with the pedigree of the Hillside Strangler killings. Two Western Washington University coeds, Karen Mandic and Diane Wilder, had been found raped and strangled in the trunk of Mandic's car.

Further investigation revealed that someone named Kenneth Bianchi, a security guard, had hired Mandic to house-sit—at a whopping $100 an hour—until his security system could be installed. Rather than spend the time alone at the house, Mandic convinced her friend Wilder to come with her.

The Bellingham police said that Bianchi was a suspect, under arrest, and that they were calling Los Angeles because he had a California driver's license on him.

Bullington checked into Bianchi's background, and he found some thrilling coincidences. First, Bianchi had lived in the same building in Glendale as one of the victims, Kristina Wackler. Second, another victim, Kim Martin, was last seen at that very building. Third, the final victim, Cindy Hudspeth, had lived directly across the street from Bianchi.

Bullington and other task force detectives headed north to speak with Bianchi.

A Man of Two Faces

Bianchi denied he was involved in any murders, but after a careful search of his house by a Washington forensics team, they matched pubic hairs that had been found on one of the girls to Bianchi. But there was something else, too. Bianchi seemed to be a man of two faces.

He kept telling everyone that he had had a wonderful child- hood in his native Rochester, New York, where he grew up in a clean residential neighbor- hood. But when they looked into it, the cops discovered that Bianchi had had a very

Red-Hot Suspect

According to Anthony Kiedis, lead singer and founding member of the Red Hot Chili Peppers rock band, the police arrested him during the Hillside Strangler murder spree because he fit one of the descriptions of the killers.

troubled childhood, dotted with trips to the reformatory. Psychiatrists detailed deep disturbances not only in Bianchi but also in his mother, a bona fide psychopath who used to scream at him constantly and who disciplined him by forcing his hands into stove burner flames. His father seemed to be a nonentity.

Bianchi was subjected to the kind of parental abuse from his mother that prepares a person for a career as a serial murderer. And he did fill some criteria in his childhood that many psychiatrists look for to spot budding serial murderers. He was a bedwetter and cruel to animals—he once killed a cat as a prank.

Bianchi's girlfriend Kelli stood by him, as did his boss at the security firm where he worked. Also, Bellingham's police chief thought Bianchi would make a good policeman and questioned Bianchi's guilt. It was a case, again, of the human "package" hiding the psychotic contents! But Bianchi's inconsistencies in his alibis for the Bellingham murders, his pubic hairs found at a crime scene, and the stunning coincidences of the victims' addresses in Los Angeles, prompted Bianchi's attorney to have a psychiatrist examine him. Maybe, the attorney figured, the only way out for Bianchi was an insanity defense.

There followed three separate examinations, one by the defense psychiatrist, one by a court-appointed doctor, and a third by a doctor hired by the prosecution. During the first examination, a bizarre new element entered the picture: A new persona emerged from Bianchi while under hypnosis: Steve Walker. Steve Walker, Bianchi claimed, emerged when he was a child hiding from his mother. Steve Walker was tough and strong and cruel and unafraid. And Bianchi made it clear that while he was not capable of murder, Steve was. In fact, Steve admitted it. Said he, as reported in *Mass Murderers*, "I killed those broads [referring to the Bellingham murders]."

The psychiatrist wanted to know why. "'Cause I hate fuckin' *cunts.*"

Kenneth Bianchi

Steve also said he had killed the women in Los Angeles, and then he introduced a new, nonimaginary player: his cousin Angelo Buono.

It was later proved beyond a shadow of a doubt that there was no Steve Walker, just a clever insanity ruse—the Hillside Strangler was two very real people, Kenneth Bianchi and Angelo Buono.

Partner in Crime

The older Angelo Buono (he was born in 1934 and Bianchi in 1951) was by far the tougher of the two cousins. Raised in Los

Angeles as a macho tough guy by an abusive mother he referred to only as "the cunt," Angelo Buono had a steel stomach—and a steel heart. He worked in a shop as a car upholsterer, but at one point he became a pimp, somehow having the ability to attract pretty young girls into his stable. He had sex with all of them but only by sodomizing them or having them fellate him. And once the women were in the stable he warned them that if they tried to leave him he would kill them. And they believed him.

Bianchi admired, even idolized, his cousin and moved to Los Angeles in 1976 primarily to be near him. He started to become a pimp himself, and the cruelty the two men displayed toward women in that profession almost naturally progressed to murder. The murders, of course, were marked by extreme cruelty. Indeed, Bianchi's Steve persona matter-of-factly and chillingly described how the two of them had murdered their first, Yolanda Washington: "She was a hooker. Angelo went and picked her up. I was waiting on the street. He drove her around to where I was. I got in the car. We got on the freeway. I fucked her and killed her. We dumped her body off and that was it. Nothin' to it." "Steve Walker" also described how the other victims had been tied to a chair in the bedroom where Buono lived, at 703 Colorado Drive in Glendale, and tortured, sexually abused, and killed.

Afterword

Bianchi rolled over, as the police say, on his cousin Angelo: In return for a life sentence, he testified against Buono. At first there didn't seem to be any hard evidence against Buono, and the prosecution was wary about going to trial with just Bianchi's testimony. However, the judge assigned to the case forced the trial—which took more than two years—and the jury found Buono guilty. He was sentenced to life, just as Bianchi was.

If Bianchi had not rolled, the men might have gotten away with the murders—or at least Buono might have. Buono was "one hard dude," a Los Angeles detective said, "a real throwback. We couldn't break him."

Bianchi has exhausted all his standard appeals and is still serving his hundred-plus-year sentence in Washington State Prison in Walla Walla, Washington. Bianchi has disavowed his confession to the crimes and supposedly has found Jesus. Buono died of heart disease in September 2002.

Crime Can Be Funny

One of the Lucky Ones

Ken Bianchi and Angelo Buono Jr. would often impersonate police officers as a way to abduct their victims. One young woman, whom they stopped on a street in Hollywood, was very lucky to escape with her life. When they asked for identification, she showed them her driver's license and a photo she carried. It turned out her name was Catherine Lorre, daughter of legendary actor Peter Lorre—the photo showed her sitting on her father's lap as a child. Bianchi and Buono thought better than to abduct a celebrity's child and let her go. Catherine only recognized the two "policemen" after they were arrested, and she wound up testifying against them in court.

Chapter 14
Dennis Rader

Notable Quotable

"He had a little shed out back of his house where he'd hidden his souvenirs, panties, jewelry, bras, etc. He'd sit in a chair by the shed, pull out his trinkets and relive the murder of his vics."

—Television writer Tom Towler, who

wrote a teleplay on the Rader case

Dennis Rader was born on March 9, 1945, in a quiet corner of Kansas, close to where Kansas, Oklahoma, and Missouri all meet. He was the first of four sons born to William and Dorothea Rader, and he was baptized at Zion Lutheran Church in Pittsburg, Kansas. His father was a member of the U.S. Marine Corps and starting in 1948 worked for the KG&E electric utility company.

When Dennis was still a boy his family moved to a home on Wichita's North Seneca Street. To paraphrase a poem by W. H. Auden, when a monster shows up for Thanksgiving dinner he looks like everyone else at the table. As a boy, Rader seemed like most other kids. He joined the Boy Scouts, participated in church youth-group activities, and attended Riverview Elementary School. He did not shine as a student, and he started to develop bondage fantasies even as a young boy. While other boys were thinking about kissing a girl or going "all the way," he was thinking about tying them up so he could have his way with them. He says Mouseketeer Annette Funicello was his favorite target for bondage fantasies. To other people, Rader seemed like a very serious, focused person, a bit withdrawn, with no sense of humor. However, when people spoke to him he would give them his full attention, and everyone liked that about him.

A Creepy Connection

When Dennis Reader was a Boy Scout leader, he taught his scouts the knots he later used to strangle his victims.

He graduated from Wichita Heights High School in 1963, and in 1965 entered Kansas Wesleyan College in Salina, too far away from Wichita to live at home. He was still a poor student, and in the summer of 1966, at age twenty-one, Rader quit college and joined the U.S. Air Force, apparently to avoid being drafted as a foot soldier in the Vietnam War.

While in the air force Rader did not demonstrate any bizarre behavior and seemed perfectly normal—in fact, years later when he was arrested for the horrendous string of murders, his fellow soldiers, like everyone else, were stunned. Dennis Rader was not an Einstein, but he was always cunning enough to conceal his true persona. Rader put in four years with the air force and was stationed stateside as well as overseas. He was honorably discharged as a sergeant. While in the air force he was unremarkable in many ways. In the summer of 1970, he returned to Wichita and served two more years in the reserves.

On May 22, 1971, Dennis Rader and Paula Dietz were married. Dennis was twenty-six, and Paula, a practicing Lutheran as was Rader, was twenty-three. They settled in Park City, Kansas, not far from the Rader home in north Wichita. He worked as a butcher for Independent Grocers Alliance for a while, then started at Coleman Company, a manufacturer of camping supplies and Wichita's largest employer at the time. He worked for thirteen months there until July 1973, when he got a job with airplane manufacturer Cessna. He was also attending Butler County Community College in El Dorado, and he earned a two-year associate's degree in electronics in 1973.

The First Kill

In the fall of 1973, Rader enrolled at Wichita State University and spent six years there before earning a degree—he was a poor student, garnering only Cs and Ds. Then, in late 1973, he was fired by Cessna. This perhaps precipitated his murders—the first on January 15, 1974, when he murdered an entire Wichita family, the Oteros. For a first killing, it was quite remarkable: a husband, wife, and two young children, and in a quite a gruesome fashion (see Part 4, "In Their Own Words").

Ironically, he then found years of solid employment with ADT Security, a company that sold and installed alarm systems for commercial businesses. While he installed security systems, he became a full-fledged serial killer known to the police and, ultimately, the public as the BTK Killer (for his MO of binding, torturing, and killing his victims). He held several positions at ADT, including installation manager. It was believed that he learned how to carefully defeat home security systems while there, enabling him to break into the homes of his victims without being caught. He was fired in 1988.

Rader killed from 1974 to 1991—ten people in all—and then he unaccountably stopped, a strange action for a serial killer. Television writer Tom Towler, who wrote an arresting, high-tension teleplay on the BTK Killer, told us "I spent time with several of the cops and others in Wichita who were involved.

The odd thing about Rader is that he stopped killing—unheard of with a serial killer. He's never given a satisfactory answer as to why he was able to stop, but several people who've spoken with him think that when he got the job as dog catcher the new-found authority took the place of his urge to kill."

Dennis Rader

Some psychologists do agree with that assessment: He stopped killing because of the job he took as supervisor of the Compliance Department at Park City, a two-employee, multifunctional department that gave him power and a sense of importance. He and his coworker were in charge of animal control, housing problems, zoning, general permit enforcement, and a variety of nuisance cases. And it was said that Rader exulted in his power and was quite strict and arbitrary.

Rader was also a religious man. He was a congregant of Christ Lutheran Church in Wichita, which had about two hundred members. He had power there, too, having been elected president of the congregation's council.

Disappearing Killer

By 2004, the trail of the BTK Killer had gone cold. Then, Rader sent an anonymous letter to the police, claiming responsibility for one of the old murders. What may have precipitated him corresponding with the police—which he had also done while he was killing—was a book about the BTK Killer. Author Robert Beattie was advised by a police officer friend to write the book as a potential way to smoke out Rader. When the book was published, Rader began once again to send notes to the police about his murders. He wanted to make sure he was the big cheese.

In one letter to the police, Rader asked whether the police could trace info from floppy disks. They said no, but of course they could. Rader then sent a message on a floppy to the police department, and they tracked it to Rader's church and then Rader himself.

To confirm Rader was the BTK Killer they lied to his daughter, telling her that to clear her father they needed a sample of his hair. Fooled, she provided it willingly and when they tested it against DNA samples from crime scenes it was a match.

On February 25, 2005, Rader was arrested near his home at 6220 Sixty-first Street in Park City and accused of the BTK killings. At a press conference the next morning, Wichita Police Chief Norman Williams flatly asserted, "The bottom line . . . BTK is arrested." Rader pled guilty to the BTK murders on June 27, 2005 (for the graphic account of his crimes that he gave in court, see Chapter 37). On August 18, 2005, he was sentenced to serve ten consecutive life sentences, one life sentence per victim. This included nine life sentences, each with the possibility of parole in fifteen years, and one life sentence with the possibility of parole in forty years. This means that, in total, Rader will be eligible for parole in 175 years. Lots of people would have loved to see Rader killed, but at the time Kansas didn't have the death penalty.

Chapter 15
Edmund Kemper

Notable Quotable

"I remember there was actually a sexual thrill . . . You hear that little pop and pull their heads off and hold their heads up by the hair, whipping their heads off, their body sitting there. That'd get me off."

—Edmund Kemper, talking about playing with his sister's dolls when he was a little boy

Everybody likes to experience new feelings, particularly teenagers, simply because they haven't experienced much. They want to feel what it's like to kiss someone they like, to fall in love, to drive a car. At the age of fifteen, Edmund Emil Kemper killed his grandparents because, he said, he wanted to know what it felt like.

During the 1970s, Edmund Kemper prowled Santa Cruz, California, and added some more folks to his kill list: specifically six coeds, his mother, and his mother's best friend. And he did unholy and stomach-wrenching things to the bodies.

A Killer's Childhood

Kemper's background was what one sees over and over again in serial and mass murderers' childhoods: chaos and abuse.

His parents were cruel in the extreme, physically and verbally. A day didn't go by that one or both of them didn't verbally flay Kemper for his inadequacies or punish him in some way. One example from his childhood serves as a horrific illustration: As a punishment, his mom made Edmund kill his pet chicken, and then his dad made him eat it. Later Edmund was to say that he cried bitterly about it.

As a young boy, Edmund gave hints that the treatment by his parents was creating a deranged personality in him. He had a habit, for example, of taking his sister's dolls, decapitating them, and amputating their legs and arms. After a while, dolls weren't enough: Dogs and cats that lived in Kemper's neighborhood would suffer the same fate as his sister's dolls.

Edmund Kemper's size would have allowed him to play noseguard in the National Football League. He was 6'9" and weighed 280 pounds. Nor was this flab; at one point during his heyday, he hung around a bar in Santa Cruz called the Jury Room, across the street from the courthouse. This was a bar patronized by lots of police officers—some in search of the so-called Coed Killer—and Kemper used to delight patrons by grasping two-hundred-pound officers by the elbows and hoisting them aloft.

He did not appear harmful, either. He wore glasses and had a face that was quite ordinary. Indeed, he appeared professorial. The one physical trait that apparently bothered him was the small size of his penis. Says John Godwin in his book *Murder U.S.A.: The Ways We Kill Each Other*, "Kemper was driven by manic sex urges but saddled with a crippling sense of inferiority. He had a small penis, which on him looked minuscule, and was quite inept as a lover."

As well as being physically imposing (except for his penis, apparently), Edmund was smart: It was perhaps this cunning that let him walk the streets despite having killed his grandparents.

After those murders, for five years he was in the Atascadero Hospital for mental treatment. When he turned twenty, no fewer than nineteen doctors there pronounced him sane and released him. Kemper was a good listener, and he likely listened to whomever he could to learn what responses and behavior evidenced a healthy personality. It's easy to imagine a guy as smart as Kemper spouting such appropriate responses and aping healthy behavior to fool the experts.

The Coed Killer

Santa Cruz is a lazy California town known mostly for the University of Southern California, a campus loaded with pretty young girls. Coeds started disappearing in the fall of 1970, and when they reappeared, they weren't all there. As John Godwin says in *Murder U.S.A.*, "The bleached skull of Mary Ann Pesce lay in a wooded mountain ravine; the torso of Cynthia Schall, minus arms and legs, was washed up on a Monterey Beach; the bodies of Rosalind Thorpe and

Edmund Kemper

Alice Liu—their heads and both of Alice's hands missing—were uncovered by road workers in Alameda county. Occasionally unidentifiable scraps turned up: a woman's hand without fingers; a female pelvic bone, one breast." Later authorities would learn that Kemper was a cannibal as well as a necrophiliac, which accounted for the missing body parts.

With the exception of one case, in which he raped a girl as she lay dying, he would have sex with his victims only after they were dead. However, Kemper was more prone to engage in sex with parts of the body. A favorite sexual activity of Kemper's was to take a victim's head into the shower with him and use it to masturbate.

Kemper made sure all the circumstances were right before he would select a victim—generally, he would pick up coeds in his car as they hitchhiked down Ashby Avenue. He used maps to plot places where he would take his victims, and he had a supply of plastic bags with him for the body parts that he would cut off and use for his bizarre pleasures. Kemper would describe later the intense sexual pleasure he derived from devouring large hunks of flesh from his victims (Albert Fish spoke of the same pleasures).

Blood Brothers

In 1972, a couple of years after the mass murderer John Linley Frazier killed five members of a family in cold blood in Santa Cruz, California, two separate serial murderers, Edmund Kemper and Herbert Mullin, began stalking that town at the same time. The combined victims of the three would reach twenty-six. These statistics would prompt District Attorney Peter Chang to say of Santa Cruz, "We must be the murder capital of the world right now."

In snaring his prey, an official parking sticker from the college aided Kemper, allowing him to use the college parking lots. Any student hitchhiker would naturally assume that the person driving the car was not dangerous—after all, they went to school together, right? Indeed, even after a number of girls had been killed and coeds had been warned not to hitchhike, the parking sticker worked: Unsuspecting girls got into his car. Kemper said that at the height of the coed killings he even discussed the murders with girls he picked up—they would talk about who might be doing it and why. He reported that he gave these coeds a free ride—for some reason he never killed any of the girls with whom he discussed the case.

Kemper followed the classic pattern of the serial murderer: He worked from fantasy to fact. For a long time he would fantasize about capturing women, holding a gun on them, and then having his way with them. Ever so gradually, he began to act out parts of it. First he put the gun under his seat when he was driving alone; then he put it there when he picked up a hitchhiker and fantasized about what he was going to do to the girl; and finally he pulled out the gun—fantasy and fact became ghoulishly and murderously one.

A rather savage irony is that the officers in the Jury Room bar unwittingly helped him kill. They gave him a pair of handcuffs and a realistic-looking police training badge. John Godwin reports that Kemper used the handcuffs to shackle the girls who put up resistance. It was a vicious turn of events that must have given more than one cop a sleepless night.

Matricide

Then Kemper did something that apparently had a profound effect on his unconscious mind: He killed his mother. Later he would state (in the documentary *Murder: No Apparent Motive*) that he realized his true rage was toward his mother. He felt that once he resolved this that he would be able to stop killing symbols of his mother. In fact, after his mother's murder he picked up a couple of girls and, instead of taking them to some lonely area to kill them, simply dropped them off where they wanted to go.

When he described the killing of his mother in the documentary, he wept. He said he had actually loved her, difficult as that was to imagine. He stated that he did not "come out from under a rock," nor was he "born to a mule"; he came out of his "mother's vagina."

Kemper said that the last night of her life, his mother, whom he lived with at 609 Ord Street, was doing her usual emasculation

147

job, diminishing Kemper more and more. Her last words to him before she went to sleep were, "I guess you'll want to stay up all night talking."

When she fell asleep, Kemper snuck up, raised a ball-peen hammer high, and brought it down on her skull, breaking it like an eggshell. Then he beat her savagely to make sure she was dead. Kemper cut off her hands and her head with his pocketknife, then cut her larynx out and ground it up in the garbage disposal. Of this act he said, "Now she won't be able to bitch at me anymore."

He stuffed the headless, handless corpse in a clothes closet and then made a call to his mother's best friend, a Mrs. Halleck. He explained to Halleck that he was going to have a surprise party for his mother and invited her over. That evening Halleck came over and Kemper promptly strangled her to death and cut her head off. Some party.

Q&A

Q. Kemper was once asked, "What do you think when you see a pretty girl walking down the street?"

A. He replied: "One side of me says, 'I'd like to talk to her, date her.' The other side of me says, 'I wonder what her head would look like on a stick.'"

Kemper then left the area for Colorado, where he did something profoundly important: He called the police and told them that he was the serial murderer they were looking for, that he had killed his mother and her best friend. He told the police, "Pick me up and put me in jail now or I will kill more." Kemper's demand was taken seriously, and it wasn't too long before they picked him up and brought him back to Santa Cruz. He was ultimately tried and sentenced to life imprisonment, serving the time in the prison hospital, a kind of mental ward within the prison.

Chapter 16

Richard Ramírez

Notable Quotable

"I love to kill people. I love watching them die. I would shoot them in the head and they would wiggle and squirm all over the place, and then just stop. Or cut them with a knife and watch their faces turn real white. I love all that blood. I told one lady to give me all her money. She said no, so I cut her and pulled her eyes out."

—Richard Ramírez

In 1983, there were five serial murders at large in Los Angeles, but the most terrifying of all was the one the media dubbed the "Night Stalker." He was terrifying—his MO was to invade homes in the middle of the night and leave dead bodies and blood all over the place when he left. He was responsible for the deaths of at least sixteen people.

As is so common with serial killers, the extent of the danger was not known in the beginning. The first victim was a seventy-nine-year-old woman in Glassell Park in June 1984. Eight months later, a six-year-old Montebello girl was abducted from a bus stop and her sexually abused body was found in Silver Lake on February 25. The next victim of the Night Stalker was a nine-year-old girl, and for some reason, his pattern differed with this crime. He abducted her from her bedroom, raped her, and dropped her in Elysian Park.

On March 17, the Night Stalker began a horrifying murder spree, entering the condo of thirty-four-year-old Dayle Okazaki and Mara Hernandez, shooting Okazaki to death and wounding Hernandez. In Monterey Park he pulled thirty-year-old Tsa Lian Yu from her car and shot her multiple times. Yu died the next day, while the Night Stalker was in the middle of abducting and raping a girl from Eagle Rock.

But something good for the police came out of this spree of violence. Hernandez, who survived, was able to provide a description of the killer. She described him as having a long, gaunt face, black stringy hair, and wide-spaced teeth that were brown and rotted out, which ultimately would be traced to the killer's subsisting on candy. The police were still playing their cards close to the vest, not saying whether the murders were related.

Things got weirder when the Night Stalker invaded the home of Vincent Zazzara and his wife, Maxine, on March 27. Zazzara was pummeled to death and his wife stabbed to death, but the killer also cut out the eyes of the woman and left with them.

Next, William Doi of Monterey Park was shot in the head, but his dying action of calling the police saved his wife. Over the summer, the Night Stalker killed eight more people of varying ages.

On August 6, Christopher Peterson and his wife, Virginia, were wounded in their Northridge home. And then there were two more killings, and the description of the killer matched the description the Petersons had given of their attacker. The police finally announced they were looking for a serial killer who was responsible for a lot of murders.

Then the Night Stalker traveled to San Francisco, and on August 17 broke into the home of Peter and Barbara Pan. Peter was shot and killed, but his wife survived the shooting and provided sketches to police of the Night Stalker.

Then, a big break came. In Mission Viejo on August 22, twenty-nine-year-old Bill Carns was shot in the head and his fiancée raped, and the Night Stalker drove away in their car. The car was abandoned and recovered by the police—along with fingerprints. The prints lead police to twenty-five-year-old Richard Ramírez, who was from Texas and had compiled a lengthy rap sheet for drug offenses. Police questioned people who knew him and learned that he was an avowed satanist who was crazed about the music group AC/DC; and one of the bands songs, "Night Prowler," had become a sort of anthem for Ramírez.

Richard Ramírez

The police spread his picture everywhere, and now the citizenry had a face to go along with the nickname. Foolishly, Ramírez stayed in Los Angeles, where he had committed most of the murders. He wandered into East Los Angeles, where he was identified by Hispanic locals as he tried to steal a car and was run down and half beaten to death before police, who had been summoned, saved his life. He was held in jail and charged with fourteen counts of murder.

Monster Beginnings

A look at his background indicates that Ramírez certainly had the right childhood environment to produce a killer. He was the youngest of five children in a Mexican American family that had immigrated to the United States. His father was a volatile man with a terrible temper. Richard kept to himself but when he was very young—in just the eighth grade, he started using marijuana and snuffing glue, obviously as anesthetics for living in a household where his father was such an unpredictable and disruptive force.

He attended Theodore Roosevelt High School in the Boyle Height section of Los Angeles but quit in the ninth grade. His diet at that time, which was to lead to the horrendous condition of his teeth, was junk food. It was a diet so rich in sugar that it rotted his teeth and made his breath foul. He continued to smoke marijuana and chalked up his first arrest for drug possession. He was also was stealing and was arrested twice for stealing cars: first in Pasadena in 1981 and then in Los Angeles in 1984.

Notable Quotable
"I gave up love and happiness
a long time ago."
—Richard Ramírez

Richard's association with his cousin Mike aided his development into a madman. Mike was a Vietnam vet and member of the Special Forces, who showed Richard pictures of the killing and torture of Vietnamese women. Ultimately, Mike murdered his wife while the twelve-year-old Ramírez watched, an event that had a profoundly negative effect on Ramírez.

Afterword
Ramírez's trial, which started on July 22, 1988, took a full year. Finally, on September 30, 1989, he was found guilty of thirteen

counts of murder and thirty assorted felonies. On November 7, 1989, he was sentenced to death. Ramírez didn't care. He said in court: "You maggots make me sick. You don't understand me. I am beyond good and evil. I will be avenged. Lucifer dwells in us all."

Right now, Ramírez is in San Quentin waiting to be executed.

Chapter 17
Robert Hansen

Notable Fact

Some (investigators) think Hansen played a kind of hunt-and-kill game with his victims, releasing them in the wilderness and then hunting them down with a bow and arrow or gun.

If Robert Hansen were murdering women today, the chances of him being caught would be a lot greater than they were in the early 1980s, when he was finally tracked down. For one thing, films, books, television, and other media have made the average person—and average police officer—much more aware of the existence of serial killers. For another, many people now know that serial killers often prey on prostitutes. Prostitutes had complained about how Hansen had treated them long before he was apprehended, but the police had a jaundiced view of them and doubted their credibility because of their profession. Also, record keeping is a lot better now. Robert Hansen's criminal record was revealing, but it was kept by separate police jurisdictions, and therefore not all the people who needed to know about his past were aware of it. And, of course, there is that remarkable new investigative tool, DNA.

The bottom line, though, was that no one put it all together before it was too late for Hansen's victims. Although he was a serial killer, Hansen was not, of course, a wild-eyed hunch-backed monster slavering at the mouth. He was a wiry, 5´ 10˝ forty-four-year-old who was married with children. He lived in a log cabin on Old Harbor Avenue in Anchorage, Alaska, and owned and operated a successful bakery there. He was even the object of sympathy: He had a severely pockmarked face, a remnant of his teen years when he suffered from very bad acne, and he stuttered.

But he was extremely dangerous. In the end, he admitted to having raped and killed seventeen women—mostly dancers

Robert Hansen, posing with some of his many weapons

and prostitutes who worked the strip joints in Anchorage on Fourth Street—but state troopers who investigated the case believe Hansen's death toll to be a lot more. Glenn Flothe, one of the state investigators, believes that Hansen killed four or five women a year from the early 1970s until police tracked him down in 1984.

Fire Starter

Hansen was raised in the tiny town of Pocahontas, Iowa. His first recorded offense against the law was in 1960, when at the age of twenty-one he and a friend set fire to the Pocahontas school bus garage, burning it to the ground and destroying three of the seven school buses. He would have gotten away with it, but his accomplice friend was seized with a surge of guilt over the act and confessed, implicating Hansen.

For this, he was sentenced to three years in the Iowa Men's Reformatory with recommended psychiatric treatment. Hansen spoke in a forthright way with the psychiatrists about his compulsion to set fires, until one day in court he got a rude awakening: Prosecutors were using the information Hansen had given the doctors against him.

Hansen said to himself, as reported much later in the Anchorage Daily News, "Wait a minute, Bob, you Goddamn fool, they suckered you . . . So right away I think, well now boy, you know you're never going to make that mistake again."

Hansen was paroled in May 1963 but had some more interaction with the law in Minnesota—he was picked up for shoplifting, an activity that he had been enjoying for a long time and one that continued even after he started to kill. In a confession to police, he explained that it aroused him sexually to steal. Once outside the store, many times he would give away the stolen articles. The stealing was its own reward. He was not incarcerated on the shoplifting charge.

He had been married for one year and then in 1967 married for the second time and moved to Anchorage, where he opened his bakery. His father had been a baker—in fact, the only one in Pocahontas—and Hansen had learned the trade from him.

Criminal Escalation

In November 1971, Hansen was arrested—he was driving in the town of Spenard, had stopped for a light, and glanced over at the woman in the car next to him. She smiled at him, and he regarded this as an open invitation to point his gun at her and demand she come with him. The woman didn't oblige him.

He was released on his own recognizance, but while awaiting trial he was arrested again, this time accused of having picked up an eighteen-year-old prostitute outside a bar in downtown Anchorage, kidnapping her, and raping her at gunpoint. But the district attorney was forced to drop this case—the prostitute who filed the complaint failed to appear in court.

Superior Court Judge James Fitzgerald sentenced Hansen to five years for drawing the gun on the Spenard woman, basing the punishment "heavily on the psychiatric evaluation." Judge Fitzgerald could clearly see that Hansen was dangerous. However, because of the way offenders like Hansen were treated in those days in Alaska, he got out of jail quickly despite objections from the prosecutor. He had immediately applied for parole and was in jail only from March to June. In June he was assigned to a halfway house, where he received psychiatric treatment until November

In December, he was let out of the halfway house on a work-furlough program. In the confession he gave to investigators later, he stated that the very first night he was free he went down to Fourth Avenue in Anchorage and started cruising the area, watching the prostitutes and fantasizing about how he would capture them again.

Then he started to hang around the strip joints, trying to lure dancers and prostitutes with the promise of money for a good time. He was always flashing a big wad of money, which was tempting to some women even though, at the time, many thought of Hansen as weird.

In 1975, another prostitute complained about Hansen to a rape crisis center, and the center reported the assault to the police. But Hansen was lucky. After a while the woman refused to cooperate—prostitutes worry about talking to the police—and he was not charged, even though officers at the time were convinced he was guilty. Hansen, however, claimed that it was merely a dispute about money. Then, in 1976, Hansen was picked up for shoplifting a chain saw from a Fred Meyer's store in Anchorage. This time the law treated Hansen's offense severely because of his two previous felony convictions, the fire in Iowa and pointing his gun at the woman in Spenard. The judge sentenced him to five years—the sentence may have been harder if the judge had known of the two rape charges that had been filed against Hansen but thrown out.

Hansen appealed to the Alaska Supreme Court, arguing that his sentence was excessive—the court agreed, setting Hansen free in August 1978. In doing so, the court cited Hansen's apparently stable family life and his job. Other than his shoplifting and two prior felonies, the court believed that Hansen lived a fairly normal life and thought that with psychiatric help he should be fine. They recommended that he be put on probation and treated, but the treatment never happened. Hansen was free again.

Also in 1978, Hansen applied for a pilot's license. On his application he said he was taking lithium, a drug used to control bipolar disorder. He was denied a license because of this. In a subsequent application he did not list any drugs—and was granted the license.

There was only one complaint on record against Hansen from that time until he was tracked down for murder, a complaint filed by a prostitute. She claimed that he held her hostage in his camper in Anchorage and that she had become convinced that Hansen was going to rape and kill her. Nude and desperate, she had broken a window in the trailer and gotten out, running down the street, screaming as she went. The police got involved, but again nothing came of the case. There was no physical evidence and it came down to the word of a respected businessman against that of a prostitute.

Finding a Suspect

Anchorage city police—and then Alaskan state police—had been receiving complaints about missing topless dancers and others who frequented the strip joint scene on Fourth Avenue, complaints that the police dismissed at first. Topless dancers tend to be a fairly transient group; when a few disappear, it doesn't necessarily mean foul play.

Added up, though, the complaints were significant. The police realized that, since 1980, six dancers had disappeared from the Fourth Avenue clubs, and Anchorage police quietly formed what they called a "dancer task force" to look into the disappearances. Then, on September 13, 1982, a female body was discovered in a shallow grave by the Knik River, in the wilds about fifteen miles northwest of Anchorage. She had been shot once with a .223 caliber bullet; a shell casing was found nearby. In late September, the police got an ID: The victim's name was Sherry Morrow, and she was a dancer at the Wild Cherry Club who had disappeared in November 1981. With the discovery of this woman—with a profile identical to that of the other missing women—the police department's fears that a serial killer was at work in Anchorage were confirmed.

Since Morrow's body was found outside the jurisdiction of city police, the state and city police combined forces to develop a list of suspects. One of the most important things they did was question again and again the women on the Fourth Avenue scene, women who had been bothered at the clubs, or who had been approached and offered money. One of the names that came up repeatedly in their questioning of these women was Robert Hansen.

Then, on June 13, 1983, a patrolman saw a seventeen-year-old prostitute running down Fifth Avenue. She was handcuffed and screaming, terrified. The patrolman, Gregg Baker, tracked the woman through two motels and found her in one of them, still wearing handcuffs. She told him a man had taken her to his house and raped her. Baker found out about Hansen's criminal history and passed it on to the task force. Immediately, Hansen became a prime suspect. Then something happened that made him the only suspect.

The remains of Paula Goulding were found in a remote area near the Knik River about twenty miles north of Anchorage. The grave site could not be reached by foot or vehicle—only by plane. Robert Hansen was the only one of the suspects who owned and flew an airplane.

The cops gathered everything they could and on October 27, 1983, brought Hansen in on the kidnapping and assault charges of the seventeen-year-old prostitute. They questioned him for five hours and were convinced that they had their perp, not only on the kidnapping and assault but also on the killings. But Hansen didn't confess, even though police were able to blow away his alibi. (The wife of the friend who supplied him with the alibi said her husband had lied.)

The trial was held for the kidnapping and assault, while the investigation into the killings continued. Police, armed with search warrants, came up with some very damaging evidence against Hansen in his home, including an aeronautical map of south-central Alaska with twenty-one sites marked off, presumably for the graves of murder victims; a gun hidden under attic insulation, which was eventually linked to the killings of two women; a bag of jewelry containing a distinctive necklace worn by a missing dancer; and business cards of two missing dancers. These things, of course, were the trophies that Hansen used to relive the killings.

A Chilling Confession

At one point, Hansen "gave it up," in police lingo (though no officer believes he gave it all up). He gave police a twelve-hour confession during which he admitted to killing seventeen women and burying their remains in the wilds outside Anchorage.

He took a plane ride with the police and pointed out the burial sites he remembered. During his confession, Hansen went to great pains to rationalize his behavior. He said he would never kill "good women," but prostitutes were something else. He could kill them with impunity. He explained that he had had problems with women since he was a teenager in Iowa and that women wouldn't go out with him because of his acne and his stutter.

He said he always "loved" women, but he made a distinction—a sharp distinction—between good girls and bad girls. Bad girls could die. In the portion of his confession that follows, District Attorney Victor Krumm is questioning Hansen. The excerpt provides some insight into the mind of Robert Hansen. The final question is from Glenn Flothe, state investigator, and Hansen's simple answer is quite chilling when one realizes its homicidal implications.

KRUMM: Why did you drive out to the road, instead of just going to a hotel or motel in town?
HANSEN: You know if you go to a motel or something with it, it's more or less like a prostitution deal. I'm going and, or I'd—I guess I'm trying to even convince myself maybe I wasn't really buying sex, it was being given to me, in the aspect that I was good enough that it was being given to me. Uh, if I can explain that a little bit better gentlemen. Going back in my life, way back to my high school days and so forth, I was, I guess what

you might call very frustrated, upset all the time. I would see my friends and so forth going out on dates and so forth and had a tremendous desire to do the same thing. From the scars and so forth on my face you can probably see, I could see why girls wouldn't want to get close to me and when I'm nervous and upset like this here; if I, I'll try to demonstrate if I can think about exactly what I'm going to say and if I talk slow I can keep myself from stuttering. But at the time during my junior high or high school days I could not control my speech at all. I was always so embarrassed and upset with it from people making fun of me that I hated the word school, I guess this is why I burned down the bus way back in Iowa . . .

I can remember going up and talking to someone, man or woman, classmate or whatever and start to say something and start to stutter so badly that especially in the younger years I would run away crying, run off someplace and hide for a day or so. The worst there was that I was the rebuttal of all the girls around the school and so forth. The jokes. If I could have faced it, I know now if I could have faced it and laughed along with them it would have stopped but I couldn't at the time and it just, it got so it controlled me, I didn't control it. I didn't start to hate all women, as a matter of fact I would venture to say I started to fall in love with every one of them. Every one of them become so precious to me 'cause I wanted their—I wanted their friendship . . . I wanted them to like me so much. On top of things that have happened, I don't want to, I'm not saying that I hate all women, I don't. Quite to the contrary, if, I guess in my own mind what I'm classifying is a good woman, not a prostitute. I'd do everything in my power, any way, shape or form to do anything for her and to see that no harm ever came to her, but I guess prostitutes are women I'm putting down as lower than myself. I don't know if I'm making sense or not. And you know, when this started to happen I wanted—you know . . . It happened the first time there, you know, and I went home and I was literally sick to my stomach . . . Over the years I've gone in many many topless and bottomless bars in town and so forth and never, never touched one of the girls in there in any way, shape, or form until they asked. It's like, it's like it was a game—they had to pitch the ball before I could bat. They had to approach me first saying about I get off at a certain time, we could go out and have a good time, or something like this here. If they don't, we weren't playing the game right. They had to approach me. I've talked to, I suppose I made it a point to try to talk to, every girl in there. Sometimes if I thought there was a possibility that she didn't say it the first time but she might come back and say it again, now I've invited two or three table dances with her and comment to her how nice she looked and everything else and I try to keep it in a joking tone, "Gosh you know, you sure would be some thing, you know, for later on," but that's as far as it would go until she, then she had to make, I guess play out my fantasy. She had to come out and say we could do it but it's going to cost you some money. Then she was no longer—I guess what you might call a decent girl. I didn't look down at the girls dancing, what the hell they're just trying to make a buck.

FLOTHE: But when they propositioned you, then it made things different?

HANSEN: Then, yes.

Afterword

In the spring of 1990, Robert Hansen was moved from the Lemon Creek Prison in Juneau to the maximum-security facility at Spring Creek in Seward, about 120 miles southwest of Anchorage. It was discovered that Hansen was collecting materials—including aeronautical maps—that indicated he was planning to try to escape from Lemon Creek.

More than one investigator thinks Robert Hansen has killed many more women than he has admitted to. He played a kind of hunt-and-kill game with them, releasing them in the wilderness and then hunting them down with a bow and arrow or rifle.

Some killers, police officers will tell you, have something likable about them. Monsters with charm, you might say. But according to ex-major Walter Gilmore of the Alaskan state police, there were no redeeming qualities about Hansen, and others have reflected Gilmore's sentiments. The house where Hansen lived on Old Harbor Avenue is still there.

Chapter 18
Harvey Glatman

Notable Fact

When his mother inquired as to what caused the welts on his neck, he said that he had tied a rope around his neck and was hanging from it—that torturing himself like this gave him pleasure.

Harvey Glatman was reminiscent of a character often seen in B movies: He looked like a harmless nerd, a baggy faced, bespectacled, slow-witted young man. But beneath this benign exterior he was sharp—his IQ, measured while he was in San Quentin, was 130—he was a genius even.

Despite this intelligence, something was clearly wrong with Harvey Glatman even at an early age. When he was twelve, for example, his mother noticed red welts on his neck. When she inquired as to what caused them, he said that he had tied a rope around his neck and was hanging from it—that torturing himself in that way gave him pleasure. In 1945, at age seventeen, Glatman started grabbing women's purses, running away, then tossing the purses back—he was more interested in scaring women than he was in robbing them. This predilection escalated further that same year when he was in Boulder, Colorado. He pulled a toy gun on a young girl and ordered her to disrobe. She screamed and he ran, but the girl was later able to pick him out of a lineup and he was arrested.

Glatman didn't hang around for the trial; he fled to the East Coast. There he was caught in a robbery, and the authorities learned that he was a fugitive wanted in Boulder. He was sentenced to five years in Sing Sing Correctional Facility.

Harvey Glatman

In 1951, Glatman was released from the prison, and he headed for the West Coast, settling in Los Angeles. He became a repairman in the burgeoning television-repair business, and he had a hobby: photography. By all appearances, Glatman appeared to have assumed his place in the community. He had a job with responsibilities, a place to stay, and a hobby. Nothing, of course, was further from the truth. Glatman was getting ready to kill.

The Inspiration for VICAP

Pierce Brooks was a Los Angeles detective who founded the Violent Criminal Apprehension Program (VICAP), a program that eventually computerized files on solved and unsolved violent crimes so that investigators anywhere could study them for similarities. The inspiration for the program was Harvey Glatman: Brooks had had a terrible time trying to check similarities among Glatman's murders, and he convinced his superiors to create it for future use.

Pretty Women

Glatman developed some methods for capturing women that seem like scenes from the movies, not real life—it doesn't seem like they could actually happen, but they did, with horrifying results. For instance, in 1957, under the alias of Johnny Glynn, Glatman made a television-repair service call to the home of Judy Dull. Dull was a very pretty, recently married nineteen-year-old. When Glatman learned that she was a model, he told her he was a part-time photographer and asked whether she would be interested in a job. He explained that a New York City detective magazine had hired him to take one of those woman-in-jeopardy photos—a girl, bound and gagged. If she accepted, Glatman said he would pay her $50. The girl agreed, and on August 1, 1957, Glatman picked her up, ostensibly to go to the photography studio.

Once in the car, Glatman pulled a gun on Dull and said that she was to obey him or he would kill her. He took her to his apartment, where he forced her to strip and took photos of her. Then he raped her and told her to get dressed. He tied her up, put a gag in her mouth, and took more photos of her. The photos

First Sex

Harvey Glatman was a virgin until he was twenty-nine years old, when he raped his first victim.

Glatman took are not overtly obscene: Dull's dress is pulled up above her knees—and, of course, she's bound and gagged.

Two of the models Glatman photographed and then killed.

Then he forced her into his car and drove about 125 miles out into the desert, near the town of Indio. He took some flash photos and then used a rope to strangle her. He buried her in a shallow grave, but the wind ultimately blew the sand off her, and her skeleton was eventually discovered. Glatman enlarged the photos of the terrified woman and mounted them on his wall.

The Lonely Hearts Club Killer

The second ploy involved Glatman becoming a member of a lonely hearts club—the potential predator that women were always warned about when they joined one of these clubs (it's like the equivalent of online dating today). There, using the alias George Williams, Glatman met a woman named Shirley Bridgford. He told her he was a plumber. They hit it off and made a date, and he told her to be sure to dress for the occasion: He was going to take her to an exclusive dance club. Once he had her in his car, he sped out toward the Borrego (now Anza-Borrego) Desert State Park near San Diego, fifty-five miles away.

Out there in the darkness, with only the stars above, he raped her repeatedly. Afterward, he tied her up and shoved a gag in her mouth and took photos of the crying woman. Like the photos of Dull, the photos of Bridgford were more suggestive than obscene. Then Glatman raped her again and strangled her to death. He left her body out in the open to decompose and be eaten by animals.

Glatman picked his next victim from the personal ads of the Los Angeles Times. It was an ad placed by the model Ruth Rita Mercado, who was looking for work. Glatman went over to her apartment, raped her a number of times, and then forced her to get into his car. He drove out to the desert and photographed her bound body, dressed only in a slip.

But Glatman had a problem with Mercado. He liked her so much that he didn't want to kill her. He debated with himself all day, and then, as reported in Jay Robert Nash's *Bloodletters and Badmen*, he decided that to protect himself he had to kill her. "She was the one I really liked," he said later. "I didn't want to kill her. I used the same rope, the same way."

At least one potential victim saw right through Glatman, a French model named Joanne Arena. She agreed to pose for Glatman, but only if there was a male chaperone with them. Glatman backed out. Said Arena, as reported in *Bloodletters and Badmen*, "I'm not so dumb . . . You know, I think he wanted to kill me . . . I knew it even then." Arena was part of a string of bad luck for Glatman—while his next potential victim, Lorraine Vigil, did not sense his homicidal intent, she was plucky, and it was his undoing.

Glatman told Vigil, as he had told other victims, that he was going to photograph her in his studio. Instead, once she was in his car he swung onto the Santa Ana Freeway. When Vigil became alarmed, Glatman pulled his gun. He stopped the car on the shoulder of the road and started to tie Vigil's hands. "I knew he was going to kill me," she told police later. "I tried to plead but I knew pleading wouldn't do any good." So she took matters into her own hands: She lunged for and grabbed the gun. A shot went off, hitting her in the thigh, but she got the gun, leveled it at him, and told him not to move. Glatman's response was to lurch for her and the gun, and they went tumbling out the door on to the shoulder, wrestling furiously.

Vigil got the better of the match and came away with the gun again. Sitting up, she trained the gun on him, and he stood transfixed, rope in hand, not knowing what to do. And just then, Harvey Glatman's luck ran out. A state police officer had spotted the fight and stopped his car. He came running across the highway, firing a shot as he did. Glatman gave up meekly, though he claimed later he could have easily killed the cop.

At the station, he gave up the details on the killings. His trial was short and, apparently for him, sweet. As Nash says in *Bloodletters and Badmen*, Glatman's lawyers tried to arrange for appeals, but Glatman refused to cooperate. He wanted to die, saying, "It's better this way. I knew this was the way it would be."

On August 18, 1959, Glatman got his way, dying in the gas chamber and perhaps leaving behind a horde of grateful movie writers for whom he had provided seeds that would grow into their fictional murderous scenarios.

Chapter 19

Ed Gein

A round five o'clock on November 16, 1957, Frank Worden returned from a day of deer hunting—it was opening day of hunting season—to the hardware store that he and his mother, Bernice, owned in Plainfield, a tiny town in northern Wisconsin. As he pulled up, he got a surprise: The store was closed. It shouldn't have been. He looked in the store window and saw no sign of his mother.

Puzzled, he went across the street to a gas station and asked the owner whether he had seen his mother or knew why the store was closed. The owner had no idea, but he said that the store had been closed for several hours. That made Worden even more anxious. He let himself into the store and called out for his mother, but there was only silence.

He searched the store, then wandered behind the counter—where he made a stunning discovery. On the floor was a mass of congealing blood. A red trail led to the back door, as if some wounded person or animal had been dragged out of the store. Terrified, Worden went out the back door, where he kept his pickup truck. It was gone. He went back inside and called the police.

A few minutes later, three investigators from the Waushara County Sheriff's Department arrived. One of the investigators called Worden aside and asked him whether he could think of anyone who might be responsible for the disappearance or who might be capable of violence.

Worden immediately blurted out a name: "Gein. Ed Gein."

Worden didn't know exactly why; it was more instinct than anything. But he did remember that, just the day before, Gein had been in the store and had asked Bernice to go out with him. To top it off, Gein had asked Worden a strange, now very troubling question: He wanted to know whether Worden would be gone all day, and Worden had said yes, that he was going deer hunting.

Then Worden thought to check the day's receipts. One was for a gallon of antifreeze, made out to Ed Gein. He had been in the store that very day.

Panic Spreads

Word started to get out that Bernice Worden was missing, and panic spread through the small town. Suddenly the police had a problem on their hands—townspeople had heard that Ed Gein was involved, and a lynch mob could form at any moment. More police called in from surrounding counties responded quickly. They knew that they must find Gein quickly to protect him.

Detective Dan Chase and the village marshal Specks Murty immediately drove the five miles to Gein's farmhouse. When they arrived, darkness had fallen and there were no lights coming from the house, which had no electricity. They knocked, then pounded, on the door. No answer. Finally they entered the house and Murty lit a match. The place was littered with papers and junk, and in fear of starting a fire they extinguished the light and left. But both men had noticed a peculiar odor that neither could place.

Back in town, the lawmen saw unrest continue to build, and Gein was at the center of it. The townspeople assumed Gein had killed Bernice—and if they found him, they were going to kill him.

Detective Chase knew that Gein sometimes hung around the house of a friend named Hill, so after checking Gein's house, Chase went over there. Gein was there, just visiting. The cops quickly arrested him and put him in their car, instructing him to lie down across the backseat so townsfolk couldn't see him. With Gein in custody, a second foray to his house was made, this time by Captain Schoephoerster and Sheriff Seley.

This time the men recognized the all-suffusing smell: decomposing flesh. Using flames to light their way, they went through the house and noticed several bowls—but not ordinary bowls. They were bowls made of human skulls, severed just below the eyebrows. It was, the men sensed, the tip of the iceberg. More officers were summoned to bring better lighting.

The cops were right—the skull bowls were the least of Gein's "treasures"; they were merely a warm-up to the discoveries in the stomach-wrenching chamber of horror. On the walls, the cops found death masks made of real flesh from real people. There was a lamp made of human skin, a belt made of women's nipples, human vests with the breasts still attached. To top it all off, the police found a fresh human heart in the saucepan.

It was all too much, and the men regularly ran outside into the November night to gulp down air and try to retain what was in their stomachs. It was horrific; what more could there be? Then, someone yelled from a back shed: There was a body, but no one could be sure whether it was Bernice Worden because it had no head. It was hanging by the feet from a ceiling beam, the body cut from genitals to chest, and it had been disemboweled and washed; the breasts were intact. The body had been prepared just like a dead deer.

Police confirmed that the body was that of Bernice Worden a little later on in the search: They found her head under a mattress on one of the beds. The mind-boggling finds did not stop with Bernice Worden. Gein had made chair seats with leg bones and dried fat. On his bedposts were human skulls preserved with salt. In a shoebox were nine vulvas.

Suddenly the sleepy little town of Plainfield—where doors were never locked and neighbors trusted neighbors—became illuminated in a worldwide spotlight that generated fear and anger. But for his part, Gein seemed unimpressed by it all. And he had hardly seemed like a monster. He was a short, slight, watery-eyed man who looked like he could harm no one.

He was given a quick hearing and sent to Central State Hospital at Waupun, Wisconsin, to determine whether the doctors there could discover what manner of creature could have done such things. Police officers and civilians alike wanted the details, an explanation, for why Gein did this. They also needed to find out whether he was qualified to stand trial—he certainly seemed legally insane.

At the hospital, Gein detailed some of his activities for the stunned doctors. Although it was never determined where all the body parts came from, Gein said that he often robbed graves for body parts and would regularly wear the parts as a human-flesh suit. He explained matter-of-factly that on more than one occasion he had donned a female scalp, secured female breasts to his body, shoved the nine vulvas into his underwear, and gone out to dance in the Wisconsin moonlight!

Ten years after he entered Central State Hospital, he went to trial, where he detailed more of his gruesome activities. He was returned to Central State after the trial, having been convicted of murder.

Gein was suspected of another murder, that of a woman named Mary Hogan, but police couldn't come up with enough evidence to indict him for it. Some of the officers also thought he had killed more people, but a lack of evidence hampered their case.

The Making of a Monster

The most fascinating question of all is, of course, why would Gein do what he did? As with most serial killers, it all starts with an unhappy childhood.

Gein's father was an alcoholic who would become enraged when inebriated. His mother was the dominant parent, the one who made all the decisions. She was hardworking and religious, with rigid morals. In high school, Gein got along well with his classmates and participated in social activities and sports such

Ed Gein

as skiing, archery, and basketball. He also enjoyed old music and adventure movies—and stories about headhunters and cannibals.

179

Gein said that he lived by his mother's rigid moral code. He was described as hardworking and always willing to help neighbors. And he was hygienic: When asked whether he was a necrophiliac, he denied it for a simple reason—the corpses "smelled bad." Gein claims that he never had sexual relations with anyone.

Gein had one brother, Henry, who died in a marsh fire under strange circumstances. It was said that Edward lured Henry into the marsh, then set it ablaze, trapping him. But nothing could be proved.

The great hang-up of his life appeared to be his mother. He was devastated by her death; despite the general disarray of most of his house, Gein kept his mother's room pristine, spotless, just the way it was on the day she died. Gein seemed to find whatever salvation and security he could in keeping the fantasy of her alive in his mind. In a sense, he denied her death all his life. Wearing female body parts and dancing in the moonlight was perhaps his way of living inside her, safe from the world—living in the only safe place he knew of, inside her strong persona.

Afterword

Gein's house no longer stands; a short while after he was charged, vandals burned his house to the ground. No one tried to find the arsonists, and many people would just rather forget it all. To this day many people will not drive by the site of the house.

In the 1970s, the asylum where Gein had been kept was closed down, and the inmate patients were distributed throughout the states, some landing in the correctional system. Gein was placed in Mendota State Hospital in Madison. He lived there quietly until his death in 1984.

Ed Gein has been featured, as it were, in two books, Robert Bloch's *Psycho* and Thomas Harris's *The Silence of the Lambs*. Both books, of course, were made into memorable and successful films. In *Psycho*, the shocker is that Norman Bates has "preserved" his mother in an upstairs bedroom. Also, Bates's identity is merged with that of his mother. Gein, of course, also outfitted himself in female parts and assumed his own mother's identity. In *The Silence of the Lambs*, the killer Jame Gumb skins his victims, just like Gein did.

Many Gein jokes have circulated. Some samples:

**What did Gein say to the lawmen who arrested him?
Have a heart.**

**What did they find in Gein's cookie jar?
Ladyfingers.**

Gein's Car

After Ed Gein was incarcerated at Central State Hospital for committing two murders, his car was sold at auction. This 1949 Ford sedan was the same vehicle he used to transport bodies during his grave-robbing abominations. An enterprising sideshow operator by the name of Bunny Clark bought it for $760—a huge amount of money at the time for an old used car. Bunny traveled to county fairs with the car, which was kept inside a tent. A big sign outside the tent read, SEE THE CAR THAT HAULED THE DEAD FROM THEIR GRAVES! ED GEIN'S CRIME CAR! $1,000.00 REWARD IF IT'S NOT TRUE! The car attracted big crowds, and during its first appearance at a two-day county fair, two thousand people paid the twenty-five cent admission price. The public uproar across Wisconsin over the morbid exploitation eventually convinced county fairs to ban the attraction permanently. Whatever became of the car after that is a mystery.

Chapter 20
Wayne Williams

Notable Fact

A woman, searching for deposit bottles along the road in a slum section of Atlanta, saw a leg sticking out of some undergrowth.

In the twentieth century, few stories equal what came to be known as the Atlanta Child Murders. In the late 1970s and early 1980s, in the city of Atlanta, one African American child after another was found murdered. Panic spread as mothers and fathers and grandparents wondered whether their loved one would be next. Nothing seemed to stop the killer.

The first two bodies showed up dumped on the side of a road, found by a woman searching for deposit bottles along the road in a slum section of Atlanta who saw a leg sticking out of some undergrowth. It was the leg of fourteen-year-old Edward Smith. She then discovered a second body, that of Alfred Evans, about fifty feet from the first. Investigators later determined that Smith had been shot in the head with a .22. Evan's body was in such a state of advanced decay that the cause of death was uncertain, possibly strangulation.

More bodies started to show up in fairly quick succession. The next body found was that of fourteen-year-old Milton Harvey, who had gone to the bank on September 4, 1979, a week earlier, and had never come back. On October 21, the body of Yusef Bell, who had gone on an errand for his mother and disappeared, was found, his body decomposing in the crawl space of an elementary school. Weirdly, his clothes were clean and it was clear that, though he had been missing for ten days, he had only been dead for half that time. In early March 1980, the body of a twelve-year-old girl was found, and just one day after that, ten-year-old Jeffrey Mathis disappeared. On May 18, yet another boy, Eric Middlebrooks, disappeared after receiving a phone call at ten-thirty at night.

At first, Atlanta police were in denial about the fact that they were dealing with a serial killer. The disappearances continued one after the other, mostly boys but a few girls also, which clouded the situation: Were they dealing with the same killer, or did someone else murder the girls? Generally, serial killers have a very specific victim type and rarely deviate from it. However, since the killings had started, there had been seven bodies of young people recovered, and three more were missing—a serial killer was on the loose.

Then, in July, the "summer of death" began. The bodies of five young boys were discovered. Not only was a serial killer on the loose but an extraordinarily dangerous serial killer—he was a prolific murderer who preyed on naive young children.

Special agents from the FBI's Behavioral Science Unit, Roy Hazelwood and John Douglas, had come down to Atlanta to help local police. After they absorbed what was going on, they tried to give Atlanta police insight into the killer—they created a profile. They told the locals that the killer was likely African American, about twenty-nine years old, homosexual, and possibly a movie producer. The killer was also unable to perform sexually, which explained why there was no sign of sexual assault. It was likely that the victims knew the killer and trusted him. Indeed, before some of the disappearances, witnesses had reported seeing some of the kids willingly getting into a blue car.

But despite what turned out to be an accurate FBI profile, the killer still roamed free. However, soon the killer began to make some changes that would ultimately be his undoing. The high mortality rate continued, but now he was disposing of the bodies in the Chattahoochee River. Then, as 1980 slipped into 1981 and the killings continued, the killer changed his MO and stopped killing kids—he began killing African American adults.

On March 20, 1981, twenty-one-year-old Eddie Duncan, a mentally and physically disabled young man, disappeared; on April 8, his body was pulled from the Chattahoochee River. The bodies of three more adult African American men were found shortly thereafter, two of them pulled from the Chattahoochee. The police started surveillance on a bridge over the river, a logical place for someone to dump a body.

Making a Splash

On the night of May 22, the surveillance paid off. Officers in a concealed location heard a big splash and intercepted a youngish, stocky African American man driving on the bridge; his name was Wayne Williams. They questioned Williams closely, and he kept telling lies, saying that he was on the way to his girlfriend's house—except he told them the wrong phone number. They took Williams to headquarters for further questioning but didn't have enough evidence to arrest him. Two days later, the body of the oldest victim, twenty-seven-year-old Nathaniel Cater, was found in the Chattahoochee River.

After further investigation, though, carpet fibers and dog hairs from Williams's home and car were found on victims—including Cater, the latest victim to be dropped into in the river—and Williams was arrested. Police also found five bloodstains on

185

the floor of his station wagon. The evidence—plus his lying—was circumstantial, but it was strong.

Williams was put on trial for two murders, that of Nathaniel Cater and another adult named Jimmy Ray Payne, in January 1982, and it took the jury only twelve hours to find him guilty. He was sentenced to two consecutive life terms. Some people believed that Williams was innocent, and others believed that the Ku Klux Klan had framed him. But there was one telling argument for his guilt: When Williams was locked up the killings stopped.

A Change in MO

One mystery in the Williams case is that, in an extremely rare departure for a serial killer, he started to murder adults. No one has been able to come up with a cogent theory as to why this might be.

Chapter 21
Gary Ridgway

Notable Quotable

"I killed so many women I can't keep straight how many."

—Gary Ridgway

One of the most notorious and frustrating serial killers in American history was the Green River Killer, so called because more than a few of his victims were fished out of the Green River near Seattle. It was years before he was caught, and over those years an astonishing number of bodies showed up. For example, between August 11, 1982, and March 21, 1983, forty bodies were found.

The police department demonstrated absolute incompetence when it came to investigating the cases. For example, in 1983 the driver's license of one of the victims, Marie Malvar, was found at an airport, and police did not even pick it up to check for

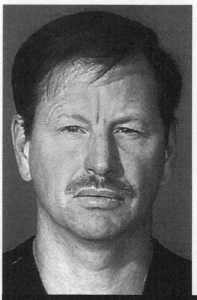

Green River Killer Gary Ridgway liked to return to his victims' bodies to watch them change color.

fingerprints. Bob Keppel, the brilliant Washington detective who did such outstanding work on the Ted Bundy case, was eventually called in to evaluate the quality of the investigation; he cited hundreds of errors. Another mistake was made in 1982: The policeman Dave Reichert came across the body of sixteen-year-old African American Opal Mills. Her body was not yet in full rigor mortis, which meant she had died only recently. Hence, if the police had surveyed the river they might have caught the killer in action—and prevented untold deaths. But they didn't, and that chance was lost forever the next day when a local television station announced to the world that the police were going to start surveillance at Green River.

As mentioned in other sections of this book, often police bring in the real killer for questioning—among a number of suspects—but he or she somehow slides though the net. This happed with Ridgway, a small, mousy-looking man who had, one writer pointed out, lips like a fish. He was interviewed because he liked picking up prostitutes and said he choked one once because she bit him.

But science marches on, and in September 2001, almost twenty years since the Green River killings had started, DNA analysis in the Washington State Crime Laboratory took a major leap forward. With the short tandem repeat (STR) procedure, they could replicate a very small sample of evidence into a sample that was large enough to test. They did, and when they tested semen found on the bodies of three early victims, Marcia Chapman, Carol Christensen, and Opal Mills, they linked them to a man named Gary Ridgway, who worked at the Kenworth Truck Plant.

They linked Ridgway to another victim, and then arrested him on November 30, 2001, and charged him with four murders. As it turned out, his body count would be astronomically higher.

Early Life

Gary Ridgway had a typical serial killer background. He wet the bed, and his mother, instead of nurturing and loving him, would march him out, nude, in front of his brothers and make him stand in a tub of cold water. In a confession he said that he killed a young boy when he was a teenager. While they were swimming, he wrapped his legs around the little boy and forcefully held him under the water until he died. He was also extremely cruel to animals, once locking a cat in a refrigerator until it died.

Afterword

Under questioning by investigators, to avoid the death penalty, Ridgway spoke about his compulsion to kill prostitutes, something he had first been aware of when stationed in the military in the Philippines. He had sex with prostitutes before he killed them, but after a while he started having sex with dead ones, too. Not that bodies were new to him. His father was a funeral director, and one detective said that he wouldn't bet against the fact that Ridgway had sex with some of the deceased who passed through the mortuary.

On May 5, 2003, Ridgway pled guilty to forty-eight murders and received forty-eight life sentences. But according to his calculations, he may well have killed up to ninety women (for portions of Ridgway's confession in his own words, see Chapter 38).

Kill His Own Son?

Once Ridgway took a prostitute to a deserted area in his pickup, and his son accompanied him. Ridgway took the prostitute into the woods and killed her. When he returned to his truck, his son asked him where the woman was, and Ridgway said she lived nearby and walked home. When asked if he would have killed his son if the boy had happened upon his father when he was killing the prostitute, Ridgway responded, "I don't know."

189

Chapter 22
Leonard Lake
and Charles Ng

Notable Quotable

"Give my baby back to me:
I'll do anything you want."

—Victim Brenda O'Connor

"You're going to do anything
we want anyway."

—Leonard Lake

Employees from a San Francisco lumberyard noticed that a young man, who appeared to be Chinese, had boldly walked out of their store with a vise without paying for it. The man had placed the vise in a trunk of a Honda parked outside, and then closed the trunk and run away, inscrutably, on foot.

The employees called police, and when they showed up, they got a surprise: Instead of the Honda being empty, there was a fortyish, bearded Caucasian man sitting blithely behind the wheel. The cops asked who he was, and he answered that his name was Robin Stapely. When asked for ID, the man produced a driver's license with the name he had given the cops. But there was a problem: the man looked nothing like the photo on the driver's license. When they opened the trunk to retrieve the stolen vise, they found a loaded .22 pistol.

He had no license for the gun, and that—plus apparently being complicit to theft—resulted in his arrest. At the station house detectives questioned him, but he didn't answer them—he didn't say anything at all. A few hours into the interrogation, he popped something into his mouth and began to convulse. He was rushed to the hospital, where he lingered between life and death for twelve days until he passed away. The medical examiner determined that he had died of self-administered cyanide poisoning, and they discovered a secret compartment in his belt where he had hidden the pill.

Why did he kill himself? For that matter, why was he carrying around a cyanide pill? The charges against him—gun possession and being complicit in theft—were not so bad, and he might have had an explanation for using Robin Stapely's ID as his own that would not end in an additional criminal charge. The investigation into these questions soon led to a horror story that would be hard to dream up.

Investigators found evidence that many different people had been murdered, including some whose last moments had been videotaped as they were tortured, and it was clear that it didn't matter to Lake—or his coconspirator Charles Chitat Ng, the man who had stolen the vise—whom they killed. For example, they murdered Harvey Dubs, a San Francisco photographer, as well as his wife and the Dubs's infant son on July 25, 1984. And police saw young women being raped and tortured and murdered, and some mutilated on camera so badly that death was the only logical result

In addition to finding horrendous videotapes that were basically snuff films, investigators also found many still black-and-white photos showing women in various stages of nudity. Later, police would try to identify the women in the photos—they eventually found six of the fifteen alive; the other nine, or at least most of them, were presumed to have been murdered.

Police also found extensive diaries kept by Leonard Lake that detailed his compulsion to enslave, torture, and murder women. And they found bodies—lots of them, and a variety of people—in the land surrounding Lake's bunker. Indeed, one of the investigators nicknamed it "Lake and Ng Memorial Cemetery." Investigators found many skeletons and skeletal fragments, which told police there were likely more victims than they knew.

Police also found a wide variety of stolen personal property; they used the vehicles and video equipment to identify the people who were missing or found dead.

Monster Mash

At the heart of Ng and Lake's crimes was a twisted desire: bondage, torture, and death. Just why Ng came to enjoy this is hard to understand. He was born in Hong Kong in 1961 to wealthy parents and was always in trouble, expelled from schools in Hong Kong and England. He was a marine, extremely violent, an expert in martial arts, and he loved guns—enough to steal $11,000 worth of automatic weapons from a marines arsenal in Hawaii with some coconspirators. That was the end of his military career: He consequently deserted and was eventually caught, jailed, and dishonorably discharged.

Lake's childhood, on the other hand, was clearly dysfunctional. He was about fifteen years older than Ng, born on July 20, 1946, in San Francisco. His mother was batty. She suggested that he glorify the human body by taking nude photos of women, but this encouraged him to become interested in pornography when young and to become involved with his sisters sexually. He also was into sadomasochism and

193

bondage by the time he was a teenager, and this interest ultimately turned to obsession.

Lake joined the marines in 1966 and served as a noncombatant radio operator in Vietnam. While there he was given two years of psychotherapy for unspecified mental maladies and was discharged in 1971. He married in 1980 and settled down in San Jose, California, where he gained a reputation as a gun lover and survivalist—and as someone who was sexually bizarre. He liked nothing better that to film women in bondage, and he was the ultimate male chauvinist pig, firmly believing that the only purpose of women was to cook, clean, and be sex slaves. He was married twice, the second time in 1981.

Notable Quotable

"If you love something, let it go. If it doesn't come back, hunt it down and kill it"

—Leonard Lake

Ng and Lake connected in 1981 when Lake answered an advertisement in a war games magazine. The two men had a lot in common—love of violence, ex-marines, and their regard for women as no more than slaves. They lived on a farm together in Ukiah, California, until police raided it for firearms violations. Ng was sentenced to fourteen years but served only eighteen months, and Lake became a fugitive, living under a variety of assumed names. When Ng got out of jail he again hooked up with Lake, who was living in a house in Wilseyville on two-and-a-half acres of wooded land. Lake built a bunker beside the house to store stolen equipment and, when he could, sex slaves.

> **Notable Quotable**
> "God meant women for cooking, cleaning house and sex. And when they are not in use they should be locked up."
> —Leonard Lake

Afterword

"Ng and Lake," one detective was to say later of them, "are as crazy as bedbugs. And killing meant about as much to them as biting you would mean to a bedbug." Ng went on the run after the authorities searched his house, and he did not receive final justice for fifteen years. On July 6, 1985, he was picked up for shoplifting in a market in Calgary, Canada. He fought extradition to the states, where he faced twenty-five felony charges, including multiple murders, and his uncooperativeness and legal maneuvers succeeded in delaying his extradition until 1991. Ultimately, he represented himself at trial and the jury convicted him of twelve murders on May 3, 1999. The jury, unsurprisingly, recommended death. He is currently in prison awaiting execution.

Chapter 23
Aileen Wuornos

One of the more interesting facts about serial killer Aileen Wuornos was that, unlike the vast majority of female serial murderers, she had an MO that men such as David Berkowitz and Robert Hansen had preferred: the gun. Women who kill tend to do it with more, well, "feminine" methods, such as poison, that don't have such an outward show of violence. Wuornos used a .22 caliber pistol and usually shot her victims at point-blank range.

Anyone reading the horrific résumé of Aileen Wuornos could have easily predicted that she was destined to murder someone someday. She was the carnal product of a teenage couple, and her father, a teenage pedophile in and out of

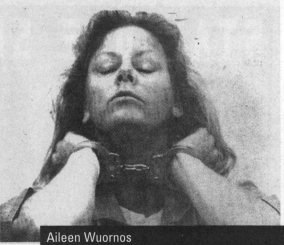

Aileen Wuornos

mental hospitals, committed suicide. Her mother, Diane Pratt, could not stand the crying of Aileen and her brother, Keith, so one day in early 1960 she left them with her parents, Lauri and Britta Wuornos. Their stay with their grandparents was tumultuous: Keith and Aileen possibly had sex and the promiscuous Aileen gave birth to an illegitimate son at the ripe old age of fourteen on March 23, 1971. The following July their grandmother died and their grandfather immediately wanted both kids out of the house.

They became wards of the court, and Aileen started to work the streets as a teenage prostitute, serving time in prison for prostitution, theft, violence, and the assumption of false identities. Although she was young, anger was already boiling inside her. Once, in a bar in Troy, Michigan, a bartender angered her and she threw a cue ball at his head, an act that might have at least put him in the hospital and quite possibly killed him had she connected.

In 1976, Keith died of throat cancer, and she got a pleasant surprise: He had left her $10,000. Rather than use the money to help straighten out her life, she bought a new car—which she wrecked—and quickly spent the rest on bars, booze, and drugs. Around this time, she grew sick of the Michigan winters and looked south toward a warmer climate and headed for Florida.

Florida was a repeat of the beginning of her life, only more so. She was constantly stealing, serving time in jail, using aliases, and working the streets. However, in June 1986, Aileen met the great love of her life in a Daytona bar—the obese, nearly toothless lesbian Tyria Moore. They started living together and seemed devoted to each other long after the sexual passion of their relationship had cooled.

As the years went by, Aileen's anger became even more out of control. She would not back down from a fight in any situation, and she did not take insults lightly. She started carrying a gun, and the rage, resentment, and terror inside of her started getting close to the surface. She told Tyria that she was just waiting for the chance to kill someone because of what people had done to her over the course of her life.

On November 30, 1989, the body of a fifty-one-year-old electrician from Palm Beach named Richard Mallory showed up in the woods northwest of Daytona Beach. He had been shot in the chest three times with a .22. After that, bodies of men were found in rapid succession: On June 1, 1990, the body of forty-three-year-old David Spears was found in a wooded area about forty miles north of Tampa. He had been shot six times with a .22. On June 6, the body of forty-year-old Charles Carskaddon was found; he had been shot nine times, also with a .22.

Cops noted the similarity in the killings but, as most police do, had not yet announced that there was a serial killer to avoid inciting panic. They did have one lead that summer: Peter Siems had been reported missing earlier in the year, and his wrecked car was found on July 4 in Orange Springs, Florida. Witnesses had seen two blonde women get out of the car, and when police investigated, they found a bloody palm print on the car's trunk. They lifted it and kept it for future reference.

Soon, however, it became clear that Florida had a real problem on its hands. The body of Eugene Burress, age fifty, was found fully clothed in Ocala National Forest on August 4, 1990. He had been shot in the back and chest. A retired police chief from Alabama was discovered next, fifty-six-year-old Dick Humphreys. His body was found in an unfinished housing development on September 12; he had been shot seven times with a .22. And then the body of Walter Antonio, a sixty-year-old trucker, was found in the woods northwest of Cross City on November 19, 1990. Now the police could no longer suppress what was going on, and the story of the murdered men exploded in the media. The police said they were looking for two blonde women in connection with the case.

The police received calls identifying Tyria Moore and Lee Blahovec—one of Wuornos's aliases—as the women they were looking for. The palm print confirmed that the blondes were involved.

Officers tracked both women down, but they were not with each other at the time—Wuornos was pawning tools and other items stolen from her victims, and Moore was at her sister's house. The investigators had a proposition for Moore: They wanted her to get Wuornos to incriminate herself over the phone. With cops listening, Tyria begged Aileen to confess to the killings for her sake.

On June 16, 1991, Aileen confessed to six murders. She denied that she had killed Siems and a John Doe. This confession, plus the belongings of the men recovered from pawnshops and storage facilities where Aileen had sold or stashed them, was enough to convict. On January 27, 1992, Aileen Wuornos was convicted of murder, and on January 28, she was sentenced to death. Later, she was convicted of the other killings and received another death sentence.

Black Widows

Aileen Wuornos was entirely unlike a black-widow killer. The nickname of such killers, of course, comes from the black widow spider, which kills its partner after mating. Human black widows are essentially the same. They usually start killing after the age of twenty-five, and for a decade or longer they systematically murder spouses, partners, family members, and indeed, anyone with whom they develop a personal relationship. They usually claim six to eight victims over ten to fifteen years, though in places where law enforcement is lax, the victim count has reached as high as thirteen or fourteen. Poison, particularly poisons that can't be easily detected, is the preferred MO.

They Should Have Known

Wuornos's only defense in the Richard Mallory case was that she had been raped, and when the jury convicted her she screamed out that she hoped the "scumbags of America!" were raped. As it happened, no one had produced any evidence that Mallory was capable of a rape during the trial, but afterward an enterprising reporter dug into his background and found through FBI computers that Mallory had indeed served ten years for rape in another state, a fact that would have given tremendous credence to Wuornos's claim.

PART III

SERIAL KILLERS WORLDWIDE

America hardly is alone when it comes to serial murders and murderers. This part of the book presents stories about some of the worst killers in the world from a variety of countries.

Chapter 24

Ivan Robert Marko Milat, Australia

Australia has some of the worst animal predators in the world—dingoes that will snatch your baby from a carriage, snakes that make herpetologists quake, great white sharks cruising the waters off the Great Barrier Reef constantly looking for their next meal. However, in the late 1980s there was a two-legged predator afoot in Australia who holds the dubious honor of being Australia's worst killer, and he was far more dangerous than any animal. His bloodlust for human victims was combined with a cunning that no animal could ever begin to equal.

In the end, like so many other serial killers, there is no telling how many people Ivan Robert Marko Milat, known as Marko, would have murdered had it not been for the raw courage of one young man, a British tourist named Paul Onions. Onions was hitchhiking near the Belanglo State Forest in Sydney in January 1990 when a silver four-wheel-drive vehicle stopped to pick him up. The driver, a well-tanned, tightly muscled man with a handlebar moustache, invited him to hop in.

Onions took off his backpack, put it on the seat, and climbed in, and the two men started down the road. The driver said his name was Bill, and everything was fine at first, the two men making friendly conversation. Then, abruptly, "Bill" changed—he began probing into Onions's life with inappropriate questions that violated his personal privacy. Gradually the man went into an enraged rant filled with racist remarks, including invectives against foreigners such as Onions—who was becoming more and more nervous with the driver's turn toward psychosis. They were half a mile north of the Belanglo State Forest when the driver suddenly pulled to the side of the road and, gun in hand, announced a robbery.

The situation hardly seemed like a robbery. Why would a man driving an easily recognizable vehicle rob someone? What was he really going to do? Rob Onions, and then let him go to the police? It didn't make sense. Onions drew the terrifying conclusion that he was going to be killed.

Abruptly, leaving his backpack on the seat, Onions burst out the door and started to run toward the forest. It was a run for his life: The man with the handlebar moustache was chasing after him and shooting, the bullets coming perilously close. Onions zigzagged his way through the forest; once inside he was able to gradually work his way to the road. He frantically flagged down a passing car and poured out the story of what had just happened, and the driver took him to the nearest police station. The police recorded all the details of what had occurred, and had Onions describe "Bill" to a sketch artist.

Onions didn't know it at the time, but his chances of dying had he not bolted from the car were 100%. Without realizing it, he had encountered the serial killer Ivan Robert Marko Milat.

Gruesome Murders

Two years after Paul Onions was accosted, the bodies of two British women, twenty-one-year-old Caroline Clarke and twenty-two-year-old Joanne Walters, were found in September 1992 at a place appropriately called Executioner's Drop in Belanglo State Forest. The decomposing remains were not too far from where the driver of the silver car had picked up Onions. The last time the women had been seen was in mid-April, when they were planning on hitchhiking to Adelaide.

Ivan Robert Marko Milat

The girls had been savagely attacked, and there were some strange elements to the murders. Joanne Walters had been stabbed in a frenzy—one wound thrust so deep that it penetrated her spine and the medical examiner thought it might have paralyzed her. Curiously, the zipper on her jeans had been pulled down but the top button fastened, almost as if the killer had raped her and then hastily buttoned her pants to somehow hide the assault.

Caroline had also been stabbed repeatedly in a manic way and shot ten times in the head. The ME theorized that the killer had actually used her head for target practice. Curiously, too, a primitive brick fireplace had been constructed at the scene of the murder, about 120 feet from the bodies. Its purpose was anyone's guess.

The media speculated in headlines that a serial killer was on the loose. The police made no progress in solving the murders over the next few weeks and eventually brought in the criminal profiler Dr. Rod Milton. He posited that the killer knew the area, was in his mid-thirties, and had a history of aggression—but that he was not a serial killer. The profiler's analysis seemed accurate; no other bodies were discovered for a year.

In 1993, two more bodies were found. The victims, James Gibson and Deborah Everist, who had been missing since 1989, were both nineteen-year-old Australians. There were similarities to the first crime scene: For one thing, the zipper on Gibson's pants was open but the top button fastened. Both victims had been stabbed in a manic way, and a small brick fireplace had been built for no apparent reason at both crime scenes. An investigator theorized that the killer was trying to simulate or symbolize some kind of family home scene.

The new discovery made it clear to the police that they had a serial killer on their hands, and the fact that these victims had disappeared four years before was a sign that there could be many undiscovered victims. A huge search was organized and police and volunteers combed Belanglo State Forest and the area around it.

Smoke and Mirrors

One piece of evidence gave investigators pause in believing that Marko Milat murdered solo: the presence of cigarette butts at the crime scenes. Milat doesn't smoke.

A month after the search started, there was another grim discovery—the body of a German woman, Simone Schmidl, who had been missing since January 1991. Like other victims, she had been hitchhiking, looking for work. The crime scene contained the same primitive fireplace and twenty-two shells. Three days later the bodies of two young Germans, Gabor Neugebauer and Anja Habschied, were discovered, bringing the total to seven known kills. The two had been savagely attacked; as in the previous cases, the pants of the young man were unzipped but the top button fastened. He had been strangled and shot many times; the woman was headless, and from rough cuts on her neck it seemed that she had been decapitated with some kind of machete or sword.

International Aid

The police had been reluctant to announce that they had a serial killer on their hands, but a victim count of seven left them with no choice. When they released the info, panic spread across

Australia like wind bending wheat. Leads poured in.

From the torrent of information that came in, several leads pointed to Ivan Robert Marko Milat. He was the son of a Yugoslavian couple who had fourteen children. Milat, a well-muscled man who loved hunting, had been in trouble with the police (as had his brothers) since he was a teenager. Sometimes, he was in big trouble: In 1971, he was tried for the knifepoint rape of two female hitchhikers, but the case brought against him was weak and he was acquitted. He had also been suspected of other rapes, but the cases went nowhere. However, the police had nothing definitive against Milat until word about the case had spread to other countries, when they heard from a Paul Onions who had barely escaped with his life back in 1990.

Onions flew to Australia from his home in Birmingham, England, and when he arrived he was shown a video lineup. Onions picked out Milat as the man who had tried to kill him. This allowed the police to get a warrant to search Milat's property at Eagle Vale, a suburb of Sydney, where Milat lived with his girlfriend. The investigators struck forensic gold at Milat's home: They found camping gear stolen from the victims and were able to connect firearms there to the killings.

Unsolved Mysteries

Police believe that Milat is guilty of many more rapes and murders than those that surfaced, including six Newcastle women and six tourists. These crimes date back to the early 1970s, a time when Milat was working in the area.

Afterword

Milat was charged and brought to trial in July 1996. His lawyer tried to blame two of his brothers, Richard and Walter, for some of the murders, but that didn't work. Milat was convicted of seven murders and received six life sentences, plus six years for trying to gun Onions down.

Who Am I?

1. I was born in Bingley, England. Considered the brightest of my parents' six children, I was also timid and something of a mama's boy who was bullied at school. I could spend hours in the bathroom preening myself in the mirror but had no interest in girls.w

2. In a strange paradox, one of my early jobs found me spending three years as a grave digger. I would quip, "I have thousands of people below me at work."

3. I was devastated to learn that my mother had been having an affair with a policeman. I worshipped her; I believe I was so traumatized by the event that it's what precipitated my becoming a serial murderer.

4. Prostitutes were my primary victims. My MO would be to cave their skulls in with a hammer, and then repeatedly stab and slash the dead body.

5. I stabbed one victim more than fifty times and gouged her back with a sharpened screwdriver. One veteran detective commented that after having seen the savagery of the attack, he was left "numb with horror."

6. All of England was in an uproar over me, and the manhunt that mobilized was the biggest ever seen in Britain. It involved 304 full-time officers who interviewed 175,000 people. I was interviewed several times myself but always released.

7. During one period of my five-year reign of terror, someone claiming to be the killer sent a cassette tape and letters to the police. It turned out to be a cruel hoax that allowed me to kill three more women while the police concentrated on the misinformation. The hoaxer was never caught.

8. One evening, in an instance of blind luck—bad luck for me—the police spotted a prostitute getting into my car (she would surely have been my next victim). In the course of being questioned about soliciting a prostitute, the police discovered I had false license plates on the car. Brought in for further questioning, I finally admitted to the attacks. My confession took seventeen hours to complete.

9. At my trial, I made claims that I had heard the voice of God telling me to rid the world of prostitutes. Several psychiatrists also stated that I was a paranoid schizophrenic, but despite my insanity defense, I was found guilty on thirteen counts of murder and sentenced to life in prison.

10. I still think about my victims. I once said, "They are all in my brain, reminding me of the beast that I am. Just thinking of them reminds me what a monster I am. Still, the women I killed were filthy-bastard prostitutes who were littering the streets. I was just cleaning up the place a bit."

Peter Sutcliffe

Answer: I am Peter Sutcliffe.

Chapter 25
Paul Bernardo and Karla Homolka, Canada

Notable Fact

Karla told Paul that she would help him implement the rape of her little sister Tammy—all they had to do was drug Tammy into unconsciousness.

With three killings under their collective belt, Paul Bernardo and his wife, Karla Homolka, hardly seem the most notorious of serial murderers—that is, until you get up close to the homicides they committed and realize that, had fate not intervened, they would have continued to kill ad nauseam.

Paul and Karla also nicely demonstrate that when it comes to killers, you can't judge by appearances. After their crimes were discovered, someone in the media dubbed them the "Ken and Barbie Killers" for their wholesome good looks. Both also had seemingly solid backgrounds. Paul, born in Scarborough, Ontario, in 1964, had graduated from the University of Toronto. When people asked him what he did for a living, he told them he was an accountant. Karla was born in Port Credit, not far from Toronto, and graduated from high school. She was employed as a veterinary's assistant at the Martindale Animal Clinic, an experience that would prove invaluable when they started to murder people.

An Unholy Union

Paul Bernardo and Karla Homolka

In mid-October 1987, Karla, just seventeen years old, attended a pet convention in Toronto. Paul, age twenty-three, was there on business for his employer, Price Waterhouse. They spotted each other in the hotel restaurant and sparks flew. Within hours they were in one of the hotel's rooms having white-hot sex.

From the beginning, Paul's handsomeness and sophisticated ways dominated Karla, even mesmerized her. They started going steady. In 1990, Paul was fired from his accounting job at Price Waterhouse. Rather than try to get a new job, he started smuggling cigarettes into Canada and engaging in other criminal activities. To make matters worse, he was also named a suspect in a series of fourteen rapes that had occurred in Scarborough. The Metro Toronto Police asked him to furnish them with blood, saliva, and hair samples for DNA testing.

Sadomasochism

Paul Bernardo and Karla Homolka based their sexual relationship on sadomasochism, or S&M. In fact, the first time they had sex Bernardo used handcuffs to shackle Karla to the bed and pretend to rape her.

Bernardo complied but there was a major screw-up: The forensic unit did not immediately test the samples. If they had, they almost surely would have come up with a match, and Bernardo would have been arrested for rape—and three young girls would likely have lived.

Even though he was unemployed and suspected of being a rapist, in Karla's eyes, Bernardo could do no wrong. Indeed, the depth of her adulation was such that Paul felt comfortable revealing a deep, sick fantasy to her: He wanted to take the virginity of Karla's attractive fifteen-year-old sister, Tammy. Excitedly, Karla told him she would help him implement the fantasy, that all they had to do was drug Tammy into unconsciousness and then Paul could have his way with her. And Karla said she had the perfect drug for it: halothane, an anesthetic used on animals.

Bernardo liked the plan, and the couple decided to put it into action on Christmas Eve in 1990. Karla cooked Christmas dinner for her family, adding halothane to Tammy's food. She also encouraged her younger sister to have a few drinks. As the night wore on, other family members retired to bed, but Paul, Karla, and Tammy went into the basement recreation room, where they continued to drink.

Eventually, Tammy passed out. Karla held a rag saturated with halothane over Tammy's mouth and nose while Bernardo brutally raped her. Bernardo also ordered Karla to engage in sex acts with her sister, which she did. They recorded the whole event with a camcorder. Then, there was a problem: Tammy awoke and started to throw up and choke on her vomit. Karla and Paul tried to clear her air passages, but they were unsuccessful—the teen choked to death. Quickly they cleaned her up, dressed her, and called 911. When the paramedics came nothing at the scene aroused suspicion, and Tammy's death was ruled accidental.

The Crimes Escalate

The death of Tammy had no chastening effect on Karla or Paul. Less than a month later, Paul picked up a teenage girl in his car, drove her to the Homolka house—which was empty at the time—and raped her in Karla's bedroom. Afterward, Paul simply drove her out of the neighborhood and dropped her off.

The young girl was so terrorized that she never reported the assault to the police.

This was followed by yet another rape; but this time, as with her little sister, Karla presented a fifteen-year-old girl to Paul as a sick, twisted gift. Karla had invited the girl to dinner in a house she and Paul had rented in the suburb of St. Catherine, where they knocked her out with drinks and halothane. Paul raped the teenager with, again, Karla videotaping the whole thing. The girl was released unharmed, but their crimes were escalating toward the inevitable: murder.

During one of his illicit smuggling trips across the border into the United States, Bernardo spotted a teenager—she was just fourteen years old—standing outside a house alone. He approached her and found that she had been locked out of her house. Bernardo then lured her into his car and kidnapped her, taking her to his and Karla's place in St. Catherine. The girl, Leslie Mahaffey, was raped, sexually abused, and beaten by both Bernardo and Homolka for an entire day, the camcorder on the whole time.

The next day, June 14, 1991, the couple realized that releasing Mahaffey would put them at risk of arrest. They decided to murder her, something Bernardo, who had the heart and soul of a serial murderer, likely had in mind all along. Bernardo strangled her with an electric cord, and then they used a chain saw to cut her up. They encased the pieces in concrete and threw them in Lake Gibson.

Another torture and murder followed just less than a year later when they lured the teenager Kristen Dawn French to their car and overpowered and kidnapped her. They took French to their home for a videotaped three-day rape and torture fest that later even hardened police had trouble viewing. Bernardo strangled her on April 16, 1992—Easter Sunday.

Blast from the Past

The beginning of the end came for both Bernardo and Homolka when police finally tested the blood, saliva, and hair samples Bernardo had given more than two years earlier, in November 1990, for the Scarborough Rapist case. The DNA proved he was the rapist, the first of those crimes having occurred in 1987, right around the time he met Karla.

On February 17, 1993, Bernardo was arrested and interrogated for eight hours. Two days later, armed with a search warrant, police invaded the rented house where Bernardo and Homolka lived. They did not find much that was incriminating during their search, but they did find a major ally in

Paul Bernardo and Karla Homolka

prosecuting Bernardo: Karla. In a fit of rage the previous December, Bernardo had beaten Karla to a pulp. Afraid for her own life, she had filed a complaint with the police. When the police came knocking after arresting Paul for the Scarborough rapes, Karla told them through her lawyer that she would lay out exactly what had happened in the house.

A kind of legal Ping-Pong followed, with both Paul and Karla denying any culpability in the rapes and deaths of the teenagers. Ultimately, Homolka plea-bargained a great deal by testifying against Bernardo. She received only twelve years, while Bernardo was found guilty of the murders and rapes and was sentenced to life without the possibility of parole for twenty-five years.

Afterword

In an attempt to discredit Karla's testimony and prove her involvement in the murders, Bernardo told his lawyers about their murder and torture tapes, and that they were hidden in the ceiling of a bathroom on the second floor of their rented house. As gruesome as they were, the tapes did not manage to derail the plea bargain Homolka made. Ultimately, because of their mind-bending content, the tapes were destroyed in 2001, when there was no further legal use for them.

Bernardo has appealed his sentence but was turned down. Unbelievably, Karla Homolka—a conspirator in first-degree murder—was released from prison in 2005.

Paul Bernardo on his way to trial.

Karla Homolka in court.

Who Are We?

1. We are American serial killers who met while we were both inmates in the California State Prison in San Luis Obispo, but we are soul brothers to killers like Paul Bernardo and Karla Homolka; one of us was a sociopathic career criminal, and the other was a schizoid sex offender.

2. While in prison we discovered that we shared a mutual fantasy of kidnapping, raping, torturing, and murdering teenage girls. We plotted a "game" in which we would kidnap seven victims, one victim for each of the teenage years, from thirteen to nineteen years old.

3. After being released from prison, we teamed up to live out our depraved fantasies. We bought a 1977 GMC cargo van with a sliding door on the side and cruised the towns and beaches along the Pacific Coast Highway. If the girls didn't accept our offer of a ride, we pulled them in through the side door. We nicknamed the van "Murder Mack."

4. We wound up with five young victims. Our savage acts included repeated rapes, shoving an ice pick through their ears into their brains, hitting them with a sledgehammer, and strangling them with a wire coat hanger. We dumped the bodies off the sides of a cliff in the San Gabriel Mountains.

5. We would sometimes record our sadistic acts using a Polaroid camera or a tape recorder. The more the girls suffered, the more we enjoyed it. We would turn up the radio

to drown out their anguished cries. We would taunt them by saying things like, "Scream, baby. Scream!"

6. Our downfall came after one of us bragged about our activities to an old prison buddy—the friend told his lawyer, who went to the police.

7. The trial was difficult to watch. Between the playing of the audiotape of a girl being tortured and the testimony that detailed the brutality, some spectators had to get up and leave the courtroom. Even the district attorney, emotionally hardened as he was from the cases he had prosecuted, wept on two occasions.

8. We were found guilty of five counts of murder and a multitude of other offenses and have been incarcerated since 1980. One of us sits on death row in San Quentin and the other, sentenced to forty-five years to life, is in Pelican Bay State Prison awaiting a parole hearing scheduled for 2010.

Answer: We are Lawrence Bittaker and Roy Norris.

Chapter 26
Pedro López, Colombia

Notable Fact
When he was released, an already disturbed mind had been damaged even more . . .

The childhood of Pedro Alonzo López is a serial killer classic. López was born on October 8, 1948, in a squalid hovel, one of thirteen children of a prostitute. When he was eight years old, his mother caught Pedro having intercourse with one of his younger sisters. His mother, a domineering, brutal person, threw him out of the house. For days, Pedro wandered the streets of Tolima, a homeless eight-year-old with no idea what to do.

After a few days, Pedro caught a break—a kindly man noticed him and asked what had happened. Pedro told him that his mother had thrown him out of house. The man commiserated and told Pedro that he could stay at his house for a while, and he promised Pedro food. Pedro went with the man, but instead of taking him to his house, the man took him to an abandoned building, where he sodomized Pedro and made him fellate him.

When he was released, an already-disturbed mind had been damaged even more, and Pedro found himself terrified of everyone, living like a rat on the run, sleeping in building entrances and empty market stalls, eating garbage. Eventually, a kindly American family found Pedro and took him into their home in Bogotá, and he was allowed to grow up like a normal boy. But the damage had already been done: When Pedro was twelve, he stole some money from his adoptive family and ran away, later claiming that he had absconded because a teacher had made sexual advances toward him. However, it's far more likely that Pedro simply felt compelled to do something like that; his mother and the man who assaulted him had irrevocably affected his personality.

Growing Up

Another trauma resulted in the emergence of the real Pedro, in all his malignant glory. When Pedro was eighteen, he was imprisoned for stealing a car. On the second day he was in prison, a new "fish" as inmates say, four other prisoners cornered him and brutally sodomized him.

Bleeding and in pain, López did not report the assault to the authorities—instead, he plotted revenge, making himself a shank. Over the next two weeks, he cornered three of the four men who had raped him and stabbed them to death. When the authorities discovered his murders, the court determined López's assaults to be self-defense and gave him just two years of extra time. What the court didn't seem to recognize was López's ability to kill with impunity.

Girl Killer

When he was released from prison, López embarked on a murderous rampage throughout three countries, killing young girls between eight and twelve years old. He began in Peru, where he would one day estimate that he killed at least one hundred young indigenous girls. To López, the young indigenous children were easy game; Peruvian police didn't really care about them and considered them substandard, not worth helping. But one day López made a mistake that almost cost him his life. He was in the process of leading a nine-year-old Indian girl from her village when some villagers spotted him, ran him down, and rescued the girl. They stripped him, tortured him for hours, and were about to bury him alive when a female American missionary happened by and begged them to spare his life. The missionary and her party promised to turn López over to Peruvian authorities. Very reluctantly, the community agreed and the missionary and her party kept their word and turned him in to the Peruvian authorities, who made an unthinkable mistake born of insensitivity: They deported him, in effect releasing a crazed homicidal pedophile.

López started to travel, dividing his time between Colombia and Ecuador. Like a seasoned predator, he learned to select victims who would be trusting and offer the least resistance. Although authorities in all three countries—Ecuador, Peru, and Colombia—were aware that there were a lot of young girls missing, no one really had a handle on just how bad it was. In fact, they thought that sex slave traders were kidnapping the girls. But then, a few coincidental events combined to ultimately bring López to justice.

Flash Flood

In April 1980, there was a flash flood near the town of Ambato, Ecuador. The local river swelled in size and brought forth some horrific secrets: the remains of four young girls. This broke open the sordid story—slave traders weren't kidnapping girls; there was a serial killer on the loose.

A few days later, a woman named Carvina Poveda saw something terrifying as she was shopping—a man was walking her twelve-year-old daughter out of the marketplace. Poveda ran

223

after them, yelling for help. People stopped the man and held him there as the police were called. When police arrived, they immediately suspected that they might have caught a big fish with this Pedro López. Indeed, they had caught a whale.

After his capture, López was mute; no matter how hard they tried, police couldn't get him to talk. Knowing that López was likely no ordinary criminal, the police came up with a plan and asked a priest to help. The priest dressed up like a convict and was put into López's cell. Using the skills he had developed in years of talking to people, the priest started to talk to López and gradually began to drag a confession out of him by trading criminal war stories. When authorities felt they had gotten López to admit enough, they halted the ruse and came at López with a withering interrogation.

López broke down and "gave it up," as police say, and what he gave up was incredible, hard to believe. López said that he had murdered more than 100 young girls in his native Colombia, 110 in Ecuador—a country he liked because of the trusting nature of the young girls—and more than 100 in Peru.

Notable Quotable

"I like the girls in Ecuador. They are more gentle and trusting. They are not as suspicious of strangers as Colombian girls."

—Pedro López

The police wanted proof of what López said, so shortly after his confession, López gave them a guided tour of an area around Ambato, Ecuador, where police eventually unearthed the remains of fifty-three young girls. López showed them many other grave sites, but the remains were gone, taken by animals. Ecuadorean authorities now believed López—they charged him with 110 murders.

Afterword

López explained his murderous method to police after his confession. He would reconnoiter crowded marketplaces looking for likely victims, and when he found one, he would wait until she came to the market again. He would follow her, then shepherd her away, and once alone he would rape and then strangle her to death. He said he enjoyed looking into their eyes as he killed them so that he could observe their agony, watch the light go out of their eyes as he applied pressure. He always found the experience sexually stimulating. He also said that he hunted in daylight so that he could be sure to see the girls' pain as they died.

He also killed as quickly as he could, sometimes more than one victim each day, and the more he murdered, the more he needed to murder.

> ### Notable Quotable
> "I lost my innocence at eight, so I decided to do the same to as many young girls as I could."
> —Pedro López

Ecuadorean authorities, of course, shared information with those of Peru and Colombia, and López provided enough details to amply demonstrate that his confessions in those countries were valid. Incredibly, following his trial in Ecuador, López was sentenced to only sixteen years, but when he gets out he is scheduled to be tried in Colombia, where they have the death penalty.

Chapter 27
Dennis Nilsen, England

Notable Quotable

"Well, enjoying it is as good a reason as any."

—Dennis Nilsen, on why he killed

There's a concept in police work called "linkage," where investigators use the sameness in the methods that a murderer employs to help find the killer—they are able to link all the crimes together and learn something about the killer from the circumstances. Unfortunately, this did not occur when police investigated the murders and assaults committed by Scotland-born Dennis Nilsen, though there were revelatory similarities. If they had, a number of lives might well have been saved.

Nilsen was born on November 23, 1945, in Fraserburgh, Scotland. His childhood was traumatic; his mother and father were constantly arguing until his father, an alcoholic, moved away when Nilsen was four. His mother and two siblings then moved into her mother's house, and Nilsen immediately bonded with his grandfather. When he was only six years old his grandfather died.

Eventually his mother remarried and had four more children, and the situation enhanced his feelings of being left out, alone, and uncared for. He was lost in a crowd. And there was something else that isolated him from his peers. At a very young age he started to feel romantically attracted to boys. But though he had the feelings, he did not act on them.

A New Country

His family moved to England when Dennis was still a boy, and in 1961, when he was sixteen, Dennis joined the Army Catering Corps. He was to learn a skill there that served him well during his murderous rampage: butchering. Following his departure from the army in 1972, he joined the police force and stayed for a year. A special treat for him certainly was access to the morgue and autopsies, which fed into the necrophiliac tendencies that had been building inside him for years, tendencies that would later manifest in some truly shocking ways.

He started acting on his homosexual urges while he was working as a civil servant at a London Jobcentre employment agency. Nilsen was attracted to a young coworker named Painter, and one day he took various photos of him while he was asleep. Painter caught Nilsen; the experience traumatized Painter, who had to be hospitalized. The police were notified and questioned Nilsen, but they released him without filing any charges.

Eventually, Nilsen could no longer control his sexual feelings, and in 1975 he started a relationship with a man named Gaillichan. After two years Gaillichan ended the relationship, and it was as if a bomb had gone off inside Nilsen's psyche. He spiraled down into an unbearable pit of loneliness and became like a child again with his feelings of abandonment. He tried to hold off the anxiety with drink, but this didn't work.

Bizarre Murders

He started to take young men home to his apartment in the Cricklewood section of London, and the homicidal urges that had been gestating in him for years finally blossomed—and then some—on the evening of December 29, 1978. He picked up a young man in a local pub and they had sex all night. When the young man got ready to leave the next morning, Nilsen used a necktie to strangle him and immersed his head in a bucket of water to make sure that he died.

The next day, Nilsen carefully and lovingly washed the nude corpse from head to toe, and that evening placed the body into his bed and lay down beside it. He spent much of the night marveling at the beauty of the corpse, and at one point he became aroused and tried to have sex with it but was unsuccessful. He spent the entire night with the dead young man. When dawn came, Nilsen decided to dispose of the body: He carefully pried up the floorboards and laid the body between the wooden frames.

Why? Why not just take the body out in the dead of night and dump it somewhere? Author Brian Masters, who collaborated with Nilsen on his biography *Killing for Company*, says that Nilsen was again warring against the abandonment of his childhood. The body under the floorboards was not dead to him; because the body was there, he was not alone. Indeed, Nilsen had what might be characterized as a very quiet roommate until eight months after the murder, when, in August, he brought it outside to the garden area and cremated the corpse in a bonfire.

A few months after Nilsen cremated his first victim he tried to kill again, this time a young Chinese man named Andrew Ho. Ho broke free and reported the incident to police. An officer who was a former colleague of Nilsen's questioned him, and Nilsen explained the assault away as a botched robbery. The cop believed his old acquaintance.

Less than two months later, on December 3, 1979, Nilsen committed his second homicide. The details of this murder were even more bizarre than the first. Nilsen met the victim, a Canadian tourist named Kenneth Ockendon, at a pub, and they hit it off. The two spent the day drinking and sightseeing, and then retired to Nilsen's apartment for a grand sexual finale to their day. Instead, Nilsen strangled the young man with an electrical cable. Then, just as he had with the first victim, Nilsen carefully washed the corpse, placed it in bed next to him and spent the night with it. This time, though, there was a variation on his ghoulish theme: Nilsen took photos of the body and this time succeeded in having sex with it. As before he stored it under the floorboards, but, even more bizarrely, in the days that followed he would periodically remove it and frequently had conversations with it.

Seven months after Ockendon's murder, Nilsen lured a nineteen-year-old homeless Irish man named Martyn Duffey to his house, and there strangled him and submerged his head in a bucket of water. Then he cleaned Duffey as he had done the other victims, placed his body on the bed, had sex with it, and placed it in a wardrobe for two weeks before storing it under the floorboards with the decomposing remains of Ockendon.

Nilsen's homicidal pattern continued, and during the next three years Nilsen murdered a total of thirteen men, storing all of them in whatever space was available—in the cupboard, a closet, under the floorboards, a shed in the garden. The stench that had been building in his apartment got worse and worse, and though Nilsen tried to control it with various sprays, he never completely succeeded. He knew he had to dispose of the bodies, so he enlisted the butchering skills he had learned in the army—he skillfully cut up the remains and incinerated them in a mammoth backyard bonfire, tossing an old tire onto the blaze to explain the stench.

During this time, a number of people that Nilsen had attacked survived, or he would attack them and then unaccountably stop. A number of these almost victims reported his assaults to the police, and this is where the linkage failed: similar complaints about Nilsen trying to garrote or drown people went unrecognized as a pattern, and no deeper investigation was done.

New Digs

Nilsen moved from his Cricklewood apartment in 1981, but his quest for new companions continued. This time, however, he used a new way to dispose of the bodies: He butchered them into pieces small enough to flush down the toilet.

Dennis Nilsen

It was the plumbing in his apartment that finally unraveled Nilsen. Although he tried gruesome means of making the human pieces pass through the plumbing—including removing flesh from skulls by boiling them—neighbors were having troubles with clogged toilets and called a company called Dyno-Rod. The technician found the clog and removed rotting pieces of human remains, some pieces clearly distinguishable by the hair attached to them, in front of horrified onlookers—including Nilsen. The police were summoned.

Police conducted a search of the entire apartment building, and it wasn't long before they got to Nilsen's apartment. They were greeted by a scene reminiscent of Ed Gein's apartment, or the future Jeffrey Dahmer's: stored all over the place was a vile assortment of heads, legs, arms, torsos, and viscera.

Afterword

When Nilsen went on trial at Central Criminal Court in October 1983 for six murders and two attempted murders there was never any question about his guilt, just whether he was innocent by reason of insanity. His lawyer, Ivan Lawrence, said that at the time of each killing he was in such an abnormal mental state that he was not capable of forming the intent needed to be guilty of murder. The trial turned into a battle royal of psychiatric experts, but in the end, Nilsen was found guilty by a vote of ten to two and sentenced to life in prison.

Chapter 28
Henri Landru, France

Notable Fact

It is said Landru was the real-life inspiration for Charlie Chaplin's black comedy *Monsieur Verdoux*.

A bluebeard is a man who kills his wives. It started with a fifteenth-century man named Gilles de Rais, who had a blue-black beard and was a child-killer. Somehow the term became attached to a folk tale about a man named Chevalier Raoul, whose seventh wife discovered the bodies of his first six in a room he had forbidden her to enter. However, twentieth-century Henri Landru seems to have taken permanent possession of the word.

One of the curious things about Landru was that, though he seemed to have no problem attracting females, he was hardly the cliché image of an attractive man. He was a short, stocky, balding man with a long red beard. (It is said Landru was the real-life inspiration for Charlie Chaplin's black comedy *Monsieur Verdoux*, in which an unattractive man supports his family by marrying and murdering rich women for their money.) But Landru appeared extremely charming and caring, and he came across as someone who had all that it took to appeal to women—a persona that was obviously a performance because he cared nothing about his victims, except for their wealth.

Perhaps his success with women was mostly a matter of timing. When World War I started in 1914, he had already been in the army, having been discharged in 1894 after four years of service. Hence, he was one of the few men available for the host of women keeping the home fires burning.

A Life of Crime

This bluebeard's career in crime kicked off in 1900, when he was thirty-one years old, when he spent two years in jail for fraud. That was followed by additional stints in jail for fraud, two years in 1904 and a little more than a year in 1906. In 1908 he was again convicted of fraud and sentenced to three years, and later managed to get himself an additional three years for having swindled fifteen thousand francs from a woman he had lured into his clutches with what would become his stock-in-trade, a lonely hearts ad. By the start of the war, he was tried and convicted in absentia of various crimes and sentenced to four years and permanent deportation to New Caledonia. Unfortunately—for a series of women—he was not captured for quite awhile.

One of these women, drawn by one of his lonely hearts ads, was Madame Cuchet, who took up residence with him in 1914. Landru told her his name was Diard. He met her family, who didn't like "Diard" and warned her against involvement, but she was smitten and set up a household with him and her sixteen-year-old son in the town of Vernouillet. By January 1915 both Cuchet and her son had gone missing, and Landru got away with five thousand francs.

Six months later, one of his ads lured a Madame Laborder Line, and she went to live with Landru in Vernouillet—but not for long. By the end of June she was missing, and the not exactly grief-stricken Landru immediately sold her securities and possessions. Just over a month later, on August 2, fifty-one-year-old Madam Guillin went to live with him at Vernouillet. Predictably, she disappeared only a few days after she arrived. Landru sold off her securities and was able to withdraw twelve thousand francs from her bank account with forged documents.

Landru waited until near the end of the year before striking again, this time luring a Madam Heon to a villa he had rented in Gambais in the south of France. Soon, he was writing plaintive letters to relatives who had inquired after her that she was too ill to visit them. Of course, she had gone way past the point of sickness. She was his fifth murder victim. The sixth victim was Madam Gambais, who met Landru in November 1916. By Christmas Day, she was missing and he was in possession of her assets.

Illicit profit was undoubtedly Landru's main motivation for killing, but he was a serial killer at heart and didn't necessarily need financial gain to murder. Buttressing this belief is the fact that he killed one female who didn't have any money. At the end of the war, he met Andree Babelay, a servant girl who was much younger than Landru. She told her mother that she was getting married, and then she left to move in with Landru. By April 12 she was gone with the wind, never to be seen again.

Landru continued his homicidal Houdini act with a number of other women, but like most serial killers, he eventually went too far. Two families, the Collombs and Buissons, who had lost daughters to Landru, applied pressure to the police to take action. Finally, on April 2, 1919, they arrested him.

It was then that Landru's meticulousness in thievery and murder backfired. Police found a notebook containing cryptic notes about all his victims—eleven in all—and they launched a full-scale investigation, including digging out the land

The Secret in the Frame

On the day he was to be guillotined, Henri Landru framed some of his drawings and gave them to his attorneys. Five decades later the frame was opened, revealing Landru's confession and explaining how he disposed of the bodies.

around his villa. The search unearthed nothing incriminating, but inside the house they found articles of clothing and other possessions that could be traced to the victims. This evidence, plus the notebook, weighed heavily against Landru; at his trial in Versailles in November 1919, and he was found guilty. He appealed, but on February 23, 1922, he met the guillotine and was no longer a threat to lonely women.

Chapter 29
Peter Kürten, Germany

Notable Quotable

"In the case of Ohliger, I also sucked blood from the wound on her temple, and from Scheer from the stab in the neck. From the girl Schulte I only licked the blood from her hands. It was the same with the swan in the Hofgarten. I used to stroll at night through the Hofgarten very often, and in the spring of 1930 I noticed a swan sleeping at the edge of the lake. I cut its throat. The blood spurted up and I drank from the stump."

—Peter Kürten

Peter Kürten was so twisted that serial murder superstars like Albert Fish would have been proud to call him brother. His life was truly off the scale of perversity. Perhaps the most telling incident is that, when he was sentenced to death by guillotine, he commented that his greatest thrill of all time would be that millisecond as

Peter Kürten

the guillotine sliced his head off and he heard the sound of his own blood jetting from his neck. If this sounds like false bravado, think again—on July 2, 1931, he went to the guillotine with an anticipatory smile on his face.

A Horrid Beginning

Like most other serial murderers, Kürten didn't have much of a chance for normalcy from the beginning. He was born in Cologne-Mulheim, Germany, in 1883. Economic circumstances forced him to live with ten other family members in a single room. His father was a sadistic drunk who forced his wife to strip nude in front of the other family members and have sex with him. His father also tried to rape his thirteen-year-old daughter and was sent to prison. Of course the psychotic, as it were, doesn't fall far from the tree; Peter also had sex with a number of his sisters.

But incest was hardly abnormal enough for Kürten. As he grew up, he also came to enjoy homicidal bestiality. A dog-catcher who lived upstairs tutored Kürten on how to torture all kinds of animals. As a teenager he had sex innumerable times with a wide variety of creatures, including goats, sheep, pigs, and dogs, either sodomizing them or masturbating with them as nature allowed. He took particular pleasure in stabbing sheep to death and watching the blood spurt from them as he had intercourse with them. Such an activity would frequently bring him to orgasm.

Kürten committed his first murder—actually two murders—at the ripe old age of nine. He was with another boy on a raft in the Rhine River, and Kürten pushed the boy into the water. A mutual friend jumped into the river to save him, and Kürten was able to keep both boys from getting on the raft, instead forcing them to go under it—and drown. Investigating authorities determined that the deaths were a tragic accident, and Kürten was free to kill again.

And as if all of this weren't enough, Kürten also dabbled in other criminal activities. He was a habitual thief, caught for the first time when he was fifteen (also the first time he was in prison, where he ultimately spent twenty-seven of his forty-seven years on earth). Kürten was also an arsonist; his specialty was barns and hayracks (frames for carrying hay). As they burned to the ground he would masturbate furiously to orgasm, not only feeling the triumph of the chaos he had caused but also hoping that there were people trapped inside.

Life of Crime

Kürten claimed that he tried to commit his first adult homicide in 1899—but he may not have actually succeeded. He was having sex with a woman near Düsseldorf and said he strangled her, but no corpse was ever found and she may have just been choked to unconsciousness and woke up after he left. He continued to commit a variety of crimes over the next few years and eventually received a prison term for theft and fraud that kept him behind bars until 1904.

Despite his extensive criminal record, Kürten was drafted into the German military when he was freed from prison. He then deserted and surfaced again in 1905, when he was arrested and sentenced to seven years for theft. It should be noted that criminal activity for Kürten hardly stopped when he went to jail. Indeed, he would later confess to poisoning a number of inmates in the prison hospital.

Kürten was free again by 1912, and he celebrated his liberty by raping a young servant girl. Soon afterward, he accosted some young women in a restaurant. When a waiter tried to intervene, Kürten pulled a pistol and fired at the man, who fled for his life. His freedom, then, was short-lived; he was back in jail for another year over the shooting incident.

In the years that followed, Kürten continued his rampage of rape, arson, thievery, and of course, murder, but he con-founded police because his victims were not from the same group, just anyone who seemed available. Therefore he had no pattern, and police couldn't figure out how the victims and crimes could be related; they didn't realize that one man was committing all of them. There had been attacks on men, young women, and children. On the night of May 25, 1913, he broke into a bar in Cologne-Mulheim. The owners, who lived in an apartment above the bar, happened to be away, but when Kürten got to the top of the stairs he discovered their daughter, thirteen-year-old Christine Klein. He sexu-ally assaulted her with his fingers and cut her throat. On the night of February 12, 1929, a drunken man named Rudolf Scheer accidentally bumped into Kürten, who responded by pouncing on him and stabbing him repeatedly with scissors, at the same time sucking up the blood that spurted from a neck wound. No one was safe. To further obscure the fact that his crimes belonged to a single perpetrator, he used whatever weaponry was available: hands, knife, hatchet, gun, garrote, and fire.

The one consistent thing about Kürten's actions was that he was capable of white-hot violence in a heartbeat, and anyone was fair game. Indeed, when he proposed to his prospective wife, a woman who had spent five years in jail for shooting her fiancé, she originally refused, but he made her an offer she couldn't refuse: Marry me or I'll kill you. She knew he would and they were soon off on their honeymoon.

The Monster of Düsseldorf

All of Peter Kürten's life as a brutal, sadistic, vampirelike murderer might be considered a mere warm-up for 1929, the year he turned forty-six years old. It was during that year that he richly earned the nickname "Monster of Düsseldorf." The carnage that terrorized the city started with the killing of eight-year-old Ruth Ohliger on the night of February 8. Her body was discovered at a construction site on March 9—she had been raped and stabbed thirteen times, including puncture wounds in the temples, which investigators noted had happened to three other recent homicide victims.

In his confession, Kürten would say that he sucked blood from Ohliger's temple. Like other serial killers, the concept of oral incorporation was very arousing to him, and he did it as frequently as possible. Small wonder that he was also known as the "Vampire of Düsseldorf."

Kürten attacked five people in August, three of whom survived and two who did not—fourteen-year-old Louise Lenzen and five-year-old Gertrude Hamacher died after being raped, strangled, and stabbed. Before the month was out, Kürten also had approached Gertrude Schulte and asked for sex in an obscene way. Gertrude said she would rather die, so Kürten tried to oblige, stabbing her several times in the chest. She survived and described Kürten to the police, who were still not able to put the case together as the work of one person.

The murderous blitzkrieg continued as the year wound down. In September, Kürten tried to strangle three more women; in October, two women were bludgeoned to death with a hammer; on November 9, the corpse of another five-year-old, Gertrude Alberman, was found. Alberman had received thirty-six frenzied stab wounds and had been strangled. And for good measure, Kürten—like so many other attention-hungry serial

241

killers—sent instructions to police on where they could find the body of Maria Hahn. Hahn had also died in August, stabbed twenty times and raped postmortem.

> ## Notable Quotable
> "The whole family suffered through his drinking, for when he was in drink, my father was terrible. I, being the eldest, had to suffer most. As you may well imagine, we suffered terrible poverty, all because the wages went on drink. We all lived in one room and you will appreciate what effect that had on me sexually."
>
> —Peter Kürten, talking about his father

The city of Düsseldorf was panicked about the seemingly random death and violence haunting the city, and as such residents were on high alert for the killer. On May 14, 1930, Kürten made a big mistake. He was on a date with Maria Budlick; while they were strolling through the woods, he pounced on her. In the middle of strangling her, he suddenly asked her whether she remembered where he lived in case he had to "help her" and she gave the right answer: "No." He released her, and shortly thereafter the police were knocking on his door.

Afterword

Kürten's trial, held on April 3, 1931, was open and shut: He had given prosecutors a highly detailed confession, and jurors came back with a guilty verdict in ninety minutes. Kürten was sentenced to death and he died on July 2, 1931, his final turn-on.

Notable Quotable

"The man Kürten is a riddle to me. I can not solve it. The criminal Haarman only killed men, Landru and Grossman only women, but Peter killed men, women, children and animals; killed anything he found."

—Dr. Wehner, Peter Kürten's defense counsel

Chapter 30
Béla Kiss, Hungary

Notable Fact
Instead of petrol each of the drums was filled with the decomposing corpse of a nude female.

There is no question that Béla Kiss, a Hungarian tinsmith who went on a murderous, undetected rampage around the time of World War I, was one of the cagiest serial killers of all time. Kiss apparently didn't start to kill people until he was in his forties, which is extremely rare for a serial killer—usually they begin in their twenties. And some people believe that a single event triggered his descent into murder.

In February 1912, forty-year-old Béla was happily taking his new bride, Marie—fifteen years his junior—to his house in Czinkota. But within weeks of taking her marriage vows, she had also taken on a lover, a man named Paul Bikari.

Kiss was not too close to his neighbors. He was a known sorcerer and had a certain weirdness about him that kept the neighbors at arm's length. Few would approach his house. However, they did observe that, within weeks of his marriage, his new bride did not seem to be around and that periodically young women would visit. Near the end of the year, someone got up the gumption to approach and ask where Marie was. Kiss's heartfelt, sad response was that she had left him for another man. The parade of women into his house was left unexplained.

The neighbors also noticed something else. As time went by, Kiss started to collect large metal drums, and when the local constable questioned him about them, Kiss said they were filled with petrol—that because World War I was looming on the horizon, gas would become scarce. The constable had no reason to question what Kiss said.

In 1914, World War I started, as Kiss and many others had predicted. Although he was forty-two years old at the time, Kiss was drafted into the army. Before he left for the service, he sealed up the house with bars and locks. But he never came back—eighteen months after he entered the service, in spring 1916, town authorities were notified that he had been killed in action. In June of that year, Hungarian soldiers came into Czinkota looking for gas supplies, and the constable directed them to the house where Kiss had lived.

They broke into the house and found seven gas drums in the attic, their weight supported by special framing. The soldiers took the drums outside and opened them up, only to recoil in horror. Instead of petrol, each of the drums was filled with the decomposing corpse of a nude female, stored in alcohol. And each had distinctive ligature marks on their neck showing how they had left the world. Among the bodies were those of Marie and her lover Paul.

The police turned the house upside down, and they uncovered not only a great variety of female clothing and jewelry but also innumerable pawn tickets for more valuables. They also found many letters from many women who had responded to someone named Hoffmann at a different address. Hoffmann claimed to be a lonely widower looking for female companionship. And there were more than seven bodies. As they searched the surrounding countryside, there was another shocker—seventeen more drums, each packed with a nude female. Kiss had killed twenty-three females and one male in all. Police theorized that Kiss had killed Marie and Paul when he had discovered their affair, and that that event had triggered his homicidal campaign to bilk widows out of their money and worldly goods.

Afterword

After such a horrible discovery everyone wanted justice, but Kiss was dead. Or was he? In spring 1919, "Hoffmann" was reputedly sighted near the Margaret Bridge in Budapest. Police swarmed over the scene, then launched an investigation to determine whether Kiss was dead. The probe extended into Kiss's military service, and it was determined that he had been shipped to Serbia, where he was wounded and died in a military hospital. But investigators found that the Béla Kiss who had died was a young man and looked nothing like the real Béla Kiss.

In 1932 the sharp-eyed New York city detective Henry Oswald, who had a reputation for remembering faces and was aware of the most wanted criminals in America and overseas, said he spotted Kiss coming out of New York City subway in Times Square. But before he could do anything Kiss disappeared into the crowd and was never seen again.

Notable Quotable

"We were so fond of him. He was kind to everyone; he wouldn't hurt a living thing. Once a dog had broken its leg, he made splints and nursed the animal to recovery. I am sure it is a mistake—he did not kill those women! Someone else did it!"

—Béla Kiss's housekeeper, defending him to police

Chapter 31
Ahmad Suradji, Indonesia

Notable Fact
And then Suradji would break out
an electrical cable and strangle them
to death. Following this he would drink
their saliva, hoping to incorporate
their power into himself.

One night in 1986, a thirty-six-year-old witch doctor named Ahmad Suradji went to bed and had a dream in which his deceased father appeared and gave him instructions on what he must do to increase and enhance his paranormal powers. In that moment, a lot of women in Indonesia were slated to die. His father had told him that to increase his supernatural powers, he had to kill seventy women.

As a sorcerer or witch doctor, Suradji had access to a lot of potential victims: In Indonesia, women and girls frequently visited sorcerers for advice and counsel and magical aid on romantic issues, particularly to cast spells to ensure that their spouses and husbands didn't cheat on them. Because the women were too embarrassed to tell their families of the visits, when they vanished no one connected their disappearances to Suradji.

His method of murder, both brutal and disgusting, was invariably the same. When visitors came to him, he would evaluate their spiritual needs and charge them the equivalent of $200 to $400. After he was paid, a woman would follow Suradji to a sugarcane field, where he claimed he had to bury them up to their waists in an already-dug hole as part of the ritual. This incapacitated them, of course, and then Suradji would break out an electrical cable and strangle them to death.

Following this he would drink their saliva, hoping to incorporate their power into himself. Then he would strip them and rebury them with their heads facing his home so that their spirits would have a direct path to him.

Sometimes, if paying customers were in short supply, Suradji would hire prostitutes to take part in the rituals that would end their lives. This was a very safe supply of victims, because, as Ted Bundy had noted, prostitutes are low-risk targets because they often do not have much family to look for them if they go missing. Prostitutes would help Suradji meet his needed seventy victims that much faster.

There is no way to know whether Suradji would have reached his goal, because on April 28, 1997, eleven years after his father had spoke to him in his dream, investigators looking for the many missing females discovered three women buried in the sugarcane field during a random search. Suspicion was cast Suradji's way.

Police questioned him—they brutalized him, his wife said—and he admitted to murdering sixteen females over a five-year period. However, when the police searched his home, they found evidence indicating many more than sixteen victims. They found clothing and personal items from twenty-five different females, the classic behavior not of a sorcerer but of a serial murderer gathering trophies of his victims. Armed with this evidence, police were able to break down the sorcerer, and he admitted to killing forty-two women and girls since his 1986 dream. The police also arrested his three wives, but after questioning, two of them were released. Only the oldest wife Tumini, age thirty-eight at the time, was charged.

The trial of both Suradji and Tumini began on April 28, 1997. They were charged with forty-two murders. The prosecution has its work cut out—the duo had taken back their confessions to police, claiming that police had beaten the admissions out of them. However, the jury didn't buy it. Both were found guilty; Tumini received a life sentence and Suradji a death sentence, an uncommonly harsh penalty in Indonesia. He was executed by firing squad in May 1998.

After the trial, Suradji lamented to reporters that he would not reach his goal of seventy deaths. Chillingly, when the case hit the limelight, police asked all families in Indonesia to report to them whether anyone in their family was missing. About eighty families responded.

Chapter 32
Yoshio Kodaira, Japan

Notable Quotable

"Four or five comrades and I entered a Chinese home and locked him in the closet. We stole the jewelry and raped the women. We even bayoneted a pregnant woman and pulled out the fetus from her stomach."

—Yoshio Kodaira

Japan, even more than most countries, has a bloody history, rife with brutality and murder—and serial killers. But the one person who stands alone as the country's most active serial killer in the twentieth century and beyond is Yoshio Kodaira. Kodaira was born in 1905. Although not a great deal is known about his childhood, at school he was combative, lazy, and uncaring. He frequently fought with his schoolmates, perhaps in part when other kids made fun of him because of his bad stutter, and he received poor grades on his schoolwork. Indeed, in his grammar school he was ranked near the bottom of the class and was lucky to graduate.

Predictably, he didn't go to high school, instead becoming an apprentice in a metalworks factory. After leaving that job, Kodaira drifted aimlessly through a series of other low-paying, blue-collar jobs, and he also fathered a child. Unable to handle the responsibility of fatherhood, he took off, ending up, at age eighteen, in the Imperial Japanese Navy.

It was a perfect opportunity for a budding serial killer. The Japanese armies were engaged in a brutal and sadistic war against mainland China in those days. Japanese soldiers raped and murdered Chinese citizens en masse. As Kodaira said of an assault on one family that he took part in: "Four or five comrades and I entered a Chinese home and locked him in the closet. We stole the jewelry and raped the women. We even bayoneted a pregnant woman and pulled out the fetus from her stomach. I also engaged in those depraved actions."

While aware that the actions were depraved, at least on an intellectual level, the experience surely didn't stop Kodaira from continuing his life in the same vein.

Killer on the Loose

When he left the navy in 1932 after a nine-year stint, he charmed a young woman into marrying him, much to the displeasure of the woman's family and particularly her father, a Shinto priest. As the family and father predicted, the marriage was hardly made in heaven, and one day it climaxed in a physical fight between Kodaira and his in-laws. The result was that Kodaira killed his bride's father with an iron bar and injured half a dozen other relatives.

He was arrested and tried for these crimes and sentenced to fifteen years in prison. But when World War II started, Kodaira and other prisoners were given amnesty so they could aid in the war effort. Kodaira, because of his navy experience, was given a job as a civilian at a navy facility where young women worked under him, something like allowing the fox to guard the henhouse. Kodaira became a Peeping Tom, spying on the young women as they bathed after work. Eventually, he started to murder them. His homicidal activities were hardly noticed because Japanese authorities were too busy trying to defend against Allied air attacks.

His first discovered murder was on May 25, 1945. The victim was nineteen-year-old Miyazaki Mitsuko, whom he had raped and strangled. He hid her corpse behind an air-raid shelter. During the rest of the year, even after Japan surrendered to the Allies in August, he killed six more women ranging in age from nineteen to thirty-two at the navy facility, finishing out 1945 with the murder of nineteen-year-old Baba Hiroko on December 30.

Postwar Murders

After 1945 Kodaira took a six-month break from killing, then started in again by raping and strangling a fifteen-year-old girl. Of course his wartime service was over, and with it the ever-ready supply of employees as victims. His compulsions demanded a fresh supply, and he devised a way to get them— at the time, postwar Japan was rife with black market activity, much of it in Tokyo. He simply trolled the area where the illegal activities took place and waited for a likely victim to come along, with the reasoning that, if the girl was involved in the black market, she wasn't likely to be missed if she disappeared. In early July 1946, Kodaira met seventeen-year-old Midorikawa Ryuko. They seemed to have something of a relationship going—he even visited her parents—but by early August, Midorikawa had vanished and so had Kodaira.

Around the same time, another young woman, Shinokawa Tatsue, had also disappeared. Tatsue was found murdered near Zojoji Temple in Tokyo, and the Ryuko girl was found in the temple itself.

Police investigated, and Tatsue's parents told police they had last seen their daughter when she went to see a man for a job interview. The name of the man? Yoshio Kodaira.

Police tracked Kodaira down, and he spoke with them freely, admitting not only the murder of the two recent females but also all of the others as well as thirty rapes. Kodaira seemed to have no interest in living, and on October 5, 1949, Japanese authorities obliged him: He was hanged.

Chapter 33
Arnfinn Nesset, Norway

A scary and surprising number of serial killers work in hospitals. The reason is twofold: some serial murderers gravitate toward hospitals because of their ready supply of potential victims, but even more than this, dramatic methods like shooting or strangling don't have to be used in hospitals. Indeed, medical serial killers can kill patients, usually fragile and weak, in a variety of ways, including poisoning, suffocating, disconnecting machines, inducing overdoses of medication, or even drowning. Medical serial killers have been doctors, nurses, and aides; they have been male and female, black and white. Such killers are more common than anyone would like to think.

Purported motives vary, at least on the surface. For example, some medical serial killers try to play hero, administering a drug to induce a crisis such as cardiac arrest and then saving the person. However, sometimes the patient dies. Others kill under the guise of mercy, or for profit, and some are likely just plain sadistic. Many of them never get caught, but occasionally one does when the sheer number of dead patients triggers an investigation or when there's a small glitch or abnormality that drives people to start looking beneath the surface. So it was with Arnfinn Nesset, a mild-looking, balding, bespectacled man in his forties who was the most prolific medical serial killer in Norway's history.

The Hospital Manager

As it happened, in early 1981 someone noticed that Nesset, hospital manager of the Orkdale Valley Nursing Home, had ordered a large amount of Curacit, a derivative of curare, a lethal poison that South American Indians put on the tips of their arrows. If administered in a large dose to a person, Curacit interferes with respiration and causes death by suffocation. However, it breaks down in a person's system and is very difficult to detect as a cause of death. Orkdale Valley had had a very high death rate among its residents since it had opened in 1977. Maybe the poison and the death rate were related?

The police were contacted and they interviewed Nesset, who claimed he bought the poison to put down a dog—a dog that, given the amount of Curacit, would have to have been the size of an elephant. On March 9, 1981, forty-six-year-old Nesset was arrested for murder: He was eventually charged with the murder of twenty-five people, eleven women and fourteen men. The victim's ages ranged from sixty-seven to ninety-four, and all had died between 1977 and 1980—the exact time frame that Nesset had worked there. Nesset denied culpability at first, but then admitted that he had indeed ended the lives of the patients. At one point he said, "I've killed so many I'm unable to remember them all."

Afterword

After Nesset's confession to the Orkdale Valley murders, police probed deaths at three other facilities where he had worked since 1962 and eventually determined that he had likely killed at least sixty-two patients. But proving it—because of the way the body breaks down the poison—was difficult, if not impossible, so police did not pursue indictments on many of the deaths.

Before his trial started in October 1982, Nesset had a surprise for prosecutors: He withdrew his confessions and pleaded innocent, using a basic defense of euthanasia. He claimed he killed the people to put them out of their misery. Prosecutors battled this by saying that the murders had nothing to do with mercy killing—a position that was easily proved, as Nesset had embezzled some $1,800 from the people he killed. The defense countered that Nesset had donated all the money to charity, but it wasn't enough. On March 11, 1983, he was found guilty of twenty-two murders and assorted embezzlement charges. Shockingly—at least for Americans—he was sentenced to only twenty-one years in jail, the maximum allowed under Norwegian law, but there is also the possibility of being sentenced for an additional ten years of preventive detention.

Who Am I?

1. I was born in Nottingham, England, in January 1946 to a working class family. I am the most prolific serial murderer Europe has ever seen.

2. I was nothing special intellectually, but my mother's favoritism of me spurred me on to become a doctor.

3. I married a very average woman named Primrose Oxtoby when she became pregnant with my child.

4. I was caught giving myself injections for depression and was fired from my job in a hospital. In 1977 I moved to Hyde, Cheshire, and opened a practice. It was there that I started to murder people with medication.

5. I was an arrogant man who thought nothing of reducing employees and sometimes patients to tears. For example, I once criticized the breasts of one young girl and she ran from the room in tears.

6. I had a quick, white-hot temper. Screw up my morning coffee and I would rip you apart.

7. My killing specialty was older people. I mocked my victims and used derogatory codes for them, such as WOW (Whining Old Woman) and FTPBI (Failed to Put Brain In).

8. I scammed money from patients who died, including three hundred thousand pounds from one elderly patient, Mrs. Grundy, who died suddenly on June 24, 1998. I came under suspicion for her death, and my colleague Dr. Linda Reynolds noted the unusually high death rate among my patients and notified a coroner.

9. Investigation disclosed that I had killed innumerable elderly patients with a morphine overdose. I was arrested and tried for killing fifteen patients, found guilty, and given fifteen life sentences.

10. I hanged myself in my jail cell on January 13, 2004. Authorities later determined that I had murdered up to 260 people over a twenty-three-year period.

Answer: I am Dr. Harold Shipman.

Harold Shipman

Chapter 34
Karl Denke, Poland

Notable Fact
Many people who stayed at Papa's rooming house went in, but never came out.

Not much is known about Karl Denke, probably the worst serial killer in Poland's history—after he was exposed as a killer, he committed suicide, taking his secrets with him. What is known, however, is right up there with the worst of the worst. Denke owned and operated a rooming house in Ziębice, Poland, from 1918 to 1924. He was well liked by his tenants and known as "Papa." Like a number of other serial murderers (such as the BTK Killer), Papa was active in his local church—he played the organ. However, there was a problem: Many people who stayed at Papa's rooming house went in but never came out.

On December 21, 1924, a coachman heard someone screaming inside an apartment in Denke's rooming house. The coachman ran to the apartment and a young man was staggering down the hall toward him, holding his head, which was streaming blood. The coachman ran up to the man, who collapsed, but before he lost consciousness he blurted out that Papa Denke had attacked him with an ax.

The coachman summoned the police, who arrested Denke and searched his house—a search that turned up some shocking things. They found ID for a dozen salesmen as well as ties, shirts, pants, and hats in different sizes and styles, which obviously did not all belong to Papa Denke. In a ledger of Denke's, they found what might at first seem like curious but harmless information: names, dates and weights of his visitors. But the ledger made horrific sense when combined with some of the other discoveries: two large tubs in the kitchen filled with pickled meat, a large pot containing fat, and bones—all human. They were able to figure out that thirty-one human beings had been murdered between 1921 and 1924 and were in the process of being eaten. While many of Papa Denke's victims were salespeople, he also preyed on tramps and beggars—anyone who wouldn't really be missed or easily linked to Papa Denke.

Perhaps worst of all, not only was Denke a cannibal but also chances are that he was feeding parts of murdered people to his lodgers. We'll never know for sure—Papa Denke wore suspenders to hold up his pants, and he used them one final time to hang himself in his prison cell before police could get any information from him.

Chapter 35
Andrei Chikatilo, Russia

Notable Quotable

"What I did was not for sexual pleasure. Rather, it brought me some peace of mind."

—Andrei Chikatilo

In late December 1978, the body of a nine-year-old girl was discovered in the Grushevka River in the town of Shakhty, Russia. She had been raped, strangled, and stabbed repeatedly in the face. The twenty-five-year-old suspect Alexander Kravchenko was arrested. He had the pedigree for the crime, having served time in prison for rape and murder. The Russian police beat a confession out of Kravchenko: He was charged with the little girl's murder, tried, found guilty, and executed by firing squad.

The only problem was that Kravchenko was innocent, and in 1981, the bodies of boys, girls, and young women started showing up in and around the woods of Rostov-on-Don, near Shakhty, where the first body was found. Despite the victim's differences in age and gender, it was clearly the work of the same killer. The bodies were all mutilated in various ways—some had nipples excised, tongues cut out, noses cut off, genitalia removed, or had been disemboweled—and almost all were stabbed repeatedly in the face. A madman was on the loose.

Andrei Chikatilo, killer of more than
100 people in Russia

As each new body was discovered, anxiety ratcheted up for both the public and the police—even though, according to the Communist regime of the time, there was no Russian serial killer. The ruling party claimed that killers like the one operating around Rostov were only part of decadent western regimes, not Russia's enlightened system. Indeed, the official government attitude hampered the police investigation because they were forbidden to put out wanted circulars on him or even admit he existed. But the police knew that the killer who came to be known as the "Rostov Ripper" was very real, and so did much of the public.

The Rostov Ripper

In August 1984, eight corpses bearing the handiwork of the Rostov Ripper were found. Right around this time, police interviewed the real killer for the second time (they had talked to him after the little girl's murder in 1978 but had let him go).

The man, Andrei Romanovich Chikatilo, hardly seemed a homicidal maniac. He was a rather bland-looking individual, married, and held a

university degree. However, he was hardly ready for sainthood—he had been employed in the late 1970s as a school dormitory supervisor and had been terminated because of allegations that he molested some male students.

After losing that job, Chikatilo worked as a supply clerk, overseeing locomotive products in Rostov-on-Don. This proved the perfect job for a homicidal maniac. He was required to make frequent trips by bus or rail, meaning he frequently shared railroad stations and bus terminals with all kinds of people, including the young women and children of both sexes whom he like to murder and mutilate.

Chikatilo's 1984 interview with the police, however, did not lead anywhere—particularly since his innocence was trumpeted by the local Communist Party, of which he was a member, who declared that a man of such fine political character could not possibly also be a murderer. Chikatilo was released to kill again. And kill he did, remaining undetected despite a massive police effort that ultimately resulted in interrogations of some twenty-five thousand suspects between 1981 and 2000.

The Monster's Mistake

In early November 1990, a policeman spotted Chikatilo in a Rostov railway station and noticed that he had blood on his hands and face. While Chikatilo was not detained, the policeman did make a mental note of this man covered in blood.

Fatal Flaws

Appearing in public with blood on your hands and face is hardly the kind of thing that will go unnoticed, but it is often the kind of sloppy mistake that ultimately leads to the capture of serial killers. Ted Bundy, when wanted for murder, drove a car at night in Florida without a taillight and was pulled over. David Berkowitz, the Son of Sam, carelessly got a parking ticket that led to his capture. Dennis Rader communicated with police via computer, trusting them after he asked whether they could track him electronically. It's easy to wonder if these are just careless mistakes, or if some part of these serial killers wants to be stopped.

Two weeks after the policeman saw Chikatilo covered in blood, a body was discovered near that same railway station. Police brought Chikatilo in for questioning, which turned into a marathon eight-day grilling, at the end of which Chikatilo confessed. Like a poisonous snake uncoiling, Chikatilo detailed how he would stalk railway stations and bus depots until he spotted a likely victim, usually a child or young person waiting for a train or bus alone. He would offer them a ride or perhaps something to eat, then lead them into the woods where he would abruptly spring on the person, overpowering and killing them and then mutilating them as his bloodlust dictated.

Chikatilo confessed to fifty-five murders and was charged with fifty-three. His trial started on April 14, 1992, in a plain courtroom. The then fifty-four-year-old Chikatilo stood in the dock like all prisoners, but he was enclosed in a large iron cage that had been constructed over the dock to protect him from parents and other angry people. The scene was chaotic, with the families of his murder victims shrieking and baying for his blood.

Unusually, Chikatilo chose to testify in front of all these people, in part to attempt an explanation of why and how he had turned into the Rostov Ripper. Chikatilo testified that he was born in the Ukraine on October 16, 1936, and that he and his family had been victims of the poverty and hunger triggered by Joseph Stalin's collectivization of Russian farms in the 1930s. Many people in his area starved. Indeed, Chikatilo believed that neighbors had cannibalized an older brother of his, and this had been seared into his young soul. There is no proof readily available to confirm that the neighbors ate his brother, but his mother constantly told him it was so, and Chikatilo came to believe it. Chikatilo believe that his mother and the fate of his brother were a large part of why he killed.

However, childhood trauma was not enough to get him off the hook for so much death, and Chikatilo was found guilty of fifty-three counts of murder on October 15, 1992, and sentenced to death. Less than two years later, following a rejected appeal for clemency from President Boris Yeltsin, the sentence was carried out and an executioner fired a single round into the back of Chikatilo's head.

Andrei Chikatilo at the end of his life.

Chapter 36
Moses Sithole, South Africa

Notable Quotable

"I force a woman to go where I want," he said, "and when I go there I tell them, 'Do you know what? I was hurt so I'm doing it now.' Then I kill them."

—Moses Sithole

Moses Sithole is hands down the worst serial murderer in South African history. Astonishingly, Sithole, when tried, was found guilty of thirty-eight murders between January and October 1995—thirty-eight murders in just ten months, or about four killings a month. That's bloodlust.

Sithole was good looking and charming, and very bold. He would approach women in broad daylight and somehow lure them into surrounding isolated fields, where he would launch his attack, which included stripping, beating, raping, and then strangling them with their own clothing. Sometimes he would tie them up; many times he would cover their faces with an article of clothing, symbolically if not actually preventing them from seeing him.

The killings had happened so fast and were so vicious that the entire country was in a state of alarm, including President Nelson Mandela, who actually canceled an important political trip to plead for the public's help in tracking the killer down. So desperate

Moses Sithole

were South African authorities to solve the crimes—dubbed the "ABC Murders" by the press, as they had started in Atteridgeville, moved to Boksburg, then continued in Cleveland—that they brought in two renowned profilers to work the case: the premier South African profiler Micki Pistorius and the famed FBI agent Robert Ressler. Their collaboration didn't result in the capture of the killer, but Ressler provided one helpful insight: He was the first to connect the murders in the three towns to one killer.

The Killer Slips

In October 1995—his thirty-eight killings all behind him—the killer contacted Capetown's *Star* newspaper and claimed to be the ABC Murderer. During the call (which *Star* recorded), he made a series of complaints that contained specific information: For example, he had been convicted of a rape in 1978 that he said he didn't do, but as a result he spent fourteen years in prison. He also said he had to endure the death of his parents and sister while he was behind bars. He said this experience built up a terrible need for revenge in him, and he took it out on women. "I force a woman to go where I want," he said, "and when I go there I tell them, 'Do you know what? I was hurt so I'm doing it now.' Then I kill them."

The *Star* reporter talking to him asked just how many women he had killed, and he had a stunning answer: "Seventy-six." This was twice as many victims as police had thought. To prove he was the killer, he finished the call with directions to the body of one of his victims.

Thankfully, however, the caller had provided more than enough personal information for police to identify him as Moses Sithole. Police soon focused on him and ultimately arrested him. When the police located him, Sithole went at them with a hatchet, but he was shot and neutralized. In the hospital it was learned that he was HIV positive.

He went on trial in February 1997, charged with thirty-eight murders, forty rapes, and six counts of robbery. On December 5, 1997, he was found guilty and sentenced to 2,410 years. It was thought that he would die within seven or eight years of his trial from HIV-related complications, but he is still alive and in prison.

273

PART IV

IN THEIR OWN WORDS

There is nothing quite as horrific as confessions straight from the mouths of serial killers. Following are the words of BTK Killer Dennis Rader, describing how he killed people, including an entire family. There is also the description of Edmund Kemper's attack on two young women one sunny day in California, and a few choice words from Green River Killer Gary Ridgway.

Chapter 37

Dennis Rader: Court Transcript of His Confession

Murder of the Otero Family

Defendant: *On January 15, 1974, said:* I maliciously, intentionally and (with) premeditation killed Joseph Otero. Count Two—

Court: All right. Mr. Rader, I need to find out more information. On that particular day, the fifteenth day of January, 1974, can you tell me where you went to kill Mr. Joseph Otero?

Defendant: Mmm, I think it's 1834 Edgemoor.

Court: All right. Can you tell me approximately what time of day you went there?

Defendant: Somewhere between seven and seven-thirty.

Court: This particular location, did you know these people?

Defendant: No. That's—*[Off-the-record discussion between the defendant and Ms. McKinnon, his lawyer.]* No, that was part of my—I guess my what you call fantasy. These people were selected.

Court: All right. So you—

[Off-the-record discussion between the defendant and Ms. McKinnon.]

Court:—You were engaged in some kind of fantasy during this period of time?

Defendant: Yes, sir.

Court: All right. Now, where you use the term fantasy, is this something you were doing for your personal pleasure?

Defendant: Sexual fantasy, sir.

Court: I see. So you went to this residence, and what occurred then?

Defendant: Well, I had—did some thinking on what I was going to do to either Mrs. Otero or Josephine, and basically broke into the house—or didn't break into the house, but when they came out of the house I came in and confronted the family, and then we went from there.

Court: All right. Had you planned this beforehand?

Defendant: To some degree, yes. After I got in the house it—lost control of it, but it—it was—you know, in back of my mind I had some ideas what I was going to do.

Court: Did you—

Defendant: But I just—I basically panicked that first day, so—

Court: Beforehand did you know who was there in the house?

Defendant: I thought Mrs. Otero and the two kids—the two younger kids were in the house. I didn't realize Mr. Otero was gonna be there.

Court: All right. How did you get into the house, Mr. Rader?

Defendant: I came through the back door, cut the phone lines, waited at the back door, had reservations about even going or just walking away, but pretty soon the door opened, and I was in.

Court: All right. So the door opened. Was it opened for you, or did someone—

Defendant: I think one of the kids—I think the Ju—Junior—or not Junior—yes, the—the young girl—Joseph [sic] opened the door. He probably let the dog out 'cause the dog was in the house at the time.

Court: All right. When you went into the house what happened then?

Defendant: Well, I confronted the family, pulled the pistol, confronted Mr. Otero and asked him to—you know, that I was there to—basically I was wanted, wanted to get the car. I was hungry, food, I was wanted, and asked him to lie down in the living room. And at that time I realized that wouldn't be a really good idea, so I finally—The dog was the real problem, so I—I asked Mr. Otero if he could get the dog out. So he had one of the kids put it out, and then I took them back to the bedroom.

Court: You took who back to the bedroom?

Defendant: The family, the bedroom—the four members.

Court: All right. What happened then?

Defendant: At that time I tied 'em up.

Court: While still holding them at gunpoint?

Defendant: Well, in between tying, I guess, you know.

Court: All right. After you tied them up what occurred?

Defendant: Well, they started complaining about being tied up, and I re—reloosened the bonds a couple of times, tried to make Mr. Otero as comfortable as I could. Apparently he had a cracked rib from a car accident, so I had him put a pillow down on his—for his—for his head, had him put a—I think a parka or a coat underneath him. They—You know, they talked to me about, you know, giving me the car or whatever money. I guess they didn't have very much money, and the—from there I realized that, you know, I was already—I didn't have a mask on or anything. They already could ID me, and made—made a decision to go ahead and—and put 'em down, I guess, or strangle them.

Court: All right. What did you do to Joseph Otero Sr.?

Defendant: Joseph Otero?

Court: Yeah, Joseph Otero Sr. Mr. Otero, the father.

Defendant: Put a plastic bag over his head and then some cords and tightened it.

Court: This was in the bedroom?

Defendant: Yes, sir.

Court: All right. Did he in fact suffocate and die as a result of this?

Defendant: Not right away, no sir, he didn't.

Court: What happened?

Defendant: Well, after that I—I did Mrs. Otero. I had never strangled anyone before, so I really didn't know how much pressure you had to put on a person or how long it would take, but—

Court: Was she also tied up there in the bedroom?

Defendant: Yes, uh-huh. Yeah, both their hands and their feet were tied up. She was on the bed.

Court: Where were the children?

Defendant: Well, Josephine was on the bed, and Junior was on the floor—

Court: All right.

Defendant:—At this time.

Court: So we're—we're talking, first of all, about Joseph Otero. So you had put the bag over his head and tied it.

Defendant: I don't know. I have no idea. Just—

Court: What happened then?

Defendant: I got the keys to the car. In fact, I had the keys I think earlier before that, 'cause I wanted to make sure I had a way of getting out of the house, and cleaned the house up a little bit, made sure everything's packed up, and left through the front door, and then went there—went over to their car, and then drove to Dillons, left the car there. Then eventually walked back to my car.

Court: All right. Now, sir, from what you have just said, I take it that the facts you have told me apply to both Counts One all of Counts One, Two, Three, and Four; is that correct?

Defendant: Yes, sir.

Court: Now, Mr. Rader— And he did not die right away. Can you tell me what happened in regards to Joseph Otero?

Defendant: He moved over real quick like and I think tore a hole in the bag, and I could tell that he was having some problems there, but at that time the—the whole family just went—they went panicked on me, so I—I—I worked pretty quick. I got Mrs. O—

Court: All right. What did you—You worked pretty quick. What did you do?

Defendant: Well, I mean, I—I—I strangled Mrs. Otero, and then she out, or passed out. I thought she was dead. She passed out. Then I strangled Josephine. She passed out, or I thought she was dead. And then I went over and put a—and then put a bag on Junior's head and—and then, if I remember right, Mrs. Otero came back. She came back and—

Court: Sir, let me ask you about Joseph Otero Sr.

Defendant: Senior.

Court: You indicated he had torn a hole in the bag.

Defendant: Mm-hmm.

Court: What did you do with him then?

Defendant: I put another bag over it—or either that or a—if I recollect, I think I put a—either a cloth or a T-shirt or something over it—over his head, and then a bag, another bag, then tied that down.

Court: Did he sub—Did he subsequently die?

Defendant: Well, yes. I mean—I mean, I was—I didn't just stay there and watch him. I mean, I was moving around the room, but—

Court: All right. So you indicated you strangled Mrs. Otero after you had done this; is that correct?

Defendant: Yeah, I went back and strangled her again.

Court: All right.

Defendant: And that—And that—that finally killed her at that time.

The Murder of Kathryn Bright

Court: All right, Mr. Rader. We will now turn to Count Five. In that count it is claimed that on or about the fourth day of April, 1974, in Sedgwick County, Kansas, that you unlawfully killed Kathryn Bright, maliciously, willfully, deliberately, and with premeditation, by strangulation and stabbing, inflicting injuries from which she did die on April 4, 1974. Can you tell me what happened on that day?

[*Off-the-record discussions between Mr. Osburn and the defendant.*]

Defendant: Well, the—I don't know how to exactly say that. I had many what I call them projects. They were different people in town that I followed, watched. Kathryn Bright was one of the next targets, I guess, as I would indicate.

Court: How did you select her?

Defendant: Just driving by one day, and I saw her go in the house with somebody else, and I thought that's a possibility. There was many, many places in the area, College Hill even. They're all over Wichita. But anyway, that's—it just was basically a selection process, worked toward it. If it didn't work I'd just move on to something else, but in the—in the—my kind of person, stalking and strolling [sic]—You go through the trolling stage and then a stalking stage. She was in the stalking stage when this happened.

Court: All right, sir. So you identified Kathryn Bright as a potential victim.

Defendant: Yes, sir.

Court: What did you do here in Sedgwick County then?

Defendant: Pardon?

Court: What did you do then here in Sedgwick County?

Defendant: On this particular day?

Court: Yes.

Defendant: I broke into the house and waited for her to come home.

Court: How did you break into the house?

Defendant: Through the back door on the east side.

Court: All right. And you waited for her to come home.

Defendant: Yes, sir.

Court: Where did you wait?

Defendant: In the house there, probably close to the bedroom. I walked through the house and kind of figured out where I'd be if they came through.

Court: All right. What happened then?

Defendant: She and Kevin Bright came in. I wasn't expecting him to be there. And come to find out, I guess they were related. That time I approached them and told them I was wanted in California, needed some car—basically the same thing I told the Oteros. Kind of eased them, make them feel better, and proceeded to—I think I had him tie—I think I had him tie her up first, and then I tied him up, or vice versa. I don't remember right now at that time.

Court: Let—Let me ask—

Defendant: Mm-hmm.

Court: You indicated that you had some items to tie these people with. Did you bring these items, both the Oteros and to this location?

Defendant: The Oteros I did. I'm not really sure on the Brights. There were some—I—When I had—In working with the police

283

there was some converserva [sic] on that. Probably more likely I did, but if—if I had brought my stuff and used my stuff Kevin would probably be dead today.

Court: All right.

Defendant: I'm not bragging on that. It's just a matter of fact. It's the bond had tau—row [sic]—tied him up with that he broke them, so that—

Court: All right, sir.

Defendant: It may be same way with—same with Kathryn. It was—They got outta—got outta hand.

Court: All right. Now, you indicated you believe you had Kevin tie Kathryn up.

Defendant: Mm-hmm.

Court: Tell me what happened then.

Defendant: Okay. I moved—Well, after—I really can't remember, Judge, whether I had her tie him up or she tied him up; but anyway, I moved basically I moved her to another bedroom, and he as already secure there by the bed. Tied his feet to the bedpost—one of the bedposts so that he couldn't run. Kind of tired her in the other bedroom, and then I came back to strangle him, and at that time we had a fight.

Court: Were you armed with a handgun at that time also?

Defendant: Yes, I had a handgun.

Court: All right. What happened when you came back?

Defendant: I actually had two handguns.

Court: All right.

Defendant: Well, when I started strangling, the—either the garrote broke or he broke his bonds, and he jumped up real quick like. I pulled my gun and quickly shot him. It hit him in the head. He fell over. I could see the blood. And as far as I was concerned, he—you know, I thought he was down and was out, and then went and started to strangle Kath—or Kathryn.

284

And then we started fighting, 'cause the bonds weren't very good, and so back and forth we fought.

Court: You and Kathryn?

Defendant: Yeah, we fought, uh-huh. And I got the best of her, and I thought she was going down, and then I could hear some movement in the other room. So I went back, and Kevin—No. No. I thought she was going down, and I went back to the other bedroom where Kevin was at, and I tried to restrangle him at that time, and he jumped up, and we fought, and—and he about—at that time about shot me, 'cause he got the other pistol that was in my shoulder here. I had my magnum in my shoulder. So—And really—

Court: A shoulder holster?

Defendant: Hmm?

Court: Did you have it in a shoulder holster?

Defendant: Yes, mm-hmm. I had the magnum in my shoulder holster. The other one was a .22.

Court: All right.

Defendant: And we fought at that point in time, and I thought it was gonna go off. I jammed the gun, stuck my finger in the—in there, jammed it; and I think he thought that was the only gun I had 'cause once I either bit his finger or hit him or something, got away, and I used the .22 and shot him one more time, and I thought he was down for good that time.

Court: All right. So you shot him a second time.

Defendant: Yes, sir.

Court: Went back to finish the job on Kathryn, and she was fighting. And at that point in time I'd been fighting her. I just—And then I heard some—I don't know whether I was lose—basically losing control. The strangulation wasn't working on her, and I used a knife on her. You say you used a knife on her.

Defendant: Yes. Yes.

Court: What did you do with the knife?

Defendant: I stabbed her. She was stab—either stabbed two or three times, either here or here, maybe two back here and one here, or maybe just two times back here.

Court: And you're—you're pointing to your lower back and your—your—

Defendant: Yeah, underneath the ribs.

Court:—And your lower abdomen.

Defendant: Yeah, underneath the ribs, up—up under the ribs.

Court: So after you stabbed her what happened?

Defendant: Actually I think at that point in time—Well, it's a total mess 'cause I didn't have control on it. She was bleeding. She went down. I think I just went back to check on Kevin, or at that basically same time I heard him escape. It could be one of the two. But all the sudden the front door of the house was open and he was gone, and—Oh, I tell you what I thought. I thought the police were coming at that time. I heard the door open. I thought, you know, that's it; and I stepped out there, and he—I could see him running down the street. So I quickly cleaned up everything that I could and left.

Court: All right. Now, Mr. Rader, you indicated that at the Oteros' you did not have a mask on. Did you have a mask on at the Brights'?

Defendant: No. No I didn't, huh-uh.

Court: All right. So what happened then?

Defendant: I tried—I had—already had the keys to the cars, and I thought I had the right key to the right car. I ran out to their car, what—I think it was a pickup out there. And I tried it, didn't work; and at that point in time I was—he was gone, running down the street. I thought well, I'm in trouble, so I tried it, didn't work. So I just took off, ran. I went down—went east and then worked back toward the [Wichita State University] campus where my car was parked.

Court: All right. So you had parked your car at the Wichita State University—

Defendant: Yes, sir.

Court:—Campus?

Defendant: The campus, uh-huh.

Court: How far away were—was the Brights' residence?

Defendant: Oh, I parked—What is that? Thirteenth? And their—I want to say their—I parked by that park, and then I walked to Thirteenth to the Brights' residence. So I basically ran back.

Court: All right. So you were able to get to your car and get away.

Defendant: Yes, sir.

The Murder of Shirley Vian

Court: Now let's turn to Count Six. In that count they claim on March 17, 1977, in Sedgwick County, Kansas, that you unlawfully killed Shirley Vian, maliciously, willfully, deliberately and with premeditation, by strangulation, inflicting injuries from which she did die on March 17, 1977. Can you tell me what you did on that day?

Defendant: As before, Vian was a—Actually on that one she was completely random. There was actually someone that across from Dillons was potential target. I had project numbers assigned to it. And that particular day I drove to Dillons, parked in the parking lot, watched this particular residence, and then got out of the car and walked over to it. It's probably in the police report, the address. I don't remember the address now. Knocked. Nobody—Nobody answered it. So I was all keyed up, so I just started going through the neighborhood. I had been

287

through the neighborhood before. I know of knew a little—little of the layout of the neighborhood. I'd been through the back alleys, knew where some—certain people lived. While I was walking down Hydraulic I met—a young boy and asked him if he would ID some pictures, kind of as a russ [sic], I guess, or ruse as you call it, and kind of feel it out, and saw where he went, and I went to another address, knocked on the door. Nobody opened the door, so I just noticed where he went and went to that house and we went from there.

Court: Now, you—you call these "projects." Were these sexual fantasies also?

Defendant: Potential hits. That—In my world, that's what I called them.

Court: All right. So you—

Defendant: They were called projects, hits.

Court: All right. And—And why did you have these potential hits? Was this to gratify some sexual interest or—

Defendant: Yes, sir. I had—There—I had a lot of them, so it's just—if one didn't work I'd just move to another one.

Court: All right. So as I am to understand it then, on [March 17], 1977, you saw this little boy go into a residence.

Defendant: Mm-hmm.

Court: And you tried another residence?

Defendant: Sir?

Court: No one was there? You tried another residence. No on was there, so you—

Defendant: Right, right, right, right. Yeah.

Court:—Went to the residence with the little boy—

Defendant: And I watched—I watched where he went.

Court: What happened then?

Defendant: After I tried this once, the residence, nobody came to the door. I went to this house where he went in, knocked on the door and told 'em I was a private detective, showed 'em a picture that I had just showed the boy and asked 'em if they could ID the picture; and that time I—I had the gun here and I just kind of forced myself in. I just, you know, walked in—just opened the door and walked in and then pulled a pistol.

. . .

Court: What happened then?

Defendant: I told Mrs.—Miss Vian that I had a problem with sexual fantasies, that I was going to tie her up, and that—and I might have to tie the kids up, and that she would cooperate with this—cooperate with me at that time. We went back. She was extremely nervous. Think she even smoked a cigarette. And we went back to the—one of the back—back areas of the porch, explained to her that I had done this before, and, you know, I think she—at that point in time I think she was sick 'cause she had a night robe on, and I think, if I remember right, she was—she had been sick. I think—I think she came out of the bedroom when I went in the house. So anyway, we went back to the—her bedroom, and I proceeded to tie the kids up, and they started crying and got real upset. So I said, oh, this is not gonna work, so we moved 'em to the bathroom. She helped me. And then I tied the door shut. We put some toys and blankets and odds and ends in there for the kids, make them as comfortable as we could. Tied the—We tied one of the bathroom doors shut so they couldn't open it, and we shoved—she went back and helped me shove the bed up against the other bathroom door, and then I proceeded to tie her up. She got sick, threw up. Got her a glass of water, comforted her a little bit, and then went ahead and tied her up and then put a blag [sic]—a bag over her head and strangled her.

Court: All right. Was this a plastic bag also?

Defendant: Yes, sir. I think it was.

Court: All right.

Defendant: But I could be wrong in that.

Court: You put a bag or—

Defendant: It was something—I'm sure it was a plastic bag, yeah.

Court: Now, you say you put a bag over her head and strangled her. What did you strangle her with?

Defendant: I actually—I think on that I had tied—tied her legs to the bedposts and worked up with the rope all the way up, and then what I had left over I looped over her neck.

Court: All right. So you used this rope to strangle her?

Defendant: Yes, uh-huh. I think—I think it was the same one that I tied her body with, mm-hmm.

Court: All right. What happened then?

Defendant: Well, the kids were really banging on the door, hollering and screaming, and—and then the telephone rang, and they had talked earlier that the neighbor's gonna check on 'em, so I cleaned everything up real quick like, and got out of there, left and went back in—to my car.

Court: Now, when you say you cleaned everything—

Defendant: Well, I mean put my stuff—I had a briefcase. Whatever I have laying around, ropes, tape, cords, I threw that in there, my—you know, whatever, you know, that I had that I brought in the house.

Court: Had you brought that to the Bright residence also or—

Defendant: Yeah, there is some—There—I—I think there's some basic stuff, but I don't remember bringing total stuff like I did to some of the others.

Court: Was this a kit that you had prepared—

Defendant: Yeah. I—

Court:—Beforehand?

Defendant: Yes. I call it my hit kit.

Court: All right, sir. You left the Vian residence, and had you parked your vehicle near there?

Defendant: Yeah, still in the same parking lot there at Dillons—

Court: All right.

Defendant:—At Hydraulic and—What is that? Harry? Lincoln. Lincoln, yeah. Lincoln and—Lincoln and Hydraulic.

The Murder of Nancy Fox

Court: All right. In Count Seven it is claimed that on the eighth day of December, 1977, in Sedgwick County, Kansas, that you unlawfully killed a human being, that being Nancy Fox, maliciously, willfully, deliberately, and with premeditation, by strangulation, inflicting injuries from which the said Nancy Fox did die on December 8, 1977. Can you tell me what you did on that day here in Sedgwick County?

Defendant: Nancy Fox was another one of the projects. When I was trolling the area I noticed her go in the house one night. Sometimes I would—And anyway, I put her down as potential victim.

Court: Let me ask you one thing, Mr. Rader. You've used that term when you were patrolling the area. What do you mean by that?

Defendant: It's called stalking or trolling.

Court: So you were not working in any form or fashion. You were just—

Defendant: Well, I don't know, if—you know, if you read much about serial killers, they go through what they call the different phases. That's one of the phases they go through is a—as a trolling stage. You're lay—Basically you're looking for a victim at that time, and that can either be trolling for months or years. But once you lock in on a certain person then you become

291

stalking, and that might be several of them, but you really hone in on that person. They—They basically come the—That's—That's the victim, or at least that's what you want 'em to be.

Court: All right, sir.

Defendant: No, no. I wasn't working sir.

Court: All right.

Defendant: No, this was—No, this was off—off—off my hours.

Court: All right. So you basically identified Nancy Fox as one of your projects. What happened then?

Defendant: At first she was spotted, and then I did a little homework. I dropped by once to check the mailbox to see what her name was, found out where she worked, stopped by there once at Helzberg, kind of sized her up. I had—The more I know about a person the—the more I felt comfortable with it, so I did that a couple of times; and then I just selected a night, which was this particular night, to try it, and it worked out.

Court: All right. Can you tell me what you did on the night of December 8, 1977?

Defendant: About two or three blocks away I parked my car and walked to that residence. I knocked at the—knocked at the door first to make sure, see if anybody was in there 'cause I knew she arrived home at a particular time from where she worked. Nobody answered the door, so I went around to the back of the house, cut the phone lines. I could tell that there wasn't anybody in the north apartment. Broke in and waited for her to come home in the kitchen.

Court: All right. Did she come home?

Defendant: Yes, she did.

Court: What happened?

Defendant: I confronted her, told here there—I was a—I had a problem, sexual problem, that I would have to tie her up and have sex with her.

Court: Mm-hmm.

Defendant: She was a little upset. We talked for a while. She smoked a cigarette. While the—While we smoked a cigarette I went through her purse, identifying some stuff, and she finally said, Well, let's get this over with so I can go call the police. I said, Yes. She went to the bathroom and came—and I told her when she came out to make sure that she was undressed. And when she came out I handcuffed her, and don't really remember whether I—

Court: You handcuffed her?

Defendant: Sir?

Court: You handcuffed her? You had a pair of handcuffs?

Defendant: Yes, sir, uh-huh, mm-hmm.

Court: What happened then?

Defendant: Well, anyway, I had her—I handcuffed her, had her lay on the bed, and then I tied her feet, and then I—I—I—was also undressed to a certain degree, and then I got on top of her, and then reached over, took either—either—either her feet were tied or not tied, but anyway, I took—I think I had a belt. I took the belt and then strangled her with the belt at that time.

Court: All right. All right. After you had strangled her what happened then?

Defendant: Okay. After I strangled her with the belt I took the belt off and retied that with pantyhose real tight, removed the handcuffs and tied those with—with pantyhose. Can't remember the colors right now. I think I maybe retied her feet, if they hadn't already—they were probably already tied, her feet were, and then at that time masturbated, sir.

Court: All right. Had you had sexual relations with her—

Defendant: No.

Court:—Before?

293

Defendant: No, no. I told her I was, but I did not.

Court: All right. So you masturbated. Then what did you do?

Defendant: Dressed and then went through the house, took some personal items, and kind of cleaned the house up, went through and made—checked everything and then left.

Court: All right.

The Murder of Marine Hedge

Court: All right, sir. Let's turn to Count Eight. In Count Eight it is claimed that on or about the twenty-seventh day of April, 1985, to the twenty-eighth day of April, 1985, in Sedgwick County, Kansas, it is claimed that you unlawfully killed a human being, Marine Hedge, maliciously, willfully, deliberately, and with premeditation, by strangulation, inflicting injuries from which Marine Hedge did die on April 27, 1985. Can you tell me what occurred on that day?

Defendant: Well, actually, kind of like the others. She was chosen. I went through the different phases, stalking phase, and since she lived down the street from me I could watch the coming and going quite easily. On that particular date I—I had a—a other [sic] commitment. I came back from that commitment. Parked my car over at Woodlawn and Twenty-first Street at a bowling alley there at the time. Before that I dressed into—I had some other clothes on. I changed clothes. I went to the bowling alley, went in there under the pretense of bowling, called a taxi. Had a taxi take me out to Park City. Had my kit with me. It was a bowling bag.

Court: All right. Now, is Park City in Sedgwick County, Kansas?

Defendant: Yes, sir, uh-huh, mm-hmm.

Court: All right. You had the taxi take you to Park City. What happened then?

Defendant: There I asked—I—I pretended that I was a little drunk. I just took—I just took some beer and washed it around my mouth, and the guy could probably smell alcohol on me. I asked—told him to let me out so I could get some fresh air, and I walked from where the taxi let me off over to her house.

Court: All right. Where does she live?

. . .

Defendant:—North Independence.

Court: All right. When you walked over there what happened next?

Defendant: Well, as before, I was going to have sexual fantasies, so I brought my hit kit, and lo and behold, her car was there. I thought, gee, she's not supposed to be home. So I very carefully snuck into the house, she wasn't there. So about that time the doors rattled, so I went—went back to one of the bedrooms and hid back there in one of the bedrooms. She came in with a male visitor. They were there for maybe an hour or so. Then he left. I waited till wee hours of the morning. I then proceeded to sneak into her bedroom and flip the lights on real quick like, or I think the bathroom lights. I just—I didn't want to flip her lights on, and she screamed, and I jumped on the bed and strangled her manually.

Court: All right. Now, were you wearing any kind of disguise or mask at this time?

Defendant: No. No.

Court: You indicated this woman lived down the street from you. Did she know you?

Defendant: Casually. We'd walk by and wave. She—She liked to work in her yard as well as I liked to work, and it's just a neighborly type thing. It wasn't anything personal, I mean, just a neighbor.

Court: All right. So she was in her bed when you turned on the lights in the bathroom?

Defendant: Yeah, the bathroom, yeah, just to—so I could get some light in there.

Court: All right. What did you do then?

Defendant: Oh, I manually strangled her when she started to scream.

Court: So you used your hands?

Defendant: Yes, sir.

Court: And you strangled her? Did she die?

Defendant: Yes.

Court: All right. What did you do then?

Defendant: After that, since I was in the sexual fantasy, I went ahead and stripped her and probably went ahead and—I'm not for sure if I tied her up at that point in time, but anyway, she was nude, and I put her on a blanket, went through her purse, some personal items in the house, figured out how I was gonna get her out of there. Eventually moved her to the trunk of the car. Took the car over to Christ Lutheran Church—This is with the older church—and took some pictures of her.

Court: All right. You took some photographs of her. What kind of camera did you use?

Defendant: Polaroid.

Court: All right. Did you keep those photographs?

Defendant: Yes. The police probably have them.

Court: All right. All right. What happened then?

Defendant: That was it. I went—I took—She went through—I tied—She was already dead, so I took pictures of her in different forms of bondage, and that's probably what got me in trouble is the bondage thing. So anyway—That's probably the—the main thing. But anyway, after that I moved her back out to the car, and then we went east on Fifty-third.

Court: All right. What occurred then?

Defendant: Sir?

Court: What happened then?

Defendant: Oh, trying to find a place to hide her, hide the body.

Court: Did you find a place?

Defendant: Yes. Yes, I did.

Court: Where?

Defendant: Couldn't tell you without looking at a map, but it was on Fifty-third, between Greenwich maybe—maybe—What's—What's the other one between Green—Greenwich and Rock?

Mr. Osburn: Webb.

Defendant: Webb. Between—I think between wed [sic] and—Webb and Greenwich I found a ditch, a low place on the north side of the road, and hid her there.

Court: All right. You say you hid her there. Did you—

Defendant: Well, there were some—there were some trees, some brush, and I laid that over the top of her body.

Court: All right. So you removed the body from the car, put her in the ditch, then laid some—some brush over the body.

Defendant: Yes, sir.

The Murder of Dolores E. Davis

Court: Now, sir, let's turn to Count Ten. In that count it's claimed that on or about the eighteenth day of January, 1991, to the [nineteenth] day of January, 1991, in the County of Sedgwick, State of Kansas, that you did then and there unlawfully kill a human being, that being Dolores E. Davis, maliciously, willfully, deliberately, and with premeditation, by strangulation, inflicting injuries from which the said Dolores E. Davis did die on January 19, 1991. Mr. Rader, please tell me what you did here in Sedgwick County, Kansas, on that day that makes you believe you're guilty.

Defendant: That particular day I had some commitments. I left those, went to one place, changed my clothes, went to another place, parked my car, finally made arrangements on my hit kit, my clothes, and then walked to that residence. After spending some time at that residence—It was very cold that night. Had reservations about going in 'cause I—I had cased the place before, and I really couldn't figure out how to get in, and she was in the house, so I finally just selected a—a concrete block and threw it through the plate glass window on the east and came on in.

Court: All right. Where is this residence located?

Defendant: It's on Hillside, but I couldn't give the address. I know it's probably 61—probably 62 something. I don't know. 62 something.

Court: North or South?

Defendant: North. North Hillside.

Court: All right. So you used a concrete block to break a window?

Defendant: Mm-hmm, plate glass window, patio door, mm-hmm.

Court: All right. What happened then?

Defendant: Noise. I just went in. She came out of a bedroom and thought a car had hit her house, and I told her that I was—I used a—the ruse of being wanted. I was on the run; I needed food, car, warmth, warm up, and then I asked her—I handcuffed her and kind of talked to her, told her that I would like to get some food, get her keys to her car, and kind of rest assured, you know, walked—talked with her a little bit and calmed her down a little bit. And then eventually I checked—I think she was still handcuffed. I went back and checked out where the car was, simulated getting some food, odds and ends in the house, kind of like I was leaving, then went back and removed her handcuffs and—and then tied her up and then—and then eventually strangled her.

Court: All right. You say "eventually strangled her."

Defendant: Well, after I tied her up. I went through some things in the room there and then—and then strangled her.

Court: All right. You say you went through. Were you looking for something?

Defendant: Mm-hmm. Well, some personal items, yes. I took some personal items from there.

Court: Did you take personal items in every one of these incidents?

Defendant: I did on the Hedge. I don't remember anything in Vicki's place. The Oteros we got the watch and the radio. I don't think I did any in Brights'. Vian's, no, I don't think so. Fox, yes. I took some things from Fox. It was hit and miss.

Court: All right. But in regard—

Defendant: Prob—Probably if it—if it—if it was a controlled situation where I had more time I took something, but if it—if it was a confusion and other things I didn't 'cause I was trying to get out of there.

Court: All right. So in regard to the Davis matter, you went around the room, took a few personal things. What did you do then?

Defendant: Strangled her.

Court: What did you strangle her with?

Defendant: Pantyhose.

Court: All right. What happened then? Did she die?

Defendant: Kind of like Mrs. Hedge. I already figured out my—I had a, you know, plan on leaving and put her in a blanket and drug her to the car, put her in the trunk of the car.

Court: So you were able to strangle her to death with these pantyhose.

Defendant: Yes, sir.

Court: All right. You put her in your car.

Defendant: In her car.

Court: Or in a car.

Defendant: Her car.

Court: Her car or trunk.

Defendant: Uh-huh, the trunk of her car, uh-huh.

Court: What happened then?

Defendant: I really had a commitment I needed to go to, so I moved her to one spot, took her out of her car. This gets complicated. Then the stuff I had, clothes, gun, whatever, I took that to another spot in her car, dumped that off. Okay. Then took her car back to her house. Left that. Let me think now. Okay. In the interim—I took her car back to her house. In the interim I realized that I had lost one of my guns. I dropped it somewhere. So I was distraught trying to figure out where my gun was. So I went back in the house, realized I had dropped it when I went in the—when I broke the plate glass window. It dropped. It fell on the floor right there, and I found it right there. So that solved that problem. Anyway, I went back out, threw the keys—checked the car real quick—quick like and threw the keys up on top of the roof of her house, walked from her car back to my car, took my car, drove it back, and I either dropped more stuff off or I picked her up and put 'em in my car, and then I drove northeast of Sedgwick County and dropped her off underneath a bridge.

Court: All right. So all of these incidents, these ten counts, occurred because you wanted to satisfy a sexual fantasy; is that correct?

Defendant: Yes, mm-hmm.

Court: Does any party desire any further matters to be put on
the record at this time?

Mr. Osburn: No, your Honor.

Court: All right. You may be seated, Mr. Rader.

Chapter 38

Gary Ridgway, the Green River Killer

Excerpts from Ridgway's confession, when he pleaded guilty to murdering forty-eight women in the notorious Green River killings, as read in court by prosecutor Jeff Baird.

"I killed the 48 women listed in the state's second amended information."

"In most cases when I killed these women I did not know their names."

"Most of the time I killed them the first time I met them and I do not have a good memory of their faces."

"I have reviewed information and discovery about each of the murders with my attorneys and I am positive that I killed each one of the women charged in the second information."

"I killed most of them in my house near Military Road and I killed a lot of them in my truck not far from where I picked them up."

"I killed some of them outside. I remember leaving each woman's body in the place where she was found."

"I have discussed with my attorneys the common scheme or plan, aggravating circumstance charged in all of these murders. I agree that each of the murders I committed was part of a common scheme or plan. The plan was I wanted to kill as many women I thought were prostitutes as I possibly could."

"I picked prostitutes as my victims because I hate most prostitutes and I did not want to pay them for sex."

"I also picked prostitutes as victims because they were easy to pick up without being noticed. I knew they would not be reported missing right away and might never be reported missing."

"I picked prostitutes because I thought I could kill as many of them as I wanted without getting caught."

"Another part of my plan was where I put the bodies of these women."

"Most of the time I took the women's jewelry and their clothes to get rid of any evidence and make them harder to identify."

"I placed most of the bodies in groups which I call clusters. I did this because I wanted to keep track of all the women I killed."

"I liked to drive by the clusters around the county and think about the women I placed there."

"I usually used a landmark to remember a cluster and the women I placed there. "

"Sometimes I killed and dumped a woman intending to start a new cluster and never returned because I thought I might get caught putting more women there."

Chapter 39
Edmund
Kemper

Kemper made the following statements to the police on the occasion of his picking two young hitchhikers, using a gun and knife to control them, and murdering them both.

"At this time, I had full intentions of killing both of them. I would have loved to have raped them. But not having any experience at all in this area, with very limited exposure to the opposite sex and I guess the learning point—fifteen to twenty-one—I was locked up with all men [for having murdered his grandparents], and there wasn't any opportunity to be with women or girls, and this is one of the big problems I had, and one of the biggest things that caused me to be so uptight. So even trying to communicate [with girls] before this happened, just casually, I felt like a big bumble butt, and I think it's just like an overaged teenager trying to fit in. They were both eighteen at the time, I think, and I was twenty-three, which isn't that much of a gap, but it was just like a million years.

"Anyway, I decided that Anita was more gullible and would be easier to control, so I told her that she was gonna go into the trunk. And she stepped right out of the car, and I had a pair of handcuffs I had purchased. I took the cuffs out and I reached for one of Mary Ann's arms and she grabbed it back. I picked the gun up like I was gonna hit her with it and told her not to do that again. I said, you know, I'm running the show here, or some such cliché. So she allowed me to put my handcuffs on her arm, and I put the other one around the seat belt, behind the lock so it wouldn't come up, and left her back there.

"I took the other girl to the trunk. Just before she got in, she reiterated something Mary Ann said—'Please don't do this,' or something like that. I said, 'What, are you gonna start in too?'"

Back in the car, Kemper found that Mary Ann was trying to get free:

"I almost stuck the gun up her nose to impress her that that was a real gun and that she kept getting me more uptight than I was. And then her lips started quivering, rather than her friend's, and I started losing control, and I told her that if she kept this up, that they were all gonna be in a whole lot of trouble. At this point, she cooperated. I handcuffed her behind her back and turned her over, and I tried to put a plastic bag over her head. I had this nifty idea about suffocating her. I was going to be really smart, and the windows were rolled up, and just normal conversation wouldn't carry—it was a fairly populated area. It was up on the hill. You couldn't hear voices or anything way off in the distance. So I didn't want anything carrying that would be conspicuous. . . . She was complaining that she couldn't breathe. I said I'd tear a hole in the bag, not intending to really, and I had a terry-cloth bathrobe with a long rope tie. I put a loop in it and started pulling it down over what I thought was her neck. I pulled it tight. That's about where I blew it."

What he meant was that he broke the rope, which had caught in her mouth, and she bit a hole in the plastic bag. Kemper, infuriated, pulled a blade.

"I poised the blade over her back, trying to decide where her heart was, and struck and hit her in the middle of the back, and it stuck a little bit; and she said something like 'ow' or 'oh' . . .

and I did it again and did the same damn thing, and I was getting mad now and I told her to shut up after the second time,
and she said, 'I can't,' and was moaning. She was struggling but
she couldn't move too much. . . . Then I started thrusting hard
and I was hitting, but apparently I wasn't hitting or the blade
wasn't long enough, which it wasn't conceivable to me because
she wasn't that large a girl, rather small in fact, about [5'2"] and
maybe 105 pounds. I struck in several places in both sides of
the back and noticed as I went further down the back that she
was a little louder and more painful in her cries, but none got
really loud. That always bothered me. I couldn't figure out why.
It was almost like she didn't want to blow up and start screaming or something. She was maintaining control. But when I
started doing this, then it got to be too much for her; she twisted
around, and I hit her once in the side with the knife.

"She turned completely over to see what the hell I was
doing, I guess, or to get her back away from me, and I stabbed
her once in the stomach in the lower intestine. It didn't have
any effect. There wasn't any blood or anything. There was
absolutely no contact with improper areas. In fact, I think once
I accidentally—this bothers me, too, personally—I brushed, I
think with the back of my hand when I was handcuffing her,
against one of her breasts, and it embarrassed me. I even said,
whoops, I'm sorry, or something like that. She was pretty cog-
nizant of what was going on, and it was getting pretty messy
there in the backseat. She turned back over on her stomach,
and I continued stabbing. I don't know how many times I
stabbed her. I'm trying to think. I usually checked something
like that—you might say, almost comparing notes—and in this
case I didn't. I did with Anita, 'cause that really amazed me.
With Mary Ann, I was really quite struck by her personality
and her looks, and there was just almost a reverence there.

I didn't even touch her, really too much, after that. That is, other than to get rid of physical evidence, such as clothing, and later the body.

"Anyway, she was across the back of the seat with her head down towards the door, towards the space between the front seat and back seat, and I don't think the bag was on. She had shaken it off. She was crying out a little louder, and I kept trying to shut her up, covering her mouth up, and she kept pulling away, and one time, she didn't, and like it was a cry, and I could have sworn it came out of her back. There were several holes in the lung area and bubbles and things coming out, and the sounds shook me up, and I backed off; at that point, she turned her head to the back of the seat and she called her friend's name, her first name. It was slow and it was not loud. That was the last thing that she said. She wasn't passing out at that point. I don't think at that point that the full impact of what had happened had really hit her. I think she was pretty well in shock or something.

"I felt I was getting nowhere, not that I wasn't getting any kicks out of stabbing her, but hoped that one would do it. When it got quite messy like that, I reached around and grabbed her by the chin and pulled her head back and slashed her throat. I made a very definite effort at it, and it was extremely deep on both sides. She lost consciousness immediately, and there were no more vocal sounds anyway."

At that point, Kemper got up in a daze and headed to the back of the car:

"I knew I had to do it to the other girl right then, because she had heard all the struggle and she must have known something very serious was going on."

PART V

TEST YOUR SERIAL KILLER IQ

Following are several questions and quizzes to test your knowledge of serial killers. Some of the questions are based on information in the text, but a few are not (we think true ghouls will know the answers).

Q&A

Q. What happened at these locations?

- 3123 Center Street, Salem, Oregon

- Forty-seventh and Hawthorn, Portland, Oregon

- Parking Garage, Meier and Frank's Department Store, Salem, Oregon

- Rest area on road leading to Santian Pass, just north of Albany, Oregon, and slightly east of Interstate 5

A. Oregon killer Jerry Brudos killed young women.

Q. What happened at these locations?

- Bridge across New York State Thruway, near 170 Dreiser Loop, Bronx, New York

- 2860 Buhre Avenue, Bronx, New York

- 33rd Avenue, 159th Street, Queens, New York

- 8331 262nd Street, Queens, New York

- Station Plaza, Continental Avenue, Queens, NY

- Dartmouth Avenue, three blocks from Sixty-ninth Avenue, opposite Forest Hills Gardens, Queens, New York

- One block from 1950 Hutchinson River, Bronx, New York

- Shore Road, near Bay Seventeenth Street Park, Queens, New York

A. The Son of Sam shot people.

Match the Killers with Their Nicknames

1. Albert Fish	A. Boston Strangler
2. Dean Corll	B. I-5 Killer
3. Bobby Joe Long	C. Lonely Hearts Killer
4. Randall Woodfield	D. Candyman
5. John Wayne Gacy	E. Machete Murderer
6. Gary Ridgway	F. Lipstick Killer
7. Juan Corona	G. Ad Rapist
8. Albert DeSalvo	H. Killer Clown
9. Harvey Glatman	I. Gray Man
10. William Heirens	J. Green River Killer

Answers: 1-I, 2-D, 3-G, 4-B, 5-H, 6-J, 7-E, 8-A, 9-C, 10-F

Match Game
Match the Killers with Their Nicknames

1. Richard Ramírez
2. Jerry Brudos
3. Richard Trenton Chase
4. Arthur Shawcross
5. Ed Gein
6. Edmund Kemper
7. Dennis Rader
8. William Bonin
9. Kenneth Bianchi
10. David Berkowitz

A. Shoe-Fetish Slayer
B. Hillside Strangler
C. Freeway Killer
D. BTK Killer
E. Son of Sam
F. Night Stalker
G. Genesee River Killer
H. Vampire of Sacramento
I. Plainfield Butcher
J. Coed Killer

Answers: 1-F, 2-A, 3-H, 4-G, 5-I, 6-J, 7-D, 8-C, 9-B, 10-E

Arthur Shawcross

Match the Killers with Their Birthplaces

1. Richard Ramírez	A. Burbank, California
2. Kenneth Bianchi	B. Brooklyn, New York
3. Dennis Rader	C. Webster, South Dakota
4. David Berkowitz	D. Kittery, Maine
5. Edmund Kemper	E. Wichita, Kansas
6. Jerry Brudos	F. Milwaukee, Wisconsin
7. Albert DeSalvo	G. Santa Cruz, California
8. Jeffrey Dahmer	H. El Paso, Texas
9. Herbert Mullin	I. Rochester, New York
10. Arthur Shawcross	J. Chelsea, Massachusetts

Answers: 1-H, 2-I, 3-E, 4-B, 5-A, 6-C, 7-J, 8-F, 9-G, 10-D

313

Match Game

Match the Foreign Killers with Their Nicknames

1. Peter Sutcliffe
2. Nikolai Dzhumagaliev
3. Pedro López
4. Lucian Staniak
5. Thierry Paulin
6. Andrei Chikatilo
7. Peter Kürten
8. John Wayne Glover
9. Clifford Olson
10. Harold Shipman

A. Metal Fang
B. Vampire of Düsseldorf
C. Monster of Montmartre
D. Beast of British Columbia
E. Doctor Death
F. Yorkshire Ripper
G. Red Spider
H. Monster of the Andes
I. Granny Killer
J. Rostov Ripper

Answers: 1-F, 2-A, 3-H, 4-G, 5-C, 6-J, 7-B, 8-I, 9-D, 10-E

Q&A

Q. What happened at these locations?

- 2900 East Chevy Chase Drive, Glendale, California

- 6510 Forest Lawn Drive, Glendale, California

- 2833 Alta Terrace, La Crescenta, California

- 4100 block of Ramons Way, Highland Park, California

- 1500 block of Landa Street, Elysian Park, California

- Los Feliz off-ramp from southbound Golden Gate Freeway, California

- 1217 Cliff Drive, Glassell, California

- 2006 North Alvarado, Echo Lake, California

- Angeles Crest Highway, California

- 703 Colorado Drive, Glendale, California

A. The Hillside Strangler (Buono and Bianchi) dumped their murder victims.

Who Am I?

1. As a child, I was bright and well adjusted. I was an altar boy and a good student. I was brought up in John Steinbeck country: Salinas, California.

2. Just after graduating from high school, my best friend was killed in an automobile accident. I was emotionally devastated and this event may have triggered the mental deterioration that was to come.

3. By my early twenties, schizophrenia had begun to manifest itself. Further aggravating my mental condition with the use of LSD and other drugs, I became a walking time bomb.

4. My increasingly bizarre behavior included echopraxia (mimicking another person's exact movements), burning my penis with a cigarette, and responding out loud to telepathic messages I was receiving.

5. I had been in and out of mental institutions, but on that final release, I began my carnage. After the fact, California Governor Ronald Reagan called my release a "psychiatric mistake."

6. Among my thirteen victims was a homeless man I beat to death with a baseball bat, a Catholic priest I stabbed to death in a confessional, and a young mother and her two children whom I shot.

7. Not only did I hear voices in my head commanding me to kill, I also heard the voices of my victims telling me they were ready to be sacrificed.

8. In my psychotic state, I believed that in committing these murders, I was preventing a cataclysmic earthquake and tidal wave from destroying California.

9. After my arrest, and in jail awaiting my trial, I was in adjoining cells with another California serial murderer, Ed Kemper. A mutual dislike kept us taunting each other the whole time.

10. Although my attorneys presented a defense of not guilty by reason of insanity, the jury found me guilty of both first- and second-degree murder, and I was sentenced to life imprisonment. I will be eligible for parole in 2025.

Answer: I am Herbert Mullin.

Match Game
Match the Serial Killers with the Correctional Facility

1. David Berkowitz
2. Edmund Kemper
3. Richard Ramírez
4. Wayne Williams
5. Dennis Rader
6. Robert Hansen
7. Herbert Mullin
8. Arthur Shawcross
9. Gary Ridgway
10. Juan Corona

A. Washington State Penitentiary, Walla Walla, Washington
B. El Dorado Correctional Facility, El Dorado, Kansas
C. Mule Creek State Prison, Lone, California
D. Sullivan Correctional Facility, Fallsburg, New York
E. San Quentin State Prison, San Quentin, California
F. California Medical Facility, Vacaville, California
G. Mid-Hudson Forensic Psychiatric Center, Middleton, New York
H. Spring Creek Correctional Center, Seward, Alaska
I. Corcoran State Prison, Corcoran, California
J. Hancock State Prison, Sparta, Georgia

Answers: 1-G, 2-F, 3-E, 4-J, 5-B, 6-H, 7-C, 8-D, 9-A, 10-I

Match Game
Name that Serial Killer

1. He had intercourse with his wife six times a day.

2. His biological father may well have been his grandfather.

3. His mother disciplined him when he was a child by placing his hand on a hot stove.

4. He cooked and ate a ten-year-old girl over a nine-day period.

5. He ground up his mother's voice box in a garbage disposal.

6. He had a partner in serial murder.

7. His mother dressed him as a girl when he went to school.

8. He probably killed John Walsh's son Adam.

9. He turned back from a planned murder spree on Long Island because of a thunderstorm.

Answers: 1. Albert DeSalvo 2. Ted Bundy 3. Ken Bianchi 4. Albert Fish 5. Edmund Kemper 6. Henry Lee Lucas 7. Henry Lee Lucas 8. Ottis Toole 9. David Berkowitz

Q&A

Q. Are there any physical differences between serial murders and ordinary people?

A. Not at all. The only differences are in their heads and hearts, and that is quite profound.

Q. What happened at these locations?

- 1940 Commonwealth Avenue, Boston
- 73 Newhall Street, Lynn, Massachusetts, Apartment 9
- 7 Grove Street, Boston
- 435 Columbia Road, Boston
- 315 Huntington Avenue, Boston, Apartment 4C
- 515 Park Drive, Boston
- 319 Park Avenue, Salem, Massachusetts
- 4 University Road, Cambridge, Massachusetts
- 224 Lafayette Street, Salem, Massachusetts

A. The Boston Strangler killed people.

Q. What percentage of serial murder victims are female?

1. 40%
2. 65%
3. 75%
4. 87%

A. 2, 65%

Q. What percentage of serial killers are heterosexual?

    1. 50%

    2. 62%

    3. 75%

    4. 86%

A. 4, 86%

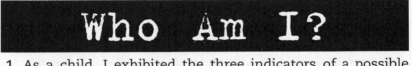

Who Am I?

1. As a child, I exhibited the three indicators of a possible future serial killer: bed-wetting, fire setting, and cruelty to animals.

2. In all likelihood I was born with a congenital mental illness, but this condition was greatly exacerbated by my constant drug abuse.

3. I developed rabid hypochondria. My delusions included thinking that my heart stopped beating on occasion, that my stomach was in backward, and that there were bones growing out of the back of my head.

4. As my psychotic behavior worsened, I began to think my heart was shrinking. I felt this could only be remedied by drinking blood. I began killing and disemboweling rabbits. I would eat the intestines raw and drink the blood.

5. I was institutionalized as a paranoid schizophrenic but eventually released. Back on the street, my craving for blood continued. I began stealing neighborhood pets. Cats and dogs became the new objects of my bloodlust.

6. In time, I graduated to human prey, killing people to get their blood. Two of my victims were women whom I savagely mutilated, pulling out their intestines and drinking their blood.

7. With six victims in my wake, the FBI was brought in to do a profile. I would turn out to be a classic disorganized killer, with little planning of the murders and even less regard for covering my tracks. The details of the profiling would prove uncannily accurate and would lead to my arrest.

8. A search of my apartment was like something out of a nightmare. A blender and glasses stained with blood. Body parts, pieces of bone, and brain tissue in jars and on plates in the refrigerator. Everything reeked of rot and decomposition.

9. The defense had asked for second-degree murder charges to reflect my obvious insanity, but the jury felt I knew right from wrong and found me guilty of six counts of first degree murder. I was sentenced to be executed in the gas chamber at San Quentin.

10. While on death row, I committed suicide in my prison cell by overdosing on antidepressant pills I had secretly saved up for weeks.

Answer: I am Richard Chase.

Q. Who was the first person executed by means of lethal injection in the state of California?

A. Serial killer William Bonin.

Who Am I?

1. I was born in Maine in 1945, but my family moved to Watertown, New York, near the Canadian border when I was very young.

2. The real truth about my childhood is uncertain, but I spoke of a turbulent family life, and of being sexually abused by an aunt at the age of nine. I had sex with my younger sister and had my first homosexual encounter at age eleven.

3. In 1967 I joined the army and served a one-year tour of duty in Vietnam. I related horrendous stories of murder and mutilation in the jungles and villages. I would claim a combat-kill of thirty-nine enemies, but army records showed that the unit in which I served in saw little if any combat.

4. Once out of the service I became a serial arsonist and was eventually arrested for trying to break into a service station. I would serve two years of a five-year sentence for this offense.

5. In May 1972, the killing began. My first victim was a ten-year-old boy whom I lured into the woods on the promise of going fishing. My second victim was an eight-year-old girl whom I lured to a deserted area while showing her a new bicycle. Both children were strangled and the girl had been sexually assaulted.

6. Eyewitnesses had seen me with the children and I was arrested. I confessed to both murders, but in a plea-bargain deal, I was charged with only one case of manslaughter. I would serve fourteen and a half years of a twenty-five-year sentence—I was released early because I was a model prisoner and the authorities thought I had been reformed and could safely return to society as a productive citizen.

7. Upon my parole, I found it difficult to find a permanent residence. When newspapers or townspeople found out about my past, there would be an uproar and I would have to move on. In an effort to settle me somewhere, the parole board made the monumentally bad decision to cover my trail and seal my records from any further investigation. This allowed me to finally settle in Rochester, New York, an upstate community situated on the Genesee River.

8. About a year after I got out of prison, the bodies of murdered prostitutes began showing up, usually dumped in the Genesee Gorge area. The women had all been asphyxiated and sometimes mutilated. As the body count kept rising and the same MO was seen over and over, Rochester police realized they were dealing with a serial killer. An intense manhunt began.

9. One winter day, the police got an incredibly lucky break. A helicopter pilot spotted a body splayed out on the ice below a bridge on the river. I was seen urinating outside my car, which was still parked on the bridge. I was followed and questioned. Subsequent interrogations and mounting evidence finally convinced me to admit to the ten murders

10. My lawyers tried a defense of posttraumatic stress disorder resulting from my Vietnam experiences, as well as an insanity defense. The jury didn't buy it. I'll be a free man in 250 years.

Answer: I am Arthur Shawcross.

Who Am I?

1. I was born in Glasgow, Scotland, the illegitimate child of a young waitress. My girlfriend was born in a suburb of Manchester, England. We met while working together at a chemical plant in the early 1960s.

2. Two of my heroes were Adolf Hitler and the Marquis de Sade. In my library I had books on pornography, sexual sadism, torture, and murder. I had intense fantasies relating to bondage and domination. My girlfriend worshipped me and my beliefs and would become a willing participant in our crimes.

3. Our victims were all children, three boys and two girls, ranging in age from ten to seventeen. We would lure them into our car using various ploys and drive them out to the moors or to our house, where we sexually assaulted and murdered them. We then buried the bodies in shallow graves on the moors.

4. We were turned in by my girlfriend's eighteen-year-old brother-in-law, who was horrified after witnessing the gory murder of my last victim, a young man whom I bludgeoned with the blunt end of a hatchet while I strangled him to death.

5. During the trial, the courtroom sat in stunned silence as they listened to a sixteen-minute tape recording we made of a ten-year-old female victim screaming and pleading for her life before she was raped and murdered.

6. Because we were considered the most hated couple in Britain, and police were fearful of a courtroom assassination, we had to sit in a three-sided enclosure surrounded by four-inch-thick bulletproof glass.

7. We were both sentenced to life in prison. I have now been behind bars for more than forty years. In 1985 I was transferred to a psychiatric hospital for the criminally insane.

8. I have made several efforts to starve myself by going on hunger strikes while in prison. While I believe I have the right to take my own life, the courts will not allow it. I am now kept alive through force-feeding. I have written my autobiography, which I wish to have published upon my death.

9. Although many people cam-
paigned for the release of my
former girlfriend, stating that she
was a changed person, she was
never released. In 2002 she died
of a heart attack at age sixty after
serving thirty-seven years.

10. Many in Britain still regard this
horrific case as the "trial of the
century."

Ian Brady

Answer: I am Ian Brady (my girlfriend was Myra Hindley).

Who Am I?

1. I was born to a mixed-race couple on the Caribbean
island of Martinique. Two days after I was born, my father
abandoned me and my seventeen-year-old unwed mother.

2. At eighteen months of age, I was sent to live with my pater-
nal grandmother. At age ten, I was returned to my mother
and eventually wound up living with my biological father,
who was then in Paris.

3. I threatened my teacher with a kitchen knife when I was
twelve years old. Although I was something of a social
outcast and a homosexual, I joined the military at age
seventeen.

4. Upon leaving the army, I began working in a transsexual nightclub. I was drawn to the glitz and glamour of the gay nightlife and I dreamed of someday owning my own club. It was at this time that I met a transvestite drug addict and we became lovers.

5. My lover and I began targeting elderly women for petty cash. We would rob and kill them, but it was the brutality of the attacks that was shocking. The women would be suffocated, strangled, or beaten to death. Our sadistic behavior included forcing one woman to drink drain cleaner when she wouldn't reveal where she hid her money.

6. As the number of victims mounted, fear gripped Paris and there were demonstrations in the street demanding that the police protect the elderly. The huge police presence and increased security prompted us to flee Paris and move to the town of Toulouse, hundreds of miles away. The killings stopped temporarily.

7. We spent the money we made from selling drugs and stealing credit cards lavishly on ostentatious parties and a wild nightlife. Our relationship eventually ended and I returned to Paris about a year later, only to resume my killing ways, but this time on my own.

8. One of my last victims, although left for dead, recovered unexpectedly and was able to give the police an accurate description of her attacker. I was apprehended while walking down the street and questioned for forty-three hours without a break. I confessed to more than twenty murders of elderly women ranging in age from seventy-one to ninety-one.

9. I was incarcerated and immediately put in isolation. There was fear that I would be set upon by the other prisoners.

10. The case would never come to trial. I died in prison from complications related to AIDS. I was twenty-five years old.

Answer: I am Thierry Paulin.

Index

About the Authors

Tom Philbin and his brother Michael have been close to crime (and its consequences) for many years. Tom is a longtime freelance writer who has written nine cop novels. He lives in New York. Mike Philbin is a musician and lives in New Hampshire.